RESTORING STUDENTS' INNATE POWER

RESTORING STUDENTS' INNATE POWER

Trauma-Responsive Strategies for Teaching Multilingual Newcomers

Louise El Yaafouri

ascd

Alexandria, Virginia USA

1703 N. Beauregard St. • Alexandria, VA 22311-1714 USA
Phone: 800-933-2723 or 703-578-9600 • Fax: 703-575-5400
Website: www.ascd.org • Email: member@ascd.org
Author guidelines: www.ascd.org/write

Ranjit Sidhu, *CEO & Executive Director;* Penny Reinart, *Chief Impact Officer;* Genny Ostertag, *Managing Director, Acquisitions and Editing;* Susan Hills, *Senior Acquisitions Editor;* Julie Houtz, *Director, Book Editing;* Jamie Greene, *Editor;* Thomas Lytle, *Creative Director;* Donald Ely, *Art Director;* Georgia Park, *Senior Graphic Designer;* Kelly Marshall, *Production Manager;* Christopher Logan, *Senior Production Specialist;* Keith Demmons, Senior Production Designer; Shajuan Martin, *E-Publishing Specialist*

All web links in this book are correct as of the publication date below but may have become inactive or otherwise modified since that time. If you notice a deactivated or changed link, please email books@ascd.org with the words "Link Update" in the subject line. In your message, please specify the web link, the book title, and the page number on which the link appears.

PAPERBACK ISBN: 978-1-4166-3075-3   ASCD product #122004   n3/22
PDF EBOOK ISBN: 978-1-4166-3076-0; see Books in Print for other formats.
Quantity discounts are available: email programteam@ascd.org or call 800-933-2723, ext. 5773, or 703-575-5773. For desk copies, go to www.ascd.org/deskcopy.

Library of Congress Cataloging-in-Publication Data
Names: El Yaafouri, Louise, author.
Title: Restoring students' innate power : trauma-responsive strategies for teaching multilingual newcomers / Louise El Yaafouri.
Description: Alexandria, VA : ASCD, 2022. | Includes bibliographical references and index.
Identifiers: LCCN 2021046042 (print) | LCCN 2021046043 (ebook) | ISBN 9781416630753 (paperback) | ISBN 9781416630760 (pdf)
Subjects: LCSH: Immigrant children--Education. | Children with mental disabilities--Education. | Psychic trauma in children. | Stress in children--Prevention. | Multilingualism in children.
Classification: LCC LC3715 .E5 2022 (print) | LCC LC3715 (ebook) | DDC 371.826/912--dc23/eng/20211018
LC record available at https://lccn.loc.gov/2021046042
LC ebook record available at https://lccn.loc.gov/2021046043

30 29 28 27 26 25 24 23 22   1 2 3 4 5 6 7 8 9 10 11 12

RESTORING STUDENTS' INNATE POWER

Introduction

Welcome! I'm so glad you're here. Your commitment to showing up for your students through continued professional learning speaks volumes about your character as an educator. Your students are so lucky to have you.

It is important to note that the information and strategies in this book can be effectively implemented in any classroom and across all strands of student demographics. However, to create the deepest level of understanding and to facilitate the most significant impact on students, we'll need to align ourselves to a specific, targeted, and shared goal.

Therefore, let's establish our central purpose. Together, we'll explore the effects of student trauma, with a focused lens on recently arrived populations, and develop a comprehensive toolkit of strategies to mitigate the adverse experiences these students often face as they transition to a new country and school setting.

Naming Our Purpose

This book isn't exclusively about trauma; it's about restoring power. The distinction is critical. Focusing on the trauma or traumatic event roots us in the past. Restoration of power moves us forward.

Unfortunately, many students have or will endure adverse life experiences, and recently arrived students are particularly vulnerable to risk factors associated with exposure to trauma as they acclimate to a new country (Anderson,

Hamilton, Moore, Loewen, & Frater-Mathieson, 2004; Gichiru, 2012; Hoot, 2011; Kreuzer, 2016). Trauma—whether it is caused by a singularly overwhelming event or the presence of persistent, ongoing aggravators—can be life-affecting. Significant stress has the remarkable capacity to restructure a young person's neural networks (Malhotra & Sahoo, 2017). This "rewiring" can, in turn, disrupt essential patterns of communication and functioning of the brain, with discouraging implications for both short- and long-term socioacademic outcomes (Bremner, 2006).

The physical aspect of transitioning into a new space and place can also spur or exacerbate stress. *Change. Uncertainty. Feeling like an outsider.* These are the kinds of words students often use to describe the overarching experience of arrival.

For many culturally and linguistically diverse newcomers, *arriving* can feel like an especially complex undertaking. In this context, entering a new school or classroom means situating oneself within a new context of language, culture, community, and shifting personal identities. Unfortunately, when viewed through a historical lens, the U.S. educational system hasn't done a great job of supporting newly arrived multilingual students through the processes of integration.

Recently arrived emergent multilinguals who are unsupported or insufficiently supported through socioacademic transition are at a higher risk for integration challenges. That is, they may have less agency in making decisions that affect their lives, less control over their education and social trajectories, and less confidence in their existing funds of knowledge (including cross-cultural and linguistic expertise). These elements, and others, speak to students' innate power. Transition—and to a greater degree, transition shock—can contribute to a sense of diminished power.

In serving our recent arrivers who may be affected by trauma, we must take these dynamics into account. We must recognize that trauma can threaten to drain a person's reservoirs of self-knowing and resilience—and that this may be compounded by the experience of recently arriving anywhere, including our schools and classrooms. We'll call this *power interruption.*

But there's promise.

If a reservoir can be exhausted, it can also be filled. Research informs us that resilience can be taught, learned, and expanded (American Psychological Association, 2019). We can have an active role in empowering (or repowering) our students. This, we'll call *power restoration*.

Let's back up for a moment, though. When we talk about empowering our students, it's important to remember that the power isn't coming from us. It belongs to our students, and they've owned it all along.

Therefore, this is a book about restoring students' power. As educators, we're signing up to facilitate that process.

Who Are Recently Arrived Emergent Multilinguals?

Recently arrived emergent multilingual (RAEM) students are those who are new to our school districts (having been enrolled in U.S. schools for less than 12 months), who have come from countries outside the United States, and who have been identified as emergent bilinguals or multilinguals. The U.S. Department of Education clarifies:

> While about 75 percent of the nation's nearly 5 million ELs [English learners] are U.S.-born, many are the children of immigrants or are immigrants themselves. Recently arrived ELs represent a growing yet often underserved subpopulation of ELs. As with all ELs, RA ELs are diverse in their levels of initial English proficiency, prior formal schooling, primary language literacy and age/grade on entry. (Linquanti & Cook, 2017, p. iv)

Centering in Student Identity

Trauma doesn't exist in a vacuum. Neither does resilience. When it comes to academic instruction, we talk about meeting our students where they are, and this also holds true in our efforts to ensure a trauma-informed learning experience.

Two individuals who are present in the same moment of adversity will process the event in separate and unique ways. Each person's brain interprets and responds to the information differently, and when exposed to the same stimuli, they each have separate capacities for restoring power (what some refer to as returning to the status quo). In short, each has a different shot at demonstrating resilience. Why is this so?

Trauma works in tandem with identity. We can't address one without acknowledging and embracing the other.

Throughout this book, trauma-informed practice might look like something you haven't seen before. Yes, we aim to restore power through trauma mitigation strategies, but the key is that we should never neglect, forget, or discount our learners' identities. From this point forward, we're centered in the idea of identity—specifically, the identity of every RAEM who walks through the doors of our classroom. Culture and language are critical aspects of this identity, and we'll focus on this space. But we need to do some work to get there.

So What's the Plan?

The first three chapters of this book lay the foundation for what is to come. They build background and forward momentum, so by the time we leap into Chapter 4, we'll have a clear understanding of

- The four pillars of transition shock and how they affect learning.
- How RAEMs see themselves and how the cultural aspects of their identities inform our work in mitigating transition shock.
- How social-emotional learning (SEL) links to trauma-informed practice.

Then we move this knowledge out of a book and into your classroom, which leads us to the remaining chapters. We'll spend time bringing the elements of culture, transition shock, and SEL together to create learning spaces that are at once culturally responsive and trauma-diminishing.

In Chapters 4–7, new information is presented in a predictable pattern. Each chapter aligns to one of the essential pillars in approaching transition shock—connect, protect, respect, and redirect—and provides a structural backbone for our learning. Chapters begin with a deeper analysis of the target pillar before diving into a series of classroom-ready strategies aligned to the topic. Every strategy introduced also includes culturally responsive cues and suggested supports for emergent multilinguals. Finally, chapters close with several SEL recommendations that correspond to the target pillar of care.

In the process, I hope you discover that these seemingly separate pedagogies are inherently linked. In order to achieve the desired outcomes for our trauma-affected RAEMs, we must consider a new approach: one that capitalizes on students' unique cultural reference points and engages their cognitive and noncognitive growth in linguistically supportive ways.

Let's get to it.

Understanding Transition Shock

All children experience stress. In fact, stress is natural and very often can be healthy. It can help us avoid danger, tackle an impending deadline, or work up the courage to audition for the middle school musical.

However, some children experience unusually high levels of tension and anxiety. This may originate from an isolated moment of intense impact or from a prolonged period of heightened unrest. In some cases, stress can become debilitating. This is when we start to see signs of trauma, which occurs when the experience of distress is significant enough to overwhelm an individual's resources to make sense of or manage it or to restore normative status (Anderson et al., 2004; Kreuzer, 2016).

Events or circumstances that may be perceived as traumatic affect different people in different ways. Not everyone who endures adverse life experiences will exhibit symptoms of trauma-affectedness. Nevertheless, for others, exposure to extreme or persistent adversity can dismantle their entire sense of belonging, safety, and self-control.

Shifting Our Language: *Trauma* to *Transition Shock*

Throughout this book, we'll lean into the idea of *transition shock*. I prefer this term over the more commonly used *trauma,* especially when we consider our work with recently arrived emergent multilinguals (RAEMs). I'd like to invite you to make the same shift. As we know, words have meaning, and the language we use is important. The distinction between trauma and transition shock is noteworthy.

We can think of transition shock as a broader, more encompassing experience. Transition shock captures a spectrum of factors that activate the fight-flight-freeze-submit response system. Various mechanisms "live" under this canopy, each with the capacity to overwhelm an individual's self-regulatory processes. They include persistent stress, transition-related anxiety, trauma, traumatic stress, high incidence of adverse childhood experiences (ACEs), vulnerability, and culture shock.

As educators of RAEMs, we can't afford to leave transition and culture shock out of our conversations about trauma. After all, how these aspects are experienced and managed can influence integration and prosocial outcomes for RAEMs. Moving away from a reliance on the term *trauma* to a more inclusive vocabulary invites recognition of the multitude of experiences that lead to students' possible power interruptions.

But what exactly is culture shock? In *The Newcomer Student: An Educator's Guide to Aid Transition* (Kreuzer, 2016), I explain it this way:

> Culture shock is elicited via exposure to social, physical, or cultural elements that are perceived by an individual to be unfamiliar, unsafe, or unpredictable. Shock may be characterized as individualized manifestations of the human experience at a particular time, under a given set of circumstances. (p. 29)

Simply, culture shock is the process of adjusting from one set of social norms to another. It can sometimes resemble grief to the extent that it generally follows a predictable cycle of transitional stages on the way to acceptance and integration. I refer to these stages—honeymoon, negotiation, adjustment, mastery—as the four corners of culture shock.

The **honeymoon** period is a romanticized one, full of awe and discovery. Stress factors may be delayed by fascination and a sense of wonder. The **negotiation** phase, which often begins approximately three months after resettlement (though every student's trajectory varies), signals reality setting in and is marked by frustration, fear, homesickness, detachment, and physical discomfort. The **adjustment** period (typically encountered 6–12 months post-transition) is one of acceptance and sense-making. Anxiety is reduced as maneuverability and self-efficacy are increased. Finally, the **mastery** (or bicultural) stage is generally achieved from one to five years post-resettlement and indicates an ability to navigate freely and successfully in the new culture.

A large number of RAEMs in U.S. schools present as or identify with the adjustment domain. This is the space where integration takes root, and it can be separated into three subcategories: isolation, adoption, and integration. If we were to place these on a spectrum, isolation and adoption would be on the two ends; they have opposite values. Of course, neither end of the spectrum is particularly healthy, although isolation tends to be more destructive. What we want RAEMs to achieve is a balance—a "sweet spot" in the middle of the spectrum we identify as integration (see Figure 1.1).

FIGURE 1.1

Adjustment: The Third Domain of Culture Shock

Isolation	Integration	Adoption
• Marked by disengagement or conflict with the new culture. • A likelihood of returning to the point of geographical origination (or staying exclusively within one's original cultural group, even in the new setting). • Feelings of separation and exclusion from both the heritage culture and the new culture are likely. • Fractured identity.	• Marked by an ability to recognize positive attributes of the origination culture (C1) and the new culture (C2). • An ability to participate fully in the new culture without loss of the old one. • Likely to experience social acceptance, emotional well-being, self-efficacy, cooperative relationships, and general productivity.	• Marked by the utter identification with the new culture at the expense of the old one. • Likelihood of complete or near-complete loss of language (L1), heritage culture, and sense of loyalty toward the origination country or culture (C1). • Social separation between the self and family members/cultural community is probable.

Integration is dynamic. Imagine you are standing in the middle of a playground teeter-totter, trying to keep the entire thing balanced with both ends off the ground. To do this, you need to have one hand and one foot on each side of the center. Constant readjustment is necessary to stay centered.

Both sides of the beam have value and worth. In fact, they are both necessary to the function of the teeter-totter. If too much weight is applied to either side of the center, one side may fall to the ground. It is possible, however, to lean into one side more than the other and still keep both sides elevated. Perhaps you take two steps left of center. The right side will rise slightly, but you'll probably still be able to keep both ends raised.

Integration is this middle space. Here, there's an agency to exercise cultural mobility, as represented by the leaning to one side of the teeter-totter. RAEMs, in particular, may lean deeper into the ethnic culture from which they originate or with which they identify—or they may shift more weight into certain aspects of the new culture. They may even toggle back and forth between the two. Most of the time, though, they'll be able to find or return to a degree of balance that feels uniquely good to them.

A student's sense of integration-related equilibrium is meaningful when we consider trauma-informed moves that are at once effective and culturally affirmative. The space on the teeter-totter that children occupy is part of their power. Do they lean further into their ethnic identity? Great! What can we connect to and capitalize on in this space? By contrast, if more weight is centered on the other end, can we more mindfully affirm the home culture and language? In either case, how a student is positioned in the process of integration can give clues about how we can tailor interventions that honor and enhance their innate power.

Meet Rujan

In August of 2019, I opened my email to a LinkedIn alert. It was a message and connection request from a student at a Colorado university, and I recognized the name immediately.

Rujan joined my 3rd grade (Newcomer Level 2) classroom a few months after the school year had already gotten underway. Despite arriving with virtually no background in English, he had progressed enough to warrant an early transfer from Newcomer Level 1 into my class.

This was my second year teaching in a newcomer-only setting, and I was still acutely aware of how underprepared I was (despite an excellent college experience and a few years of "regular" teaching under my belt) to meet the dynamic learning needs of each of my students.

A firm relationship with Rujan's family was in place before Rujan joined our learning group since his cousin was already in my class. Still, the relationship began with a home visit, and I started volunteering with an adult ESL group where Rujan's mother was a member. We took a number of field trips with the adult group—mostly to museums and local attractions—and as a result of those experiences, Rujan's mother revealed more of herself and her family's story.

My bond with the family grew. Often, I'd pop by their apartment complex to say hi and end up drinking tea with the entire extended family, grandmother, aunts, uncles, and cousins included. Hospitality was embedded into every part of their existence. We'd pore over family photo albums, and they'd share (typically through one of the children as translator) the rich history of the family—of Nepal, Bhutan, the beauty of the countries, and the simple ease of being . . . and then of refugee camps, fires, flooding, and airplanes to the United States.

Now Rujan was a grown young man studying philosophy, on a med track, and hoping to pursue neurological sciences. His LinkedIn message was incredibly well spoken. I zoomed in on his picture and saw a confident smile, Western-style business suit, and a Nepali *tilak* on his forehead. He'd made it.

Let me clarify, though. By "made it," I mean that he'd not only managed resilience and academic accomplishment but also achieved integration. Rujan had learned to navigate the world of his new home without compromising the integrity of his personal and cultural identity.

This, I believe, is what we most want for our students. A checklist of academic "can-dos" is not the goal. Those skills are important, but they are just conduits through which students' fullest selves can be expressed. Without question, Rujan needed to learn how to read and speak English, understand biological life cycles, and solve mathematical equations to move toward graduation and successfully engage with the world. These are all essential skills.

Rujan undoubtedly learned the skills we taught him, but what is the larger, combined goal of these content objectives? Is it to pass benchmark tests? No. Is it to enable greater access toward becoming whatever it is the child aspires to be? Perhaps.

I've embedded the stories of various students throughout this text, yet we'll return to Rujan in each chapter, leading up to his thoughts on resiliency.

Here's Rujan:

My life message (or perhaps it is more fair to say my family's message) is deeply rooted in the upbringings back home in Nepal. Amidst constant struggle with corruption in government, civil distress, and our very own battles with poverty, we saw hope, an immigrant ambition for better. My parents, though uneducated by today's metrics, had profound understanding that if there was any way to escape this generational cycle of life and death muddled by inhumane poverty in Nepal, it would have to be a life of proper education and opportunity elsewhere. Their wishes seemed hollow and unrealistic to many, but that is what we all were taught growing up. A life of better requires Herculean undertaking and was filled with constant worries. It was better to be content with how little we had, or so we were told.

In my early education in Nepal, life took a turn for my family. A fire burned our whole village and rendered us with only a few blankets and no place to call home. This marked the end of a chapter in my family's story in Nepal. We were not the writer of this chapter though. We had little say in how it would end and to describe its suddenness. Nevertheless, we told ourselves that this next and new chapter in our life, which we were about to embark on, would be written by us and us entirely. Thus, the journey to a better life ensued; my parents left what they knew and called home to fly over an ocean to uncharted territory. That in itself brought forth daunting challenges.

Transition Shock and the Brain: An Overview

Significant stress affects the human brain at the molecular level, resulting in explicit physiological, psychological, and emotional changes (Teicher et al., 2003). How the brain is affected by stress can have implications for social, academic, and economic well-being (Anderson et al., 2004; De Bellis & Zisk, 2014; Frater-Mathieson, 2004). Let's explore a snapshot of this process.

First, we'll talk about the brain stem and limbic system. Together, they comprise the emotional center of the brain. The thalamus, hippocampus, and amygdala are all parts of the limbic system. These elements work together to activate our fight-flight-freeze-or-submit response (Bremner, 2006; Himelstein, 2016). Here's how it works, in brief:

- A stressor (say, a door slamming loudly) comes in. It gets picked up by the outward senses (the slam is heard; responses and expressions on others' faces are seen and interpreted).
- The message is instantly transported to the brain stem and limbic system, where the thalamus captures the signals and consolidates them into one of two categories: *emergency* or *nonemergency*.
- Nonemergency messages are routed to the prefrontal and cerebral cortexes for closer examination and more deliberate problem-solving.
- Emergency messages are sent to the amygdala, which fires up its "alarm," initiating a fight-flight-freeze-submit response (Harvard Health, 2017; McEwan & Gianaros, 2010). Once activated, this defense circuitry dominates brain functioning. If you've heard about the brain being "hijacked," this is where and when it happens.

Transition shock confuses this built-in alarm system. The thalamus of a trauma-affected person is more likely to skip over this sorting process. Instead, it simply sends *all* incoming messages directly to the amygdala. The amygdala, now receiving both emergency and nonemergency information, becomes hyperactive. Its fight-flight-freeze-or-submit switch is left on—even in situations where no immediate threat exists (Blue Knot Foundation, 2020).

The amygdala is part of the limbic system, which is largely responsible for integrating sensory input, regulating emotions, storing and retrieving memories, ensuring focus, and producing responses to various stimuli. When this region of the brain is compromised, the lower-level functions it controls are disrupted.

This is critical in the context of learning. Limbic stress frequently manifests as emotional outbursts, incontinence, toe-walking, a lack of balance and coordination, "*W*-sitting" (i.e., sitting on one's knees with shins splayed to the side), fine and gross motor lapses, and a lack of organizational skills. RAEMs (and especially refugee newcomers), as a demographic whole, are particularly vulnerable to issues related to limbic dysfunction (Arnetz et al., 2020; Schauer & Elbert, 2010).

There's another part of the brain that's important to this conversation: the cerebral cortex. The cerebral cortex, which wraps around the limbic system, occupies a considerable amount of territory within the brain and is subdivided into right and left hemispheres.

The right hemisphere, along with the amygdala, oversees lower-hierarchy behaviors that become automatic with training. Adhering to social norms, sitting on cue, or raising a hand to ask a question are behaviors that fall into this category. The right brain reads observable cues, such as body language, gestures, and facial expressions; it also identifies with negative responses and stimulates withdrawal (American Speech-Hearing-Language Association [ASHLA], 2020). Right-brain functions are best observed in small children where curiosity, creativity, and elementary automaticity are usually evident.

The left hemisphere of the brain is linked to higher-level functions. It's often associated with logic and organizational factors and has been demonstrated to process and respond to positive stimuli (Kelley, 2018). Relevant to RAEMs, left-brain functions are also critical to language development. Scientific mapping of the brain reveals that words and word meanings are filtered and digested through the left hemisphere and throughout the wrinkly outer layers of the cerebral cortex (Rosen, 2016).

Socioacademic success depends on the functionality of *both* brain hemispheres. However, research suggests that traumatic stress may disrupt typical growth patterns (Bremner, 2006; Rauch et al., 1996). Disruptions to the cerebral cortex are particularly relevant in conversations around trauma-informed planning for RAEM populations. That's because the right- and left-brain hemispheres are so closely tied to prosocial communication, such as the ability to read facial expressions, interpret social cues, recognize contextual norms, and acquire new linguistic skill sets (Henry, 1993; Rosen, 2016).

What does this mean for RAEM education? Simply, it means we can have a top curriculum and the best instructional moves, but if we're not meeting our students where they are in managing and mitigating transition shock, we'll always be one step behind. In looking to the long-term integrative well-being of recently arrived multilinguals, this creates a new (or renewed) sense of urgency for our work.

How Does Transition Shock Affect Learning?

Data on the effects of trauma show that students who have experienced significant or ongoing adverse life experiences are at an increased risk for school absence, behavioral suspensions or expulsions, and dropping out. Meanwhile, they are less likely to excel in school, having lower reading levels and GPAs than their peers (Porche, Fortuna, Lin, & Alegria, 2011).

One reason for this is that transition shock can impair cognition. The frontal cortex—the region of the brain responsible for executive functioning such as memory, planning, organization, and self-regulation—is especially hard-hit by stress (Aupperle, Melrose, Stein, & Paulus, 2012). If we think about it, these executive functions are central to a successful learning day. They help us remember where we left our backpack, make it to the bus stop on time, understand instructions, problem-solve, exercise our creativity, anticipate successes and failures, and reflect on the day or the moments within it. Power interruptions that get in the way of executive functioning will negatively affect one's school experience.

Here's another reason to consider. Unresolved transition shock can manifest in outwardly observable ways that impair concentration, motivation, and social integration (De Bellis & Zisk, 2014; National Child Traumatic Stress Network, 2019; Wodzenski, 2017). For someone dealing with transition shock, these manifestations can command a great deal of time and energy, and the effort required to manage them can take away from academic learning.

In a classroom setting, transition shock may be observed as physical symptoms (e.g., appetite changes, nausea, incontinence) or bodily ailments (e.g., joint or bone pain, toothaches, rashes) (Substance Abuse and Mental Health Services Association [SAMHSA], 2014). It may also show up as excessive tidiness or its opposite: extreme disorganization (Dykshoorn, 2014). Speech impediments, poor coordination, and a difficulty concentrating can be linked to transition shock, along with detachment indicators, such as defiance, poor attendance, and an inability to accept adult guidance (Ferfolja & Vickers, 2010; Kreuzer, 2016; National Child Traumatic Stress Network, 2019). Of course, any combination of these indicators could detract from one's ability to meaningfully engage in the learning day. See Figure 1.2 for a breakdown of the various manifestations of transition shock.

However, before we read too far into this, let's keep in mind that any of us can—and will—demonstrate these indicators from time to time. My own sons can be weepy or clumsy or compulsive in any given moment. They sometimes lack motivation or demonstrate clinginess. I see myself on this map, too. I can be extremely disorganized in some areas and hyperorganized in others. I can sometimes have a poor memory, act compulsively, or be too sensitive.

Therefore, when I notice a student presenting manifestations of transition shock at school, I'm not immediately concerned. There are two key exceptions to this, though: (1) when a child demonstrates four or more indicators in a singular moment or situation, and (2) when a child demonstrates one, two, or three (or more) indicators routinely and over a prolonged period of time.

In either scenario, my built-in teacher red-alert flag raises. This is when I start paying closer attention, taking notes, and asking questions. I am likely to seek advice from specialized school staff, such as the counselor or nurse, I work to ensure the classroom is a safe place, and I make sure I have the right tools to enact interventions as appropriate.

FIGURE 1.2

Manifestations of Transition Shock

Physical	Internalized	Externalized	Emotional	Social	Detachment
• Physical pain • Nausea • Nightmares • Sleep apnea • Uncontrolla-ble bladder/bowels • Appetite changes • Clumsiness	• Extreme tidiness • Disorganiza-tion • Stimuli sensitivity • Boredom • Hoarding • Stalled creativity • Diminished motivation	• Impeded speech • Concentration difficulties • Toe-walking • W-sitting • Coordination challenges • Poor memory • Categorizing difficulties	• Guilt • Anxiety • Anger • Weepiness • Sensitivity • Reflective challenges • Problem-solving difficulties	• Repetitive play • Self-talk • Clinginess • Inability to trust or main-tain relation-ships • Self-regulation challenges	• Defiance • Delinquency • Poor attendance • Compulsivity • Disengage-ment • Inability to accept adult guidance

As teachers, we sometimes witness the effects of childhood trauma in the classroom. Nevertheless, it is not advisable to step directly into the role of psychologist or student counselor unless you happen to be explicitly trained and licensed to do so. (Thanks, all you school psychologists and counselors out there!) However, we *can* do our best to take proactive measures that mitigate significant stressors—and the resulting power interruptions—in the classroom.

The Four Pillars to Approaching Transition Shock

The four pillars of trauma-informed care form the scaffolding that will support our practice moving forward (Hummer, Crosland, & Dollard, 2009). These pillars offer a cohesive and comprehensive way to sort concepts related to trauma (see Figure 1.3). Here, they'll be used mainly as an organizational structure. We'll add to them with additional research and insights from my work with students, and you'll finish this book with a guiding framework that examines each pillar through the lens of transition shock.

The pillars are as follows:

- Connect
- Protect
- Respect
- Redirect

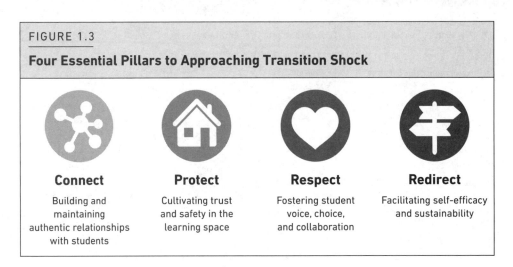

FIGURE 1.3

Four Essential Pillars to Approaching Transition Shock

Connect	**Protect**	**Respect**	**Redirect**
Building and maintaining authentic relationships with students	Cultivating trust and safety in the learning space	Fostering student voice, choice, and collaboration	Facilitating self-efficacy and sustainability

Let's break these down. **Connect** centers on the idea of relationship-building. It calls for authentic and meaningful exchanges with our students that are rooted in receptivity, empathy, constructive conversations, and partnership. True interpersonal connectivity requires individual investment, which, in turn, demands a combination of positive risk-taking and healthy social-emotional engagement.

Protect calls for the cultivation of trust and safety within the classroom, school, and larger community. This is where the "Maslow's before Bloom's" talk comes into play. In other words, in order for students' brains to be open to learning new things, they must first have their most basic needs met, including the need for safety. Then, as we work to remove some of the fight-or-flight distractions students face throughout the school day, we make space for new energy and cognitive availability for learning.

Respect draws on and enhances the values of connection and protection. Feelings of respect are catalyzed by connection and flourish in physically and emotionally protected spaces. In these environments, all parties can be safely seen and heard, and transformative dialogue can occur. Respect harnesses student voice, choice, and collaboration—elements that facilitate equity.

The final pillar, **redirect,** champions the learned ability to reframe unproductive thought and behavior patterns and to channel this energy into constructive outcomes. Principles of redirection include self-efficacy, accountability, and sustainability. Redirective ability is also a critical 21st century skill and one that crosses over all content-learning areas and the domains of social-emotional efficacy.

From an instructional perspective, each of the four pillars—connect, protect, respect, and redirect—has standalone value. However, it is important to note that these principles are inherently linked. Together, they provide the framing for trauma-informed practice.

Connect

Idrees Al-Abbas arrived in my classroom as a 5th grader from Iraq. For the entire first week of school, he'd lay his head down on his desk or hunch behind the classroom door and cry. With time, he became more participative. In a RAEM context, we are prepared for the possibility of a "silent period" as students move from absorbing to producing in a new language. However, after three weeks in class, Idrees still wasn't talking.

In his case, there was evidence to support a need to explore barriers to verbal output that reached beyond language acquisition. Idrees demonstrated a number of potential manifestations of trauma, including extreme disorganization, clinginess, and sensitivity to stimuli. What especially stood out was the fact that Idrees was both a *W*-sitter and a toe walker. Both of these indicators are regularly evidenced in children. However, persistent displays have been linked to underlying sensory processing issues, including those that are rooted in or exacerbate transition shock (Williams, Tinley, & Curtin, 2010).

I implemented several trauma-informed interventions for Idrees in the classroom, including reduced sensory stimuli, grounding practice, and art-based tools. My paraprofessional (who also shared Idrees's home language) and I took careful notes on his progress. Halfway through the year, I also requested that Idrees be evaluated by our site-based mental health team. Their findings aligned with my suspicions: Idrees did, in fact, demonstrate significant trauma impact.

Involving Idrees's family in a conversation around the young boy's mental health proved difficult. His family, like many from the Middle East, adhered to the culturally normative value of saving face. This principle is a feature of many collectivist societies and appeals to the idea that upholding the individual's outward reputation (and, by extension, the reputation of the family or clan name) is of critical importance. When an individual is associated with mental health–related labels, certain implications are applied to the image of the larger family unit. Thus, acknowledging trauma, which has close associations with one's mental well-being, is not commonly encouraged.

Idrees did eventually receive the full spectrum of services he required. However, it took nearly three years of working closely with the family, building trust, and visiting Idrees's home before his parents were on board with an approval to move forward. With time, they became tremendous advocates for their son's academic and social-emotional well-being.

Protect

It was already late in the school year, and I was sitting backstage with a small group of 8th grade newcomers before our end-of-the-year musical rehearsal. We sat in a loose circle, running lines from the script and waiting for other cast members to make their way to the theater.

As we waited, I asked, "So, what was the best piece of advice you were given before you came to the United States or right after you got here?"

Maung was the first to contribute. "Learn to ride the city bus. You can get anywhere and have more freedom." Lots of nods of agreement.

"Don't buy a cell phone on the street," Kigi added. "You'll probably get ripped off. At home in Uganda, we get any phone and then just buy, like, a little card with a number that you kind of scratch off. You buy a number of minutes, like 60 or 3 hours or whatever, and you can use it on any phone." More nods.

Then Mohammad said, "Don't ever call the police."

And there it was. The uncomfortable truth of living in the United States as a person of color. Mohammad was a Muslim, black male, but his comment was unanimously acknowledged within our small group.

The realization was harsh and instantaneous. Protection is not a universal—or an equitable—realization. Here, my own privilege screamed out. From my vantage point, the police represented protection to the highest degree. I wasn't raised to fear them. I was taught to recall the magic numbers 911 at will.

In that moment, it was difficult to have empathy for my students. The truth is that I couldn't understand more than what they had expressed to me. I lacked the personal experience, was poorly educated on the subject, and had not yet reckoned with the magnitude of my own socially and economically constructed privilege. I fumbled over how to proceed with the conversation in a way that was both supportive and appropriate.

In the end, I dropped the ball. I changed the subject.

I bailed on what could have been an incredibly profound teachable moment—or, at the least, an opportunity to deepen the relationships with my students that I was so proud of. In short, I perpetuated the problem, making Mohammad's desire and right to feel protected all the more elusive.

That afternoon has stayed with me. I experience a feeling of loss and disappointment each time the memory replays in my mind. Nevertheless, that perceived failure has also pushed me forward. It forced me to ask questions, read about the issues my students were talking about, and seek out mentors of color (including some of my own students) who helped me grow in this area.

Today, much of my work involves professional development that focuses on understanding issues of race and cultural identity—and on supporting educators in facilitating these tough conversations. Transformation can be awkward and uncomfortable, but our students depend on us to make a valiant, authentic attempt. We cannot stand as allies in the protection of young people without seeing them in full light.

Respect

Angelina had lived in Cambodia her entire life, but her family immigrated to the United States right before her 4th grade year. Both of her parents were highly educated, and both had enrolled in advanced degree programs at universities in Colorado.

Angelina herself had not experienced a specifically defined traumatic event in her lifetime. However, her family carried a deep burden of historical trauma. *Historical trauma* is a phenomenon that occurs when an entire social group is exposed to significant adversity, and the processing of that adversity is passed down generationally. Like Angelina, her parents had also been inheritors of historical trauma as lived by the previous generation during the Khmer Rouge regime.

The presence of historical trauma, also called *intergenerational trauma,* created a unique dynamic in Angelina's home. All of her basic needs were met to high standards, but the unresolved grief her parents carried with them interfered with their ability to forge deep bonds with their child (as was later explained to me by Angelina's aunt). Consequently, the relationship between Angelina and her parents was detached and marked by limited emotional exchanges or physical contact.

At school, Angelina did well. However, she could become easily upset. When this happened, she'd put her head down on her desk and cry. It was difficult for Angelina to move beyond these moments and, once started, they could last an entire school day. This resulted in an incredible loss of valuable learning time.

We initially tried a variety of approaches and began by engaging Angelina in conversations about the presented behavior. We embedded restorative justice (an approach to discipline that strives for active solution-seeking over punitive consequences) into the learning day. We also engaged in visits with the school counselor, pop-ins with the school principal, and phone calls home. Eventually, Angelina and I became frustrated. Many days, I floated between losing my temper and giving up on Angelina's behavioral episode to resume the class lesson.

However, during this time, I was working to increase my own knowledge and efficacy around culturally responsive pedagogy. Eager to apply these principles, I attempted to gain a deeper understanding of Angelina's cultural lens. I learned that a common value in Cambodian culture is *collectivism,* a social construct that emphasizes group belongingness over individual gain. As a part of this, it's not uncommon for people to avoid all forms of confrontation.

I quickly realized that all the mitigation strategies I'd tried with Angelina up to that point involved some element of confrontation. Although it is imperative for students to develop interpersonal problem-solving skills, Angelina was not yet prepared to launch into that. As Geneva Gay (2014), a pioneer in culturally responsive instruction, explains in an interview with *Learning for Justice,* my outgoing message didn't match up to Angelina's receptors. I had not responsively acknowledged her cultural reference points; as a result, my prescribed solutions were a terrible fit.

Together, we eventually discovered power-restorative strategies that were better aligned to Angelina's collective unconscious (explained further in the next chapter)—the same area where culturally responsive teaching and learning occurs. Art therapy and blackout poetry became her go-to practices for recentering and reestablishing a safe space. With time, we inched our way back toward the interpersonal approaches we'd started with.

As an educator, this experience provided a valuable lesson for me. Sometimes, truly respecting a student means stepping back. I needed to do a better job of listening—in this case, to Angelina's deeply rooted cultural cues. I also needed to offer and honor the element of student choice on the road toward collaboration.

Redirect

Hset Sar Oo was a first-year RAEM in my 5th/6th grade combination class. She was a bright, charismatic girl with an abundance of curiosity and a drive for learning. But she had one daily habit that stood out.

Each day, she'd arrive to class with a new ailment—a hurt toe, a tummy ache, a suspicious red dot on her arm. Some days, she'd have multiple physical woes—a headache in the morning, a "broken" ankle after lunch, and a bump on her tongue during math. They all required a full investigation (some involving a trip to the nurse's office) and a nod of clearance before she was able to return to learning.

As the year went on, the origin of her complaints became more focused and concentrated around her heart space. She'd express feelings of heaviness, pinching, biting, and squeezing in and around her chest. Hset Sar Oo's fixation on these maladies also became more frequent and a more significant obstruction to her learning.

Eventually, she was recommended for medical evaluation. Taking note of her symptoms, the hospital team set to work. They listened to her heart, ran an EKG, and took chest X-rays. They reported back to the family that they'd found nothing wrong with her.

At that point, we began to consider the possibility that Hset Sar Oo's symptoms might have been tied to transition shock. At school, we devised a plan to collect background information from the family that might help us create an appropriate approach to trauma-informed instruction that would meet her needs. Through a series of meetings and at-home visits with the young girl's family, several realizations emerged. The first came from the Burmese translator who stumbled over our remarks about trauma and mental health. As it turns out, there is not a direct translation for these ideas as they exist in our Western framework (Acharya et al., 2017).

The second realization came from the parents. As we talked about what the family had experienced, both parents held their hands to their hearts and bellies, expressing various forms of physical discomfort, including those that Hset Sar Oo had shared with me in the classroom. This very physical description of emotional turmoil, it turns out, is a culturally normative value. From the Burmese perspective, it is socially acceptable to describe the physiological aching of hurt, but it is not common to express emotional implications such as anxiety, fear, or sadness. Of course, this cultural reference point was misaligned with a Western approach, which automatically called for an investigation into the physiological health of Hset Sar Oo's heart.

Working with our school counseling team, we devised a trauma-informed intervention plan that focused on redirecting techniques. Each tool was designed to help Hset Sar Oo learn to recognize when her thought energies were moving toward a hyperfocused concentration on her physical well-being. Then we introduced and practiced strategies that empowered her to shift those thought patterns and reduce her flight-or-flight stress responses—ultimately increasing her ability to be cognitively present and receptive to new learning. Ultimately, this plan has had wider applicability and has been used as a template for addressing similar scenarios with other learners.

The Nonnegotiable 4

When I walk into any classroom, school, or organization, there are four specific indicators I'm looking for. Each of these "nonnegotiables" speaks to elements of security, trust, and safety. Combined, they facilitate power restoration.

- A calm, organized environment
- Moderated sensory stimuli
- Routine and predictability
- Robust stakeholder partnerships

The first three elements are specific to the spaces in which students spend their learning days. These indicators are important because they transcend all language and cultural orientation barriers. They are the proverbial actions that speak louder than words. They are also essential avenues to trust, which is critical to students who have experienced trauma (and is beneficial for all learners). The last two indicators highlight collaboration and connection—aspects that are paramount in negotiating transition shock but that also appeal to key tenets of culturally responsive teaching and learning.

The Nonnegotiable 4 create a foundation of safety. Once firm ground has been established and trust has taken root, we can begin to explore any number of trauma-informed practices.

Calm, Organized Environment

A calm, organized setting can help students feel a sense of control related to their environment and the ability to safely maneuver within it. Security is power restorative. With fewer outside stressors to manage, learners can focus on, well, learning! A well-managed space can bolster self-trust, self-efficacy, agency, ownership of space and time, and classroom community building.

What elements contribute to a calm, organized learning space? My guess is that it's a lot of the things you're already doing! For example, consistently storing supplies in labeled bins (or icon-labeled bins for early emergent multilinguals) can relieve some of the pressures of "not knowing." Having systems in place for repeated daily activities or providing step-by-step instructions for a task has a similar effect. Of course, calm teacher behaviors and designated "safe spaces" in the school or classroom also go a long way in fostering a power-restorative environment.

Moderated Sensory Stimuli

Moderating sensory stimuli is an ongoing process that engages students in recognizing and advocating for their own unique sensory needs. Unwanted or stressful sensory stimuli act as power interrupters; precious energy is used up in order to cope with these distractions. When external stimuli are effectively managed, these energies can be redirected, effectively restoring power to students. As an added benefit, as students learn to name their own stimuli preferences, they also learn to respect the learning needs of others.

The interesting thing about sensory stimuli is that each child's senses are unique. Some learners with trauma backgrounds require more stimulation, and others less. Some crave sensory engagement in some areas (sound, for example) but less with others (say, touch). Sometimes, something that wouldn't normally be bothersome can suddenly become overwhelming. For some students with trauma histories, too much of any one thing can lead to shut down. It's important to keep a pulse on who these students are and what their needs are.

Practitioners in clinical settings who work with identified trauma survivors often introduce a "sensory diet." Essentially, these types of programs eliminate most of the stimulation in someone's environment and then reintroduce sensory activities in a slow and scheduled way, providing time for individuals to practice modulating, or self-regulating, their responses.

To a lesser extent, this approach also works well in the classroom. For example, I tend to start the school year with a sensory-minimized classroom. I strive for a clean and inviting classroom, but I'm also careful not to overdecorate my walls. I keep a careful eye on curriculum-embedded screentime. As the weeks progress, I might try turning off the lights during a quiet reading time or introducing background music while we engage in group work. During these periods, I am especially receptive to my students' reactions (if any) and use them to inform my next moves.

In working with older learners, I've created sensory input inventories (which I have translated in multiple languages or adapted to work with icon cues). Information is solicited in the same way as a reading inventory; they're brief, direct, and provide insight into a learner's unique preferences. This is also a great way to remind students that they have the power to advocate for their own learning needs.

Here are a few other things to keep in mind when thinking about moderating stimuli:

- Consider limiting (or further limiting) teacher talk time. Too much of it can be overwhelming. Not to mention, learning is often amplified when we get out of students' way!

- Discuss overtly intrusive sounds (such as fire alarms) in advance and have a plan to work through them. For younger students, a bucket of small stuffed animals is helpful in the event of a lockdown or shelter-in-place drill. In classes with older students, we've made our own pressure squeeze balls to have on hand during these events. Watch for episodes of self-pressure (e.g., poking/scratching oneself with pencils, paper clips, or other sharp items), and strive to model self-regulating techniques.

- Avoid abrupt changes, such as bringing another adult into the classroom without warning or turning on a video at full volume.

- Consider adding sources of sensory stimuli that can be made available to specific students who may need it. As an example, I had one student, Mu Eh, whose self-regulating activity involved sitting directly under a lamp in our reading corner where she could feel the warm heat on her skin. Weighted vests, headphones, or sensory bags (I fill a zipper storage bag with a small variety of items, such as a wax candle, piece of felt, smooth stone, and square of sandpaper) are useful tools to have on hand.

- Be intentional about tech time. Technology can be an incredibly useful classroom tool, but it has also become an inescapable daily stimulus. Most tech-based applications are designed to engage the user's senses. For trauma-affected students, this can be overwhelming (especially when combined with other "plugged-in" periods during the day). This may hit RAEMs especially hard, as access to these devices in students' countries of origin may have been limited. Go slow, note signs of overwhelm (e.g., restlessness, behavior changes, "deer in the headlights" looks), and modify use accordingly.

Routine and Predictability

Routine and predictability in the school setting strengthen anticipatory skills (including anticipation of purpose, success, and failure). Trust and safety are supported in these spaces, as learners are better able to imagine next steps and learn to plan and organize accordingly (thus strengthening frontal cortex/executive functioning skills).

What can we do to ensure routine and predictability in the school day (and from one day to the next)? The good news is that, once again, you probably already have many of these features embedded into your practice. I'd suggest adding or becoming more mindful about, for example:

- Posted daily schedules.
- Advance warning for schedule shifts (when possible).
- Preemptive practice and advance explanation of nonroutine events, such as inclement weather drills and lockdowns (when possible).
- Consistency in teacher voice and demeanor.
- Clear norms and expectations.
- Evident and equitable consequences for undesirable choice-making.

Robust Stakeholder Partnerships

Stakeholders, in this sense, are people in the school community who hold a particular student's best interests (including mental health) in mind. Collaboration among stakeholders is power regenerative. It contributes to a sense of belonging and positive self-worth, facilitates relationship-building skills (which are often compromised by the presence of transition shock), and supports executive skills development. Partnership-centered environments also invite self-management skills practice and opportunities to "test the waters" of stimulation in a controlled setting.

Multifaceted collaboration works to engage all key stakeholders at the school, including staff members, students, and families. Let's explore examples in three critical areas:

- *Adult-to-adult collaboration* might include whole-school goals and working agreements, vertical and horizontal team planning, meaningful partnerships between teachers and mental health resource personnel, or working partnerships between the school and community stakeholders.
- *Adult-to-student collaboration* might involve daily/weekly check-ins, 2x10 meetings (i.e., spending 10 high-quality relationship-building minutes with two students each learning day), the worry box strategy (introduced in Chapter 5), or mentorship programs (including those that occur outside the learning day).
- *Student-to-student collaboration* could make way for collaborative structures (e.g., inside-outside circle, four corners, or partner-think-pair-share), small-group problem-solving, cross-grade relationships (e.g., 5th grade students reading aloud to 1st grade students), whole-class projects or goals, class roles/jobs, and team sports.

Robust partnerships are also evidenced in the welcoming process. A school that comes together to create a welcoming and inclusive environment for newcomers is likely to place value on the power of RAEM students and their families in other ways, too. These include

- Strategic and consistent school-to-home communication systems.
- Culturally responsive outreach and engagement.
- Purposeful solicitation of parent/family participation.
- Identifying and capitalizing on existing funds of knowledge that exist in the classroom, school, home, and community.
- Intentional and ongoing partnerships with key community stakeholders.

Where Do We Go from Here?

In this chapter, we

- Embraced transition shock as the broader value that encompasses trauma.
- Explored how the brain interprets, processes, and responds to emergency or adversity.
- Identified the four pillars of transition shock.

- Named and investigated the Nonnegotiable 4.

In the next chapter, we shift the focus to transition shock in order to lay a foundation for trauma-informed care. Then we introduce a collection of strategies designed to best meet the diverse intrapersonal, interpersonal, and linguistic needs of RAEM students.

Inviting Culture into the
Trauma-Informed Conversation

Transition shock isn't a neat and tidy element that can be contained in a box. If it were, dismantling it would be a simple task, and we wouldn't need to have this conversation. The truth is that transition shock can be unruly, messy, and difficult to tease apart from other areas of life. Let's talk about this intersectionality. Transition shock overlaps and interacts with other aspects of students' identities. These junctions (where they do and do not exist) influence how adverse experiences are acknowledged, communicated, processed, and managed.

Intersectionality is especially relevant when considering trauma-informed moves for RAEMs. These include history, race, gender, location, language, and culture (National Child Traumatic Stress Network, 2019). Here's a closer look at each of these.

History: Historical (or intergenerational) trauma is a phenomenon that occurs when an entire social group encounters significant adversity, and the processing of that adversity passes from one generation to the next. Students who live in a home where intergenerational trauma is present may not have experienced a singular or specific adverse event themselves. However, the persistent presence of underlying trauma in a child's home or community environment can lead to observable power interruptions in the school setting (Kaplan, Stolk, Valibhoy, Tucker, & Baker, 2015). Historical trauma is well documented among specific populations of newer Americans, including those who resettled from

Vietnam and Cambodia during the 1980s and 1990s (Mohatt, Thompson, Thai, & Tebes, 2014). Intergenerational trauma can also have domestic origins. For example, it is frequently evidenced in communities that are historically or systemically affected by high levels of crime, poverty, and subversive public policy (Conner, 2020).

Race: Race-based trauma includes the impact of racial profiling, bias, and explicit prejudice on the psyches of those who face discrimination. It is insidious by nature, and it frequently becomes embedded into historically normative social values—and perpetuated in ways beyond the control of those experiencing the trauma. Race-based trauma is highly likely to intersect with historical (intergenerational) trauma (Conner, 2020).

My friend and colleague Dr. Lisa Collins (2021), whose work on the topic is trailblazing in its own right, explains it this way:

> Racial trauma is traumagenic and has long-term effects. [It] requires tremendous energy on the part of the person who is experiencing it. The minoritized person must continue to function while carrying the memory of shame, discrimination, weakness, and vulnerability. While the individual may want to move on, the rational brain does not do this easily. The slightest hint of danger interrupts the brain circuits and massive amounts of stress hormones are released. (p. 98)

Gender: How society views the role of gender concerning mental health–related issues and the expression of emotion can influence an individual's manifestations of anxiety. It can determine how a person deals with the energy of distress in a public space. Most cultures assign specific emotive qualities to the separate genders (Parkins, 2012). These complex communal norms also influence projections and perceptions of mental health, including trauma.

Location: *Location* refers to the region where a person is from and the space and place in which trauma occurred. It also encompasses the worldview of the community and generational group to which an affected person belongs. For example, half of my family is Lebanese, Arabic is the primary language in my home, and we spend a significant amount of time each year in Lebanon. In this region (as in much of the Middle East), trauma is not a common talking point. In general, matters related to mental health tend to be dealt with discreetly—or not at all. My husband (who is wholly Lebanese) is often bewildered by my work and alarmed at both my directness in speaking to the subject and the terminology I affix to it. From his reference point, mental health concepts are expressed using one or two general (and potentially offensive) terms. Meanwhile, I'm taking an entire book to portion out one term—*transition shock*—into a myriad of dimensions.

Trauma-aware and trauma-informed care are ideas that are gaining momentum in regions such as Lebanon. Still, the notion of "saving face," which serves to uphold a family's name and reputation, is dominant within the social narrative, especially among older generations. This frame of reference influences how an individual's mental well-being is perceived and cared for and what resources are available for this purpose. My perspective and the tools I use (which are swayed by my space and place) are not superior to my husband's. Similarly, the ways in which most educators address trauma in U.S. schools is not necessarily better than the way RAEM students' families might be inclined to address it at home. It's key to keep in mind that these perspectives are not in competition with one another. Instead, they are simply different lenses on power interruption and power restoration.

Language: Language is, in part, what sets trauma-informed practice for newcomers apart from more global applications. For example, teachers may encounter fundamental translation issues since trained interpreters are not always available in a parent's language of preference. In addition, for some of the sociolinguistic communities we serve, the language around mental health—especially as it relates to trauma—*simply does not exist.* There is no direct way to translate school-based communications on the topic because there is no accurate vocabulary for it (Acharya et al., 2017; Thiele, 2018).

This is true with many resettled Burmese populations, for example. Many social groups of the region, including the Chin, Karen, and Karenni, are likely to describe mental and emotional distress as physical symptoms (as I saw with Hset Sar Oo, described in Chapter 1). Traumatic distress might be described as a somatic symptom, such as sleeping troubles, headaches, stomach pain, or chest discomfort (Schweitzer, Brough, Vromans, & Asic-Kobe, 2011; Thiele, 2018). In other cases, the language around mental health depicts the most extreme cases of mental disorder, and this vocabulary is often highly charged and deeply stig-matized. I've seen this in the Nepali language and some dialects of Arabic.

As another example, studies on the Somali language and culture shine a light on cultural idioms of distress (e.g., Im, Ferguson, & Hunter 2017). Essen-tially, mental health is only discussed indirectly within the generalized Somali society. Usually, it's communicated via the use of idioms and abstract descrip-tors. We can see how sophisticated these intersections between language and transition shock can be. Language itself is intertwined with vastly different approaches to the human experience and how that experience is perceived within a society.

This is only one reason that it is so imperative that we explore trauma-informed programming within students' unique cultural contexts. In addition, multilingual learners who are new to English require dedicated supports and scaffolds designed to bolster language acquisition. Trauma-informed practice that reaches RAEM students must include appropriate tools and strategies for effectively engaging culturally and linguistically diverse populations.

Culture: The element of culture looks to an individual's deeply embed-ded worldview, which is inherent to that person's core identity. Cultural ref-erence points can sway an individual's encounters with adversity, activating or deactivating specific coping mechanisms used to make sense of that adversity. Thus, culture—and the other points of identity with which culture intersects—profoundly influences intrapersonal and interpersonal mental health concepts.

Here's Rujan:

To a typical citizen who has the comfort and luxury of life in Amer-ica, my life's journey may be viewed as tumultuous and traumatic as it deviates from their traditional standards. For me, my struggles in the past are only a figment and minuscule in size relative to the constant defining battle between life and death many others face out there in the world. From these battles come powerful stories of human suffering and strength.

From a cultural perspective on stress, the concerns of Nepalese people are hardly ever about discussing trauma or stress. It [doesn't serve us] well, or so many people think. To think about these problems does not provide any food on the table or a source of income. In the eyes of many, it certainly does not change your current situation to think about trauma or stress encountered. In short, it is almost taboo to discuss these stresses, and it can be ignored or dealt with very privately.

At the Intersection of Transition Shock and Culture

Although we will touch on all six points of intersection in this book, we'll spend most of our time at the junction of culture and transition shock. RAEM populations are unique in that cultural orientation is a contributing determinant for long-term integration and well-being. Since the cultural backgrounds of newcomer students and their families can be very different from the dominant norms of the new community, misalignments between students' worldviews and educators' perspectives constitute a persistent challenge.

The message here isn't that culturally different views are an unfortunate phenomenon—or even that such discrepancies should be avoided. Quite the opposite. Diverse insights and experiences bring high-powered learning spaces to life.

But there's a caveat. Suppose we fall short in acknowledging and responding to culturally influenced socioacademic cues. In that case, we circumvent the goal that is at the heart of excellent education: to reach and teach all students effectively.

Just as cultural reference points inform the way we approach academic instruction, they also influence ideas related to mental health. For example, culture plays a critical role in how students and their family members identify with, process, and manage intrapersonal well-being. More specifically, a person's worldview—and the language that defines it—shapes how that person processes stress, negotiates with adversity, and self-regulates responses to trauma.

This brings us to the focus of our work together. To best serve all RAEM students, we need to stitch together the pieces of culturally responsive practice and trauma-informed care. We need to become practitioners of stress-mitigating strategies that empower newcomer students by effectively engaging them at their unique cultural-linguistic points of intersectionality.

Before we get there, though, we need to create a foundation of understanding. We can't dive into culturally responsive approaches to trauma-informed care unless we're clear about the very idea of culture itself. So let's take a moment to make sure we've got it right.

As a note, I typically use the following organizers in a professional development setting. However, I've also put them to work in the classroom with kids and young adults. If you have the capacity to have these conversations with students, I'd certainly encourage it. After all, taking time to thoughtfully consider one's own cultural identity can be tremendously power restorative. As Esther Usborne and Roxanne de la Sablonnière (2014) explain:

> Having a clear and confident understanding of one's cultural identity is important for psychological well-being, as it clarifies one's understanding of personal identity. [A] clear cultural identity clarifies one's personal existence by providing a clear normative template, reducing personal uncertainty, providing an individual with a sense of continuity, and buffering an individual against fear. (para. 1)

The Onion of Self-Concept

For a moment, I invite you to zoom out from culture to take in a larger view of student identity. We'll capture this in what I refer to as the "onion of self-concept." The ideas and definitions that make up the onion of self-concept are grounded in the work of sociological scholars, including those who worked extensively with culturally responsive pedagogy: Gloria Ladson-Billings, Geneva Gay, and Zaretta Hammond.

When students enter our schools and classrooms, they each present a richly layered cultural-ethnic identity. Specifically, newcomer students commonly enter our learning spaces with highly dynamic personal identities—and vast funds of knowledge that come with them. As a classroom practitioner committed to a culturally responsive approach, I encountered fragmented pieces of students' cultural-ethnic identities in various aspects of their instructional engagement. The challenge, for me, was in putting those pieces together to create a deeper awareness of the whole child.

To make sense of this, I utilize a graphic organizer made up of concentric circles (Figure 2.1). When I work with adults in a professional development setting (or with students in a class setting), I ask participants to cut out and build this organizer by stapling the bases of the circles together. There is a purpose to this. Performing small, repetitive tasks (such as cutting out the five circles) is one tool for diminishing trauma and anxiety. Meanwhile, the organizer itself is a terrific tool for language learners and is helpful across a wide range of grades and content areas.

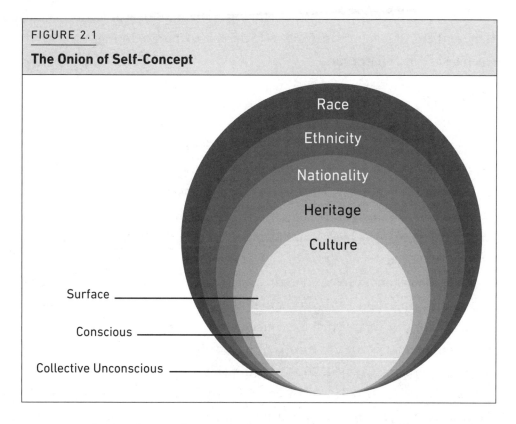

FIGURE 2.1

The Onion of Self-Concept

Let's consider the vocabulary that appears in this organizer. Conversations about identity frequently employ the words *race, ethnicity, nationality, heritage,* and *culture* interchangeably. Of course, this is problematic. After all, they're incredibly different ideas.

When identity values stand in for one another, we end up with a muddled concept of self. This habit also reinforces the human tendency to lump distinctions into tidy categories based on a series of checkboxes. Not only is this type of mental sorting the seed of implicit bias, but it is overly simplistic. Identity is not a tidy tick mark.

Race is vastly different than ethnicity, and heritage is not always a lead-in to culture. Working toward whole-group clarity around these concepts requires a common working language. Although I recognize that this organizer falls short in capturing the extensive and nuanced details of the human experience, I think you'll find that it provides some level of clarity. Most important, it returns us to our main point: that the language of students' cultural-ethnic identities is meaningful and worthy of deeper conversation. Hang in there; this "map" also leads us to the space where culturally responsive teaching and learning occurs.

Race

Race, which occupies the largest circle of our graphic organizer, is a complex concept. There is no consensus about the term's precise meaning (James & Burgos, 2008; National Research Council, 2004). Nevertheless, here's the definition we'll use for *race:* the composite perception and classification of an individual based on physical appearance and assumed geographic ancestry; a mechanism used to facilitate social hierarchies (James & Burgos, 2020; National Research Council, 2004; Snellman, 2007).

Race, then, is an invented construct designed to enhance the social maneuverability of some and diminish that of others (Smedley, 1998). If we look at human history, we can see that the concept of race has been effective at achieving this aim, but the idea of race is at once subjective and overly simplistic (National Research Council, 2004). Historically, majority parties create arbitrary social categories that label those who are different from them. As a result, those categories are filled with identifying descriptors of "otherness," usually based on outward physical characteristics.

Race is also malleable. Racial categories (and their descriptors) differ from one society to another and change over time (Hochschild, 2005). They are susceptible to shifts in power, demographics, and sociopolitical climate. In the United States, race has historically been defined in terms of color, which serve as neat boxes we can check off during an enrollment process or on an application.

There is so much more to our students' stories.

Ethnicity

The idea of ethnicity gets us a bit closer to understanding students on a more authentic level. Ethnicity is more expansive than race, and it both captures the many elements that link a community together and encompasses past and present values of a social group. We describe *ethnicity* thus: an individual's ties to a broader social group as defined by shared language and value systems, including nationality, heritage, and culture.

Ethnicity introduces the element of choice. Even though individuals may be "born into" certain features of ethnicity, they may choose to abandon, adjust, or add to their ethnic identification (Bhopal, 2004; Ruixue & Persson, 2021). The self-determining nature of ethnicity also leaves room for *and:* Cherokee *and* Lakota. Latina *and* Korean. Palestinian *and* French. Igbo *and* Yoruba. Black American *and* white American. Multiethnic. Bilingual. Polyethnic. Multilingual.

This singular aspect of *choice* is what sets race and ethnicity apart. Both are invented concepts, but race often exists as an external social construct placed on individuals by other members of society. These assignments are usually based on outward physical features or behaviors and may be imposed on others without consent or merit. Ethnicity, meanwhile, is often viewed as an internal construct (with external influences) and is more evidently marked by mechanisms of personal choice and affiliation.

Language is also housed here, within ethnicity, and represents an interpersonal exchange between peoples of a country or community. It is also the conduit through which elements of ethnicity (including nationality, heritage, and culture) are expressed (Fought, 2006; Kubota & Lin, 2009).

Nationality

Nationality, heritage, and culture can be viewed as ideas that live under the umbrella of ethnicity and rely on some element of choice. *Nationality* refers to the country where an individual was born, holds citizenship, or identifies as home. This last part of the definition is critical, and it is where the element of personal decision is observable. For example, a student born in Russia but who has lived in the United States since the age of 6 is likely to have a very Americanized worldview and may identify primarily as American, even if her citizenship status does not reflect this. The element of choice also applies to resettled refugees and DREAMers (immigrant children and young adults who may qualify for the Development, Relief, and Education for Alien Minors Act). Second- and third-generation family members who identify with the heritage country as home and Americans who have lived abroad for an extended time may also have complex nationality identities.

Heritage

The idea of heritage has much to do with the place(s) from which one's ancestors originated. Specifically, it looks to the unique cultural and linguistic traits those ancestors subscribed to and includes genetic ties and the values sustained by that group. Thus, an individual may have strong, weak, or neutral links to their ancestral heritage.

To illustrate this, let's meet Rustam, Sara, and Fatima. The three share a Tajikistan heritage connection. Rustam spent his formative years in Tajikistan. He resettled to the United States with refugee status as a young man. In his new Colorado home, he cooks the foods he grew up eating as a child. He regularly video chats "home" to check in with family members who still live there. Although he speaks four languages, including English, he considers Tajik his most vital tongue. Rustam's heritage and ethnicity are deeply intertwined.

Sara is 16 years old. Her grandmother was born in New Jersey, months after Sara's great-grandparents immigrated to the United States from the northern region of Tajikistan (then part of the Turkestan Autonomous Soviet Socialist Republic) for work opportunities. Sara has heard stories about her great-grandparents' adventurous new start, and her friends compliment her "unique" features, but she's never been asked if she's from a different country or culture. Sara isn't familiar with Tajik customs or traditional foods, nor does she speak Tajik. However, her home holds reminders of her heritage: the flag that hangs outside her house, the maps in her father's home office, and the ceramic trivets in the kitchen. Sara and her family take great pride in their ancestral roots but are removed from the day-to-day aspects of their heritage.

Fatima is the youngest of five children. She and her brother are the only two siblings in her family born outside Tajikistan. Her brother Sami was born in a refugee camp in Greece after they fled their home country. Fatima, now 13, joined the family after they'd resettled in Des Moines, Iowa. Fatima's parents have embraced their new surroundings but also hold tight to their Tajik identities. Tajik is spoken freely among Fatima's parents and oldest siblings, but Fatima and Sami prefer English and struggle to communicate in their parents' native language. Fatima understands she has a strong responsibility to honor her parents' wishes, including their Tajik community's social customs and expectations. However, Fatima is accustomed to U.S. cultural norms and often views her parents as strict and old-fashioned. She finds it extremely difficult to balance the traditional expectations of her home and family with what she thinks of as a "normal" American experience. Fatima is closely linked to her heritage, even as that identity intersects and overlaps with her experiences as a teenager in the United States.

As another example, I invite you to peek inside the doors of my home. My heritage is, to an extent, Irish. However, I do not speak Gaelic. I can't name a traditional Irish meal, know very little about the daily norms of Irish cultures, and do not follow the same religious practices as my ancestors. A disconnect is evident. On the other hand, my children hold a solid link to their heritage on their father's side. Both have traditional Arabic names. We speak Lebanese (the Levantine dialect of Arabic) at home; it is, in fact, our kids' first (and so far only) language. We prepare traditional Lebanese foods frequently, observe typical social norms and customs, and spend a significant amount of time in Lebanon. For my children, ethnicity and heritage stand side by side.

Culture

Finally, we arrive at culture. In many ways, this is the most complex value represented in our organizer. Culture is often confused with ethnicity, but if we look carefully, we see that cultural indicators are nested *within* the dynamic of ethnicity. I sometimes think of them as the architectural beams of one's ethnic identity.

Before we move further into this idea, let's take a moment to acknowledge that culture plays out in innumerable ways in the United States. Therefore, we need to sharpen our focus and center RAEMs in our lessons and discoveries regarding culture. Yes, the concepts we're examining can be applied widely (and optimally once we're in the habit of meeting *all* students as their culturally authentic selves). For now, though, let's become great at affirming the cultural integrity of our newcomer students.

With that in mind, *culture* relates to the specific combinations of socially acquired ideas, arts, symbols, and habits that make up one's day-to-day existence and influence social interchange. Whereas ethnicity captures overarching themes that define a society, culture refers to the specific markers and material emphases of that ethnic group or its subgroups (Ladson-Billings, 1994; Prinz, 2020).

Culture has other attributes that set it apart from race, ethnicity, nationality, and heritage. Namely, it is not exclusively defined by outward physical features. Culture is also a fluid property and primarily determined by personal choice. Cultural alignments may be changed, shared, or acquired. Any person may pick up another's culture at any time; and a person's culture is highly likely to change over time—in whole or in part—based on new experiences, interests, and social influences.

Hip-hop culture is one example of this. What combination of socially acquired ideas, arts, symbols, and habits are collectively unifying within this space? A shared code of music? Fashion? Styles of greeting or interacting with one another? A language that is unique to the group? With an enormous global influence, hip-hop is arguably one the most "picked up" cultures.

This, of course, also opens doorways to cultural appropriation—or the adoption of one person's culture by another, especially when that culture is assumed by a member of the dominant social majority. Fordham law professor Susan Scafidi (2005) defines *cultural appropriation* as

> Taking intellectual property, traditional knowledge, cultural expressions, or artifacts from someone else's culture without permission. This can include unauthorized use of another culture's dance, dress, music, language, folklore, cuisine, traditional medicine, religious symbols, etc. It's most likely to be harmful when the source community is a minority group that has been oppressed or exploited in other ways or when the object of appropriation is particularly sensitive, e.g., sacred objects. (p. 9)

Let's walk back for a moment and recall how we got here. In exploring cultural identity, we moved from the external social construct of race into the areas of ethnicity, heritage, nationality, and culture. Now, to reach the space where culturally responsive teaching and learning occur, we must tunnel down deeper still and portion out elements of culture into three distinct layers: surface, conscious, and the collective unconscious (Hall, 1977; Hammond, 2014; Hollie, 2011).

Surface culture is tangible and refers to observable markers inclusive of fashion, food, slang, art, holidays, literature, games, and music. In our classrooms, surface culture commonly manifests in the use of multicultural artifacts. Generally speaking, the intended outcome is to appeal to diverse groups of students, draw them in, and create a sense of welcoming and inclusivity.

Conscious culture looks to the governing rules and norms of a community. These values are usually explicitly taught and evoke social repercussions if not adhered to. Examples of conscious culture include expectations regarding eye contact, concepts of time, personal space, accepted emotions, and gender norms.

Collective unconscious culture is at the very core of one's worldview. It houses mechanisms used to process time, people, spaces, and events that constitute one's existence. Essentially, the collective unconscious helps us make sense of the world and our place within it. Spirituality, kinship, norms of completion (e.g., the sense of urgency assigned to work over social engagement), and the importance of group identity are all part of this layer.

We're here! We've made it!

This—the collective unconscious—is where culturally responsive teaching and learning occurs. And it is where a culturally relevant approach to trauma-informed care is born (Gay, 2018; Hammond, 2014).

Collective Unconscious Culture and RAEM Populations

In many schools and districts across the United States, RAEM students are underserved or inadequately served (Ruiz-de-Velasco, Fix, & Clewell, 2000). This is due, in large part, to gaps in teacher preparedness. Even as classroom landscapes are becoming more diverse, relatively few teachers possess the specialized training and cultural awareness to engage multicultural student populations effectively (Ballantyne, Sanderman, & Levy, 2008; Henkin, 2019). Historically, educator training programs have not placed much urgency on RAEM programming—a trend that has left many teachers underprepared to address the demographic realities of their classrooms (Gay, 2002; Henkin, 2019; McHugh & Doxsee, 2018).

Helena Henkin (2019), writing for the University of San Francisco, provides some background:

> Many American teachers are white, middle-class, and lack cultural awareness," she explains. "This poses a problem because such teachers are not able to 1) build on students' prior knowledge, 2) build relationships with students of different cultures, or 3) understand the diversity of social identities among their students. When teachers lack these skills, there is a cultural mismatch, and students will not learn. (pp. 9–10)

This mismatch is the central focus of culturally responsive pedagogy (CRP), which was introduced by Gloria Ladson-Billings more than two decades ago. The strategy is two-fold: train teachers to recognize students' unique cultural frames of reference and use that knowledge to shape the messaging of instruction so it can be better received by the students for whom it is intended to reach (Ladson-Billings, 1994).

One of the pioneers of the culturally responsive approach, Geneva Gay, describes *culture* as a set of filters that we apply in making sense of even our most mundane experiences. In a video interview with *Learning for Justice* (formerly Teaching Tolerance), Gay (2014) explains a central focus of CRP: "It is [the] incompatibility between the cultural filters that are used to *send* instructional messages to students—coming from the school's frame of reference—and when kids from different ethnic backgrounds are trying to *receive* what we send from school from *another* set of cultural filters." If these filters don't match up, we may not be getting anywhere.

More specifically, culturally responsive pedagogy looks to those deeply embedded elements of worldview—group identity, kinship, norms of completion, spirituality, and so on—to effectively reach and teach students. Dr. Jacqueline Jordan Irvine, a professor of urban education at Emory University, appears alongside Gay in the *Learning for Justice* video series. She urges us to remember that every student enters the learning space with existing cultural identities and embedded cultural funds of knowledge. Effective practice builds on this prior cultural knowledge, "making connections between what is known and what is to be taught or understood."

Gay (2002), who has long championed culturally responsive education, explains that culturally responsive teachers learn to recognize the internal structure of ethnic learning styles, which include at least eight key dimensions. They are

- Preferred content.
- Ways of working through learning tasks.
- Techniques for organizing and conveying ideas and thoughts.
- Physical and social settings for task performance.
- Structural arrangements of work, study, and performance space.
- Perceptual stimulation for receiving, processing, and demonstrating comprehension and competence.
- Motivations, incentives, and rewards for learning.
- Interpersonal interactional styles.

As you can see, CRP has a broad and influential reach. Here, we'll pull out some specific elements of these dimensions that are most relevant to the unique cultural identities and experiences of recently arrived learners. These five culturally influenced learning structures frequently appear in RAEM classrooms:

- Transmission of information through storytelling and language. *Key dimensions: techniques for organizing and conveying ideas and thoughts; ways of working through learning tasks.*
- Orientation of oneself to others. *Key dimensions: interpersonal interactional styles; ways of working through learning tasks; structural arrangements of work, study, and performance space.*
- Social standing. *Key dimensions: interpersonal interactional styles; motivations, incentives, and rewards for learning; structural arrangements of work, study, and performance space.*
- Recall devices. *Key dimension: techniques for organizing and conveying ideas and thoughts.*
- Education of the young. *Key dimensions: preferred content; perceptual stimulation for receiving, processing, and demonstrating comprehension and competence.*

Transmission of information through storytelling and language refers to the practice of communicating important information through the processes of speaking and listening. Vocal tradition and storytelling, for example, are highlighted within this learning structure. Information transmission is one of our oldest and most reliable cultural attributes. For as long as we've had language, humans have been communicating and making sense of the world through the use of stories.

Many of us are, to some varying degree, removed from this aspect of our deep culture. However, many newcomer students maintain strong connections to an oral tradition and storytelling (even though they may rest at the unconscious level). Let's look at the lives of three 6th graders in a Phoenix classroom to see how and where culturally influenced transmission of information shows up for them.

Aya has always wanted to be a storyteller like her *teta* (grandmother). She grew up hearing passed-down tales at home, but Aya most loved watching her teta's performances in the community. In Syria, storytelling is considered an art form and a valuable living tradition (Cartier, 2018; Cultural Heritage Without Borders, 2020). Aya's teta remains in Syria, hoping for reunification with her children and grandchildren in the United States. In the meantime, the family has established bonds within Phoenix's Arab community. Once a month, they attend a storytelling circle, where women from the community narrate traditional stories for an audience. These events are the one thing that most remind Aya of her home in Syria.

Shar Min's family is originally from Myanmar, although his only memories before settling in Arizona are of a refugee camp in Thailand. Shar Min recalls shopkeepers telling stories in the hopes of drawing potential customers inside. Additionally, much of Shar Min's early education was verbally relayed by his mother, older siblings, or the teacher who sometimes set up inside the camp. Lessons were often delivered via folktales, rote memorization, or apprenticeship (Charmarik, 1999). Shar Min's parents held to a belief that other members of their cultural community reinforced: that storytelling is a skill of the laboring class, such as the shopkeeper drawing in customers. In Phoenix, Shar Min's parents expressed disapproval of their son writing fiction stories at school, as they did not perceive it as having educational value. Even though a verbal tradition is a deeply embedded facet of their culture, their lived experiences within that culture influenced their views.

Josephina's family immigrated to the United States from Nigeria so her father could pursue a master's degree at Arizona State University. Three months after the move, each family member appeared to have readily adjusted to the new home and community. They had jobs, went to school, and had established a circle of American friends. Inside their home, the Nigerian cultural influence was still very much alive. One part of Josephina's home experience always stood out to her. It seemed to her that virtually every aspect of her life was imprinted with a proverb. Her father, especially, seemed to have a saying for every occasion: a lesson, an explanation, a joke, a piece of advice. At school, these short messages would often come to mind as her teacher lectured in class. *Make hay while the sun shines. Add up the miles after the race is finished. The wheat can't grow taller than the farmer.* Josephina often wanted to share these proverbs as a way of demonstrating understanding, but she hadn't heard anyone else in class speak like this and was shy about responding in this way. Still, this culturally infused path to comprehension was inseparable from her school experience.

Orientation of oneself to others speaks to how social traditions or expectations influence interpersonal behaviors. Collectivism—rather than individualism—is one such orientation that is common in RAEM settings. The African continent, as one example, is made up of thousands of cultural subsets. Speaking broadly, "The Africanist perspective is more about community; it's more about collaboration," explains African American literary professor Neal Lester. "It's less about what we can do individually. [This is] a certain worldview that challenges Western individualism" (Goldberg, 2016).

In U.S. classrooms, we may see a student's collectivist nature play out in a tendency to favor group work over independent study or as a desire to participate in "jobs" or responsibilities that benefit the whole class. Collectivism can also deter students from wanting to stand out or feel like they are the center of attention. By paying attention to the various ways students (and their families) orient themselves to others, we are better equipped to shape the learning experience in culturally responsive ways.

Social standing has to do with perceptions about a person and/or that person's aligned networks based on socially held norms and values. As one example of this, the concept of "saving face" references a binding, unspoken code of honor within a shared social group. Each individual, in essence, acts as an agent of the whole. Thus, perceived individual failures reflect poorly on the cohesive family name—or even on the broader community group. Similarly, excellence and recognition usher in respect and high social standing for the entire unit. Students who hold this lens may be less likely to volunteer information in class and may feel uncomfortable being put on the spot for fear of negatively representing the broader social unit to which they belong.

Recall devices are deeply embedded aspects of culture that enhance memory and preserve critical funds of knowledge, including key historical events and records of lineage. Traditional recall devices differ among societies, but certain features frequently appear across multiple cultures. These include, for example, the use of rhythm, song, gamification, mnemonics, and vision boards to aid in retention and recollection.

The first time I saw recall devices authentically at work was at a high school in Morogoro, Tanzania. It's a school I founded in partnership with local residents and teachers in 2011. It continues to graduate students (all of whom face economic barriers that prevent them from attending government school) each year.

Though the curriculum introduces elements of West-based learning, such as group work and project-based learning, the school's headmaster has opted for a traditional operations model. Students spend most of the day seated in tidy, differential rows with a teacher at the front of the classroom. These blocks of desk learning are broken up by spurts of highly interactive engagement. Much of this time occurs outside, with students clapping, stomping, drumming, and singing together.

In my earliest days at the school, I mistakenly read these sessions as break time. Yet, despite outward appearances (from my West-based lens), it is also a time of incredible productivity. For example, students might recall steps to a problem through song or act out a story through dramatic play, poetry, art, or call-and-response. Remarkably, students lead much of this process and make the day's learning concrete in their minds by creating and sharing recall devices. Teachers or administrators do not interrupt these creative sessions—even impromptu dance competitions—except to correct knowledge or misinformation.

Weeks after a taught lesson, I'd revisit a previous topic of study. Within seconds, the group would be in chorus, recalling the pertinent information in the unique form they'd preserved it (say, by stomping out a pattern or reciting a poem they'd created together). This was an incredible learning experience for me—one that I carry into each learning group I enter.

Take a moment to consider: Where do recall devices already exist within the learning landscape of your classroom? Where else could they fit in meaningful and relevant ways?

Education of the young includes ideas and practices that take different shapes across cultural and subcultural landscapes. For example, inside this area of ethnic influence, we may encounter concepts such as perceived levels of rigor, norms around coed learning, the school's role in ensuring discipline, parents' roles in their child's education, and expectations for what the school experience should look like. "Wander-and-explore" emphases, which rely on curiosity and inquiry as valid mechanisms for growth and learning, are an illustration of this.

Return with me for a moment to that school in Tanzania, and I'll explain. Walking around the community, I'd see young people of all ages engaging freely with the world around them. They'd bind and kick a homemade soccer ball, invent games, investigate lizards and broken radios, and build towers out of found materials. By and large, this exploration carried on without the direct and persistent supervision of an adult.

I'm not at all suggesting that these children were irresponsibly neglected. Indeed, the agency and freedom these young folks had to move about their environment was grounded in knowing they were fundamentally cared for. Should someone fall and become injured, a passing *mzee* (village elder) would pick the child up and dust them off. Should someone behave poorly, an auntie (by relation or otherwise) would step in to correct the negative behavior. Should someone become hungry or thirsty, there were no reservations about entering the nearest friend's home and eating what was (almost certainly) offered.

Of course, this all requires community investment. In Swahili, this is explained as *goti moja halimlei mtoto* ("One knee doesn't bring up a child"). No matter who a child's parents are, everyone is responsible for their upbringing. When young people feel safe and protected by the adults in their sphere— even adults with whom they do not have a direct personal relationship—they are freer to engage in discovery without compromising their self-preservation. This also requires a social pact, of sorts, that places value on learning through doing.

Many world cultures place high regard on exploration and experience as a pathway to and through learning. As we'll see, when viewed through an asset lens, these reference points can be invaluable learning strengths. They can also inform some of our culturally responsive practices, including those we employ to restore trauma-interrupted power.

Where Can I Use CRP in My Classroom?

Culturally responsive teaching and learning engage students in ways that draw from critical cues of the collective unconscious. The good news is that you likely already implement some best practices that speak to deep-level culture. What may be less evident is where and how those practices align to effective culturally responsive teaching. Moving forward, we should aim for greater clarity and intention as we craft meaningful learning experiences for RAEMs.

Take a moment to review the learning structures discussed in this chapter, as well as the corresponding instructional moves (Figure 2.2). We will refer back to this figure as we progress through our work together.

FIGURE 2.2
Culturally Influenced Learning Structures

Structure	Instructional Moves
Transmission of information through storytelling and language	cooperative structures, journaling, extended listening, animated retelling, digital storytelling, story-based word problems, guest speakers
Orientation of oneself to others	small-group work, flexible seating, shared group success, helpfulness, "jobs"
Social standing	team problem-solving, anonymous responses (e.g., PearDeck), "ready-to-respond" cues
Recall devices	gamification, rhythm, song, "memory palace," mnemonics, *lukasa*
Education of the young	inquiry, project-based learning, STEM, mind mapping, sensory learning

Where Do We Go from Here?

In this chapter, we

- Took time to clarify who RAEM students are.
- Created a common language around student identity.

- Established a baseline understanding of culturally responsive practice.
- Examined what culturally responsive teaching might look like in the classroom.

Chapter 3 continues to lay the foundation for our strategies and activities and helps us better understand social-emotional learning (SEL) and its relationship to trauma-informed practice.

Understanding the Link to
Social-Emotional Learning

So far, we've established an understanding of transition shock and explored some of how culture can influence our approach to trauma-informed care. Now we'll explore one final component: social-emotional learning (SEL).

Successful trauma-informed interventions weave SEL skills into their fabric. However, it is imperative to note that SEL and trauma-informed care are separate pedagogical concepts. The differences between the two are reflected in the processes, tools, strategies, and intended student outcomes associated with each.

A trauma-informed approach focuses on creating safe spaces in which all students—especially those affected by adverse experiences—can learn and grow. Trauma-aware educators actively manipulate the environment to minimize the chances of initiating the brain's alarm system. Meanwhile, SEL focuses on improving students' intrapersonal and interpersonal relationships by developing targeted skill sets. Although SEL strategies can enhance efforts to mitigate transition shock in the classroom, a SEL approach primarily concentrates on students' internal management systems, including those that enable them to engage in meaningful, cooperative relationships.

In a whole-child context, trauma-informed care and SEL share considerable overlap. Both pedagogies are rooted in the idea that students learn when their core intrapersonal needs are met. Additionally, both approaches endorse the ideals of safety, trust, and personal development, which in turn foster self-regulation and healthy social interchange. Ultimately, both trauma-informed instruction and SEL drive academic, prosocial, and intrinsic well-being, even as they take separate paths toward this outcome.

What Is SEL?

At its core, social-emotional learning "focuses on a set of social, emotional, behavioral, and character skills that support success in school, the workplace, relationships, and the community" (Frey, Fisher, & Smith, 2019, p. 2). Tim Conklin, author of *Social and Emotional Learning in Middle School* (2014), condenses these ideas. "It's based on a fairly simple idea," he writes. "Students who are better able to understand and manage their own emotions while interacting constructively with others will be better learners" (p. 5).

Many schools and districts look to the definition of SEL introduced by the Collaborative for Academic, Social, and Emotional Learning (CASEL), which has been championing the academic integration of social-emotional learning since 1994. CASEL defines SEL as "the process through which children and adults understand and manage emotions, set and achieve positive goals, feel and show empathy for others, establish and maintain positive relationships, and make responsible decisions" (CASEL District Resource Center, 2020).

CASEL, as part of its framework for social-emotional teaching and learning, identifies five core competencies students should have opportunities to practice and observe at school, at home, and within the community. "These competencies are thought to facilitate students' academic performance, positive social behaviors, and social relationships during the school years; reduce behavior problems and psychological distress; and help to prepare young people to succeed in college, work, family, and society" (Mahoney, Durlak & Weissberg, para. 4).

The five core competencies, according to CASEL, are

- **Self-Awareness:** A developed cognizance and understanding of one's thoughts, emotions, strengths, shortcomings, and value systems, as well as the ability to manifest confidence and operate from a growth mindset.

- **Self-Management:** The capacity to set and pursue goals, harness motivation, practice self-discipline, negotiate stress, and self-regulate thoughts, emotions, and behaviors in various situations.
- **Responsible Decision-Making:** The ability to identify, analyze, and evaluate situational elements—including culture, context, safety, consequences, expected norms, and possible implications for others—and to modify behaviors and interactions accordingly.
- **Relationship Skills:** The capacity to establish and maintain positive and diverse social relationships by implementing elements of healthy prosocial exchange, including proficient communication and collaboration skills, conflict resolution techniques, and the ability to ask for help when needed.
- **Social Awareness:** The ability to acknowledge multiple perspectives, experience empathy for others, recognize and honor diversity, consider social and ethical norms, and assess existing and potential systems of support.

Why SEL?

The research on SEL is promising. Studies show that as students develop proficiency across the five core competencies, they are more likely to experience improved behavioral outcomes (Shechtman & Yaman, 2012). In addition, consistent, high-quality SEL programming in schools also correlates with reduced incidences of bullying, truancy, aggression, substance abuse, and documented behavioral infractions (Durlak, Weissberg, Dymnicki, Taylor, & Schellinger, 2011; Organisation for Economic Co-operation and Development [OECD], 2015, 2018).

Social-emotional literacy can also improve cognitive functioning and lead to long-term academic gains (Greenberg, 2006; Mahoney et al., 2018). Unfortunately, the reverse is also true: SEL skill deficiencies can impair cognitive operation (OECD, 2019).

Students with a robust command of SEL skills are more likely to demonstrate grit, or the ability to persevere through adversity (Aronson, Fried, &

Good, 2002). This may be due, in part, to the fact that targeted social-emotional learning emphasizes problem-solving and responsible decision-making. Learners with highly developed SEL skill sets are highly likely to set high academic goals, have self-discipline, motivate themselves, manage their stress, and organize their approach to work, learn more, and get better grades (Duckworth & Seligman, 2005; Elliot & Dweck, 2005). Further, new research suggests that SEL practice may improve cognitive-affect regulation in the prefrontal cortex, effectively boosting central executive cognitive functions, such as inhibitory control, planning, and organization (Greenberg, 2006).

Let's quickly revisit the distinction between SEL and trauma-informed instruction. The former is directly concerned with helping students manage their internal environment so they are better equipped to engage in productive relationships with others. The latter focuses on eliminating external triggers and creating safe spaces to avoid power interruptions or restore power where disruptions have already occurred.

Here's how they fit together. The *processes* involved in developing social-emotional learning can enhance the *practices* that facilitate trauma-informed care. Students who are successful at regulating their emotions have more agency to engage with others in constructive ways. Of course, collaborative and prosocial behaviors also lend themselves to a productive learning environment, which circles back to the objective of trauma-informed care.

It may be easier now to see how the two approaches are complementary. Together, they are particularly effective at activating coping skills, enhancing a healthy school culture and climate, and promoting equity. Pawlo and her team write, "To a large extent, the basic tenets of SEL overlap with the principles of trauma-informed instruction. Where they have differed are on questions of intensity—both the intensity of the stress children are experiencing and the intensity of the instruction required to help them" (Pawlo, Lorenzo, Eichert, & Ellis, 2019, para. 3).

Establishing a SEL Focus for This Work: Self-Regulation

Social-emotional learning is a vast landscape. It is beyond the scope of this book to explore all that SEL has to offer. Instead, as mentioned, I've narrowed the field of vision to embrace the area of competency that best highlights and supports our work in mitigating transition shock. Each of the SEL strategies introduced in this book supports power restoration. More specifically, they promote self-regulation—or governing oneself within the parameters of social norms and expectations (without external intervention).

I've chosen this element of SEL with my mind on the understanding that power interruptions can short-circuit one's ability to self-regulate (Dvir, Ford, Hill, & Frazier, 2014). Fortunately, internal governance strategies need to be explicitly taught, modeled, and practiced. And, as we've already mentioned, when young people can self-regulate, the classroom environment (the focus of trauma-informed practice) becomes more power restorative.

However, keep in mind that self-regulation may be exhausting, especially for kids with limited prior exposure to self-regulation strategies. Students may need to build up self-regulatory stamina gradually within a secure, stable environment. We can also help youth grow their social and emotional reservoirs by scaffolding the use of self-regulation strategies. Eventually, kids learn to activate these "powers" independently.

The Four *R*s of Self-Regulation

In a school context, internally managed (though sometimes externally activated) self-regulation falls into four broad categories. We'll refer to these as the four *R*s of self-regulation: root, resource, reach, and reduce.

Root: Rooting (or "grounding") techniques attract and keep individuals in the present. Trauma-affected students are highly likely to spend large portions of their thinking day either in the past or the present, reliving old traumas or imagining new ones (SAMHSA, 2014). Grounding exercises help to restore power by "rooting" down into the present moment.

Rooting is one of the ways we can work to counter dissociation, which is common in those with histories of complex transition shock. For example, the National Child Traumatic Stress Network (NCTSN) describes dissociation in this way:

When children encounter an overwhelming and terrifying experience, they may dissociate, or mentally separate themselves from the experience. They may perceive themselves as detached from their bodies, on the ceiling, or somewhere else in the room watching what is happening to their bodies. They may feel like they are in a dream or some altered state that is not quite real or as if the experience is happening to someone else. Or they may lose all memories or sense of the experiences having happened to them, resulting in gaps in time or even gaps in their personal history. At its extreme, a child may cut off or lose touch with various aspects of the self. (NCTSN, 2019, para. 10)

Once dissociation gains traction as a learned defense mechanism, it can quickly evolve into an automatic response to stress. This "checking out" may be perceived as a lack of interest, inattention, aloofness, defiance, or daydreaming—states of being that can adversely influence school performance and relationship building. The NCTSN (2019) reminds us that "dissociation can affect a child's ability to be fully present in activities of daily life and can significantly fracture a child's sense of time and continuity" (para. 11) Rooting activities, therefore, help restore psychological and physiological self-awareness.

Resource: Perceived danger activates the stress response. In the broadest context, this is a regular and natural occurrence. Once the stimulus has ended, the brain sends a message to the physiological self to resume a state of normalcy. Breathing slows, a rapid heartbeat subsides, and the focus moves away from the perceived threat.

Neuroception is a term used to describe how neural circuits distinguish between people or situations that are safe, dangerous, or life-threatening. Trauma-affected individuals may experience disruptions in these circuits (Porges, 2004). Either the "all clear" message fails to send or it gets lost in translation, creating the dilemma of being stuck in the flight-flight-freeze-submit state. As a result, the physical body remains agitated while the mind becomes hyperfocused on the element of threat.

Neuroceptive strategies help "turn down" the threat dial through practiced self-awareness. Resourcing is a neuroceptive strategy. That is, it empowers an individual to (1) identify and choose from viable calming options and (2) learn to access and implement those tools during periods of anxiety. Ultimately, these capacities are associated with resilience (Roipel, 2021).

What does resourcing look like? A resource is anything, anyone, or any-where that lights you up, helps you feel safe, helps you calm down when you are stressed, makes your belly happy, warms your heart, or feels like home. In short, "resources" are internal or external safe spaces that can be accessed throughout the day and that bring a sense of calm order, especially in moments of distress. In a classroom, these can be physical safe spaces or areas of the room that are intentionally purposed zones for calming and refocusing. They can also be inward-focusing strategies that are explicitly taught and practiced at school.

Here are some guiding questions for resourcing:

- Is there a place in the classroom or school that makes you feel calm or safe (e.g., by a window, close to a door, in the classroom library)?
- Whom in the school building do you trust or feel relaxed around?
- What types of activities make you feel happiest and most free from stress?
- What habits or routines help you manage anxiety (e.g., counting to 10, rocking, listening to music, writing, engaging in physical exertion)?
- Can you think of a positive memory or people in your life who bring you to a place of calm, safety, or happiness?
- What physical objects signal relaxation or joy for you (e.g., an article of clothing, a special rock, a memento)?

Reach: Reach calls for physical movement or ways to reach for something tangible to help mitigate stress. Some power interruptions respond well to an intentional, self-selected physical stimulus (e.g., self-holding, Velcro strips under the desktop, exercise balls in place of a chair, small tactile objects to hold or manipulate while working). Exercise can also counter the negative effects of trauma (Rosenbaum et al., 2015).

Movements that incorporate "crossing the midline" are especially benefi-cial (Tripp, 2016). In crossing midline (also called *the bilateral coordination*), we have a set of imaginary lines that divide the body into horizontal and vertical halves (Spokane Regional Health District, 2019). Crossing midline movements cross over from one quadrant to another (say, right elbow to left knee, left hand to right shoulder, or right hand to left foot). Some studies show exceptional promise for exercise and bilateral coordination in resolving transition shock among refugee populations (Budde, Akko, Ainamani, Murillo-Rodríguez, & Weierstall, 2018).

Reduce: Reducing is a slowing-down process that allows individuals to self-manipulate the pace at which they process their trauma. Reducing minimizes the intensity and momentum of specific triggers, creating a space to negotiate small, bite-sized pieces of distress. In this way, it may be possible to process upset in manageable strides. Heidi Hanson (2018) writes, "Titration / Slowing and Portioning is so important because—if you think about it—one key characteristic of trauma is having *too much* come *too fast*. So, titration is doing the exact opposite of what trauma does; it deliberately reverses *too much, too fast* by enacting *a little bit, slowly*" (para. 7).

Titration, or the conscious act of slowing down, offers a range of benefits (Khan 2014). It requires a physical reaction to a stimulus—which automatically engages the senses. When the senses are engaged, mind/body integration is within reach. Slowing also helps constructively direct this state of heightened alertness. Often, we begin by focusing on a single, repetitive movement and eventually progress to concentrating on a specific thought or problem. Expected outcomes of reducing include

- Increased focus and concentration.
- Diminished responses to external stimuli.
- Increased openness to new thoughts and ideas.
- Negotiation of unresolved trauma.
- Protection against retraumatization.
- Reparation of neural functions and rhythms.

Does SEL Overlap with Culturally Responsive Practice?

It's an often-asked question. The honest answer is no.

Let me back up. It *can* overlap but very often doesn't. Unfortunately, social-emotional learning, "done poorly and without a deep understanding, can be not only ineffective but actively harmful" (Devaney, 2020, para. 3). Before we go any further, I'd like to introduce a few different experts on the subject who offer plenty for us to consider. I invite you to think and reflect critically about these passages as you read them:

> Social-emotional learning (SEL) skills can help us build communities that foster courageous conversations across [human] differences so that our students can confront injustice, hate, and inequity. . . . However, educators often teach SEL absent of the larger sociopolitical context, which is fraught with injustice and inequity and affects our students' lives.
>
> Recoiling from topics that divide us—when SEL skills could help us get along better—diminishes SEL's promise. . . . We can no longer avoid discussing topics that make us uncomfortable. Our students, incessantly inundated with divisive rhetoric and reports of premeditated acts of violence (or even themselves targets of violence), don't have that luxury. (Simmons, 2019, paras. 3–4, 6, 8)
>
> Many resources designed to promote students' social and emotional learning (SEL) do not take race into account. By failing to acknowledge students' racial and cultural diversity, "colorblind" SEL programs, which are de facto grounded in the norms and expectations of white culture, can imply that the differences that emerge from students' diverse backgrounds are deficits. Further, by ignoring the ways that systemic racism can affect students' development of SEL skills, these programs imply that the social and emotional challenges that students do encounter are the result of individual shortcomings, rather than the byproduct of oppression. (Caven, 2020, para. 2)
>
> We can't tell Black kids to take 10 deep breaths when people who look like them are dying because they can't breathe. . . . To create the impact they desire, schools must face a clear reality. It is not possible for a person to be racist and socially emotionally well. If schools acknowledge the systemic bias in our country, they have a unique opportunity to use social emotional learning as a tool for social justice and racial equity. (Weaver, 2020, paras. 11, 14)

I have been noticing an unfortunate trend among some of the educators—and other practitioners and scholars in the SEL field: When they describe how students of color behaved before they participated in an SEL program, they tend to use words like "rowdy," "misguided," "disengaged," and "violent," as if to highlight the urgent need for SEL programs for "these kids."

In other words, they frame SEL as a sort of savior—one that transforms students of color from being unmotivated, loud, lazy, and uninterested students into motivated individuals suddenly enthusiastic about school and quiet enough to learn. (Simmons, 2017, paras. 2–3)

What comes to mind when you read these passages? What holes or contradictions do they reveal about the implementation of social-emotional learning in our classrooms and schools? I think we can agree that there's a lot of work yet to be done. Many of these conversations are still very fresh—there's no rule book yet. As we work together toward more culturally affirmative interpretations of SEL, I propose we begin with these first steps:

- **Check our narrative.** Look for broad, sweeping statements about students or student groups, disempowering words or phrases, and patterns of thinking that perpetuate attitudes inconsistent with sociocultural affirmation. Keep in mind that SEL practices are not a targeted approach to "fixing" certain groups of students. Instead, they are tools to help *all* students engage in proactive ways with others across the various platforms, issues, and social constructs that are persistent in their actual lives.

- **Challenge our biases.** Implicit and explicit biases color the way we see students. They can also drive how we show up in the SEL space. This means that "teachers really need to understand themselves, recognize their power and privilege and identity, and what that means in the work that they do and the people with whom they often work" (Madda, 2019, para. 19).

- **Clarify our context.** Much of the criticism related to current SEL implementation has to do with its lack of a sociopolitical context. When SEL is taught in isolation from the events that shape students' day-to-day lives, it loses relevance and becomes less applicable within the context of their lived experiences. When SEL is taught in ways that only reflect the perspective of the teacher or school, the content of those lessons is at risk of becoming harmful to the cultural identities of RAEMs and other marginalized populations. In short, SEL devoid of culturally affirming practices and understanding is not SEL at all.

SEL skills must be taught in a relevant context, especially when uncomfortable conversations about systemic racism, gun violence, homophobia, xenophobia, and white supremacy are likely to occur. By teaching SEL alongside students' authentically lived experiences, we can "not only prepare our students to engage civically and peacefully across [our] differences, but also to become the change makers and leaders we need" (Simmons, 2019, para. 8).

- **Forge new pathways toward culturally affirmative SEL practices.** Pedagogically speaking, culturally affirmative SEL is still in its infancy. This means we all need to have our eyes on the topic; we are all responsible for shaping it into something that better aligns with the actual lives of diverse groups of students, including newcomers. Elizabeth Devaney (2020), director of the Whole Child Connection at the Children's Institute in New York, details the organization's internal conversations and reflections about expanding CASEL's five social-emotional competencies:
  — Should SEL's self-awareness features explicitly address concepts related to racial identity to the extent that students of color understand the implications of systemic oppression, and white students recognize both the positive and harmful implications of inherent privilege?
  — Should self-regulation make space for examining how lived experiences of racism, discrimination, and oppression influence our students' root thoughts and behaviors?
  — Do the ideas of "appreciating diversity" and "perspective-taking" reach far enough in cultivating true respect for one another's cultural and ethnic diversity and an urgency to dismantle racist systems?
  — Should a focus on building relationship skills also explore how our own biases can influence intersocial exchange? Are students truly prepared for the types of courageous conversations that lead to deep relationships?

Culturally Affirmative Check for the Four *R*s of Self-Regulation

As you strive to implement SEL practices that are relevant to the lived experiences of your students, consider the following as you work through the four *R*s:

- Who is centered in our work when we teach SEL skills?
- Teaching students of color and speakers of other languages self-regulation strategies cannot will away the challenges of systemic injustices they face in their daily lives. How can we begin to think more critically about SEL curricula with regard to relevance, access, and equity?

Where Do We Go from Here?

In this chapter, we

- Differentiated between trauma-informed care and social-emotional learning.
- Grouped SEL strategies into categories, which we named the four *R*s.
- Opened the door to exploring inequities and injustices that seep into SEL work.
- In the coming chapters, we'll put together everything we've learned so far. We'll take what we know about best practices for serving RAEM populations—including culturally responsive pedagogy—and apply it toward our goal of restoring students' innate power in the classroom setting. Let's go!

Connect:
Beginning with Relationships

Social connection is not only power restorative; it's central to the resolution of transition shock (NCTSN, 2018; Siegel, 2012). Therefore, our goal should be to introduce more opportunities for social connection. It's a simple solution, right?

Sort of.

I mean, the intent is certainly reasonable, except for one troublesome hurdle: power interruptions complicate social connectivity. Why? Because the presence of transition shock (and its effects) interferes with one's ability to establish and maintain positive relationships (Beck, Grant, Clapp, & Palyo, 2009; Nietlisbach, Maercker, Rössler, & Haker, 2010).

When we talk about social connections, we're speaking to the idea of relationship-building. We're talking about authentic and meaningful exchanges with (and between) students that are rooted in receptivity, empathy, constructive conversations, and invested partnerships. To enjoy this level of connection, a person has to exercise vulnerability, positive risk-taking, and a whole set of prosocial skills.

Exactly how does transition shock disrupt social connectivity? First, students with a history of adverse life experiences are more likely to struggle with ambiguity (Hamm, 2017). In fact, "unknowns," such as new people or situations with unclear outcomes, can trigger survival mechanisms (those physiological reactions we refer to as fight-flight-freeze-or-submit). Additionally, power interruptions can leave kids feeling discouraged, self-defeated, or angry with others.

Trust also has a hand in connectivity. Unfortunately, some trauma-affected youth do not receive robust and consistent adult support necessary for healing. Some of their interactions with adults have even been damaging. Relationships with adults or authority figures that are nonexistent, inconsistent, inauthentic, unpredictable, or toxic can diminish a young person's ability to engage in trusting connections with others.

Additionally, unresolved traumas evolve in complexity. As this happens, kids and teens may detach themselves from existing bonds with adults without forming new ones to replace them. Every unstable or unhealthy tie a young person has with an adult attachment figure embeds this message into the child's thinking: *Do not trust or put your faith in other people, especially grown-ups. They will let you down.*

What's the path to power restoration? "In the science of resiliency," writes Ron Huxley (2018), "the relationship is how we tip the scale from negative to positive outcomes. One healing relationship in a chaos of trauma can provide enough emotional strength for a child or adult to survive" (para 11). In fact, across the vast landscape of research on child trauma and healing, relationships take center stage. They are often referred to as the "agents of change" in shifting the momentum from an orientation of loss to an orientation of hope and possibility (Perry, 2011; Werner, 2013).

According to NCTSN (2019), "The importance of a child's close relationship with a caregiver cannot be overestimated. Through relationships with important attachment figures, children learn to trust others, regulate their emotions, and interact with the world; they develop a sense of the world as safe or unsafe, and come to understand their own value as individuals" (para. 3). Key attachment figures include parents, caregivers, and those whom the child admires or spends a significant amount of time with: teachers, coaches, community mentors, or role models.

Howard Bath (2015) summarizes it this way:

There is solid scientific evidence about the therapeutic value of trusting relationships. Decades of research on psychotherapy shows that it is not specific
treatment models or techniques, but positive relationships (i.e., a therapeutic
alliance and empathy) that drive change. Research on resilience reaches similar conclusions: caring relationships between children and caregivers, teachers, or mentors are foremost. (p. 8)

The Case for Friend-Making

Close friendships are among the most important social connections in a young
person's life. Unfortunately, these relationships aren't exempt from the challenges transition shock creates. In fact, power-interrupted youth are less likely
to enjoy deep and lasting friendships.

One reason for this is that power interruption stifles prosocial behaviors
(such as sharing space or physical objects). In fact, individuals with a history of
adversity tend to score lower on the prosocial behavior scale (a measure that
explores patterns, skills, and behaviors that contribute to happy, well-function-
ing friendships). Lower scores may mean fewer healthy bonds. Meanwhile, the
absence of positive peer relationships deepens isolation.

This can be a double whammy for RAEMs. After all, many are already navigating the precarious terrain of cultural and linguistic inclusion. For many newcomers, friend-making in a new place is no small feat. And that's before tacking
on the added complexities of transition shock.

Friend-making is important for all students, but it is vital to power restoration and long-term integration success. In fact, the presence of valued
friendships boosts positive intrapersonal and academic outcomes among
trauma-affected youth (Powers, Ressler, & Bradley, 2009; Treismen, 2018).

Learners who feel they have friends (or who, at a minimum, are largely
accepted by their peers) are more likely to demonstrate a healthy self-view
(APA, 2019). Students who self-identify as partners in a friendship or friendships tend to have more robust self-esteems, and learners with this type of
confidence are more likely to perform well academically. The reverse is also
true. Youth who face challenges making friends are also likely to experience difficulties in learning and participating at school (University of California, 2010).

> My biggest worries about starting school in the United States were that I would never make friends that liked me and that I would get bullied. One of the things that helped me the most was learning how to introduce myself to other people and practicing it a lot, even though I was scared to do it. I'd also tell the teachers that they shouldn't give [newcomers] special treatment because other students might bully them for being a teacher's pet. But for other kids who speak a different language, I'd tell them: Never let what other kids say to you keep you from achieving something greater in life.
>
> —*Saphina, age 14, arrived in the United States at age 11 from the Democratic Republic of the Congo (first languages: French, Lingala, Swahili)*

Here's the bottom line. RAEMs who establish and maintain healthy relationships are more likely to experience better physical and mental health—and they're better positioned to realize more fulfilling integration outcomes (United Nations High Commissioner for Refugees [UNHCR], 2020). A power-restorative approach supports student connections, including peer friendships. The following are culturally responsive recommendations for supporting friend-making for trauma-affected RAEMs.

Facilitate safe, predictable opportunities for social engagement. For example, try scheduling "interaction appointments" in advance so students know who, when, and how they are meeting—and what will be discussed. This can help manage anticipatory anxiety and return more control to the student.

For example, Hamad demonstrates visible anxiety when transitioning from one activity to another, when trying new things, or when events occur that are outside his predictable daily schedule. Consequently, Hamad's teacher begins using transition cards (see Chapter 7) as a way to help him prepare and engage in periods of cooperative learning. At the beginning of the school day, his teacher hands Hamad the following note:

Good morning, Hamad! Today in math, you will have a partner-pair-share with Carl to discuss parallelograms.

At 2 pm, we'll leave science early for a choir concert in the auditorium! You'll sit between Amilie and Htoo Lin.

Fifteen minutes before the partner-pair-share activity, Hamad's teacher puts a sticky note on his desk:

Almost transition time! In 15 minutes, you'll meet with Carl to talk about parallelograms.

Start with small but purposeful exchanges in small blocks of interaction time. In the initial stages, pair groupings are optimal. These scenarios can encourage talk and decrease the chances of a student feeling left out. From here, build toward small-group interactions. Then, as students build confidence, trust, and stamina, they can work toward more extended frames of engagement.

For example, during the first two months of school, Hamad engages in cooperative learning structures with his classmate Carl. They begin with two-minute partner-pair-share activities and slowly move toward longer work periods. Eventually, Hamad switches (with advance warning) to working with a new partner. Several weeks later, another participant is added to the dynamic. The triad begins with five-minute intervals and eventually works as a project learning team, often meeting for 45-minute sessions. The following month, Hamad's teacher engages Hamad and his classmates in a relay learning activity that involves quad groupings. The teacher has a goal for Hamad to participate in a whole-class cooperative structure by the end of the school year.

Practice intentionality when selecting the focus for these sessions. Activities and conversation topics should support interaction and highlight the various strengths of students within the groups.

Listen to interactions and note when individual students appear uncomfortable, disengaged, or unsure of what to say. Work closely with these learners to create "social scripts" that can serve as anchors or guideposts through tricky spots in a conversation.

To illustrate this, let's check in on Hamad and Carl's partnership in those early weeks of school. The teacher has just expanded the pair to include Amalie. A week after this addition, the teacher notes that every time Carl or Amalie asks Hamad a question, he quickly lowers his gaze, tucks his hands under his legs, and replies, "I don't know." Hamad's teacher is aware that he does know the response; he had correctly written about the same prompt just moments before. So the teacher asks the trio to create a group graphic organizer to align with the subject under discussion (a Venn diagram comparing and contrasting earthquakes and volcanoes). Then they return to the original conversation prompts, using the new organizer as an anchor chart.

Explicitly teach the meaning of facial expressions, body language, volume/tone, and gestures in a relevant context. Provide students with low-stakes opportunities to practice interpreting these features. In culturally diverse settings where trust is already established, encourage learners to discuss similarities and differences in facial expressions or gestures from one country or social group to another.

For example, Hamad and Carl explore a series of photos showing people exhibiting various thoughts and emotions. Together, they look at each image and name what the person in the picture is thinking, feeling, or communicating. Some are straightforward. The people are happy, sad, or stressed out. But others—such as a picture of a teacher curling her pointer finger to summon a student—spur conversation. Hamad seems perplexed and asks, "Why would she do that thing to the kid? Does she think he is a dog?" As they talk over the picture, Hamad insists that everyone he knows would consider the gesture an insulting one. He explains that beckoning should be done with all the fingers—not just one—and that the palm should be facing down. Carl, meanwhile, isn't particularly concerned with the gesture. After the pair has completed the exercise, the class comes back together to share out. Hamad and Carl choose to share the picture of the finger beckoning. Others in the class had a similar response to Hamad's, to varying degrees of annoyance or insult. As the year progresses, the teacher and other students become more aware of their body language, facial expressions, and gestures—and how they perceive and react to nonverbal cues in their environment. These small moves help reduce opportunities for unintended distress.

Replace competitive exchanges with activities that promote teamwork, sharing, gameplay, and structured conversation. Each of these elements draws from the well of deep-level (or collective unconscious) culture. Meanwhile, they diminish some of the risks involved with inter-personal exchange.

Invite students to enter interactive settings empty-handed. Leaving personal items behind minimizes the risk of conflict between members of the group or partnership. Slowly incorporate activities that require sharing or taking turns.

To illustrate this, Hamad and Carl's first exchange was mostly wordless. Both students left their pencils and other personal items at their desks and met at a separate workspace. Their teacher met them there and introduced a deck of cards. Each card displayed an image (in this case, nonacademic icebreaker images), and each picture had a matching logical pair. The teacher held up an image of a shoe and then a sock. He put the cards together and set them in the center of the workspace. Then he nodded at the pair of students and walked away. Carl and Hamad picked up where their teacher had left off. Salt, pepper. Hammer, nail. Eventually, the pair ended up with six unmatched cards. Here, they began to talk. In shy, broken phrases, they negotiated the final solutions, which relied on more culturally nuanced points of reference. Peanut butter . . . jam? Baseball . . . glove? Completing the activity as a team helped alleviate some of the pressures of engagement while honoring those students who tended toward "orientation of self to others." When the students returned to the pair workgroup later in the day, Hamad seemed slightly less reserved and demon-strated less anxiety than he did at the start of their initial work session.

Provide relevant exemplars. For example, if students watch a video of other students working in groups of three at various classroom stations and then rotating between stations in a calm, organized way, they will have a better idea of the anticipated norms and expectations in that context. The same considerations apply to play, conversation, or working toward a class or schoolwide goal.

Establish a foundation of structure and routine, but work toward student agency by introducing the element of limited choice. Providing a limited range of three or four options to choose from reduces stress while still promoting a student's internal locus of control. Anticipate that students will demonstrate self-efficacy in productive ways, and redirect as necessary.

Model healthy conflict. Let's face it: we won't all agree all the time. That's not necessarily a bad thing. Kids can actually grow from conflict when it is presented and constructively resolved in real time. This sends a clear message: It's OK to disagree, but there are ways to handle disagreements that minimize hurt and maximize solution-seeking. For students with a history of trauma, take care to introduce these scenarios in a safe, controlled setting (e.g., a read-aloud from a story that centers on conflict resolution). Offer sentence stems and invite students to practice these exchanges in a monitored environment.

Let's return to Hamad to see how cooperative conversations, an integral part of his classroom's culture, can demonstrate this. At the beginning of the school year, his teacher introduced and modeled the idea of "I statements" (e.g., I think/feel that . . .). Each week, the class learns and practices a new cooperative sentence stem. One day, Carl and Hamad work together to read and discuss a text on an important social justice issue. They'd previously practiced using the stems *I agree because* and *I (respectfully) disagree because,* so they each begin the activity with a handheld anchor chart containing these cooperative stems (and others that are already part of their cooperative repertoire).

Prepare students to be active listeners. Friendships require listening and empathy. Emphasize the important role that listening plays in a conversation. Ask students to engage in discourse and then recall details about what their partner or groupmates shared. Model facial expressions and gestures that indicate active listening.

Here's Rujan:

I [was] distraught for our move to America initially. I hated it here, socially; thinking back now, it felt like my family gave up everything [that] we ever knew and made us comfortable in hopes that we would see a better future here. Initially, the picture of a better future was not all too clear in America either. My parents struggled to find jobs, but they did well as usual to hide these tiring struggles. I struggled socially and emotionally; I recall, even as I am typing this, the words of outcry letting my mother know that if we had the hospitals and buildings like we had in America in Nepal, it would be better there.

Perhaps those sentiments of my younger self highlight a fundamental challenge of relocation and refugees like me: the isolation and sense of not belonging that comes with moving to a new country. Nevertheless, my battle with social aspects (i.e., understanding the Americanized way of living and lack of friends) made me struggle in a classroom setting in one way; it never fully allowed me to express myself and embrace the language. Thinking back now, this may have been one of the reasons that explain my early fear of public speaking.

Reciprocity

Reciprocal interaction is a power-restorative factor in building and maintaining social bonds. *Reciprocity* is the mutual and caring engagement in a shared activity, interest, or common aim. Howard Bath (2015) shares, "When two parties are involved in reciprocal interactions, a positive connection is created. It is almost impossible to dislike someone while you are rhythmically in sync with them." These seemingly "everyday" interactions go a long way in creating bonds, growing a safe environment, and building students' innate power. "Respectful connections," Bath continues, "are necessary as we help children cope with their challenging circumstances and unruly emotions" (p. 9).

Reciprocity can be challenging for youth with a history of adverse life experiences. Fortunately, we can embed reciprocal behaviors into content-area learning, language instruction, extracurricular activities, and structured play. The following are a few examples:

- Tossing a ball between partners or group members.
- Learning a dance or challenge together.
- Creating and listening to a class playlist while working together.
- Playing mimicking games or activities, such as Simon Says.
- Reading passages of a story with a partner.
- Exchanging a special artifact and describing its meaning while a partner is holding it/looking at it.

"We're going to go outside together as a class. Your assignment is to find a stone."

This was my college professor, and it was the last class I would take on campus before starting my student teaching placement. I was anxious to get into the "real world" of teaching and wasn't particularly interested in spending my day looking for rocks.

"Take as much time as you need. Make sure it's the right stone for you. Understand why that is so. This is your only task for the day."

I let out a slow, exasperated sigh and thought of the million and one other things I needed to be doing at that moment (which, in retrospect, was foreshadowing professional development sessions years later). We set out and then met up 45 minutes later with stones in our palms and pockets.

"Great! Don't forget your stones for the next class period. They are part of your grade."

Two days later, we reconvened. We sat in a circle on the floor. Everyone in the class shared the stones they had collected. They talked about why it represented them, why it stood out, and why it was special.

"It reminds me of going to the beach with my mom," said one student. "She died last year of cancer."

Another classmate shared, "I like the way the moss wraps around it, like a mini forest. We always used to hike as a family when I was a kid. We don't have any pine trees here, and I didn't realize that I actually miss them."

Yet another: "It was the only smooth stone of all the rocks in the area. I feel like I stand out like that, too. It relaxes me when I touch it."

After each stone was introduced, it was placed in a basket, and the basket was passed on to the next person. The activity was designed as an example icebreaker for the early days of school with students. The idea was that the rocks represented what was special and unique about each of us—and that all those pieces came together in a collective that would become the classroom community.

I put the strategy to work with my first class. It was a 4th/5th grade newcomer classroom. That year, we had a fluctuating number of students, with eight or nine languages present at any given time. It was the first year this particular refugee magnet school was in operation, and we had influxes of students from Yemen, Eritrea, Myanmar, the Democratic Republic of the Congo, Iraq, and Libya. Although not all students identified as having experienced trauma, all were in the throes of culture shock.

The stone icebreaker failed. Or I failed in implementing it. At least, that's how I perceived it.

The collecting part went off without a hitch. No one complained about leaving the classroom for some outdoor exploration. I had to convince a few students to choose a rock they could actually carry or narrow down a handful of stones to two main contenders. Otherwise, I was feeling pretty good about my first-year teacher prowess.

Then came the basket. With our sentence frames in tow, introducing and explaining our stones wasn't an issue. Leaving them in the basket was. Almost half the class just could not let their stones go.

"OK," I told a student. "We'll go around the circle and then send the basket back to you to place your stone inside."

Except that didn't happen. I was perplexed. This wasn't in my professor's playbook. We talked more about the class's goal of coming together, sharing ourselves with our team members, and having a safe place for all the stones to be together. Nothing.

This was my first experience with the concept of reciprocity. For some of my students, giving up (or even placing into safekeeping) the thing that was "theirs" required an enormous amount of vulnerability. It required trust, and we hadn't established that yet.

We worked on filling up that basket until February, when the last stone finally dropped in. Some students were even able to let their classmates touch or hold their stone or ask more detailed questions about it. Ultimately, we celebrated when students reclaimed their rocks at the end of the year and took them home for good. Those dang rocks became an integral part of our classroom culture. In a way, they were us. I imagined this is what my college professor had had in mind; we just took our own scenic route to get there.

In the years that followed, 8th grade students would occasionally pop by to show me their rocks from 3rd grade. They had made an impact. Of course, sometimes things don't go according to plan in our classrooms. In my case, at least, it's more than just occasionally. In the case of those rocks, the perceived failure became one of my most enduring classroom activities—and my first big lesson in reciprocal behavior.

Connect: Into Practice

From here on, we'll be putting what we've learned to work. Each of the following strategies highlights the pillar of connection. In addition, all exercises speak to one or more culturally responsive elements and can be adapted to engage learners across the language-learning spectrum. Here we go!

Strategy 1: Student Connection Board

The student connection board is a tool for taking ownership and responsibility for all students. It is also helpful in creating an awareness of those who may benefit from more purposeful connections at school. In this case, we're looking at bonds that exist (or do not exist) between students and staff. Remember, focusing on relationships is the most effective action schools can take to mitigate transition shock.

Student connection boards can be completed for a single class, but ideally, this strategy is employed schoolwide or by vertical teams. Once a grade-level team has constructed and completed its board, folks from outside the workgroup are invited to visit that board. Visitors can include the previous year's teachers for that cohort of students; the school librarian(s); educators who specialize in music, art, physical education, and other subjects; coaches; office staff; and auxiliary team members.

A few notes. First, it's best to house whole-school student connection boards in an area that's accessible to all adult stakeholders at the school. Also, this strategy can be overwhelming if you take the entire student body into account (but it's highly recommended to include all learners if you have the time and resources to do so). For our purposes, we'll focus only on RAEM students.

Here's who's empowered:

- Teachers and educators in a professional learning setting or as independent learning

Here's what you'll need:

- Class- and/or grade-level rosters with identified RAEM students
- Whiteboard, chart paper, etc.
- Markers
- Sticky notes (in two colors)

Here's what you'll do:

1. Organize by grade-leveled staff (or a committee of representatives from each grade level).
2. Each team receives a premade chart or makes one following an established template.
   - Prepare the whiteboard or arrange the chart paper horizontally.
   - Create a two-column chart. The first column should be narrower and take up less space; the second should be as wide as possible. (See Figure 4.1.)
3. Working with your group, list students who have been identified for consideration (in our case, RAEMs) in the first column. If the board is created at the beginning of the year, these will be the *incoming* students.
4. Now, get the sticky notes ready. There should be two colors. The first color will indicate that you know the student and the student is already familiar with you. The second color will signal that you know this student and have a strong relationship of trust. Write your name or initials on each sticky note you use.

5. Working alongside your team, mark the board with your color-coded labels.

6. Once your team's board is completed, visit the boards of other grade levels (especially those that include students you've taught in previous years). Repeat the process, adding sticky notes to the names of those students you know or have established relationships with.

7. Return to your board as a grade-level team. Where are the critical gaps? Which students appear to be most in need of purposeful relationship-building attempts from adults? Once that has been identified, which adults will focus on which students? What will that look like?

It is a good idea to revisit your student connection boards periodically (at least four times per year). How are they shifting? Where are gaps still present? If there are gaps, why do they persist? Could students benefit from strategies that focus specifically on relationship-building, or is it a matter of the teacher(s) becoming more focused in their efforts?

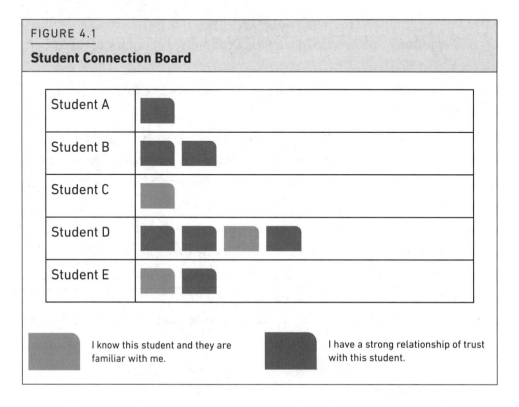

FIGURE 4.1

Student Connection Board

Strategy 2: Glasses On/Glasses Off

Often, when we interact with students who present as "difficult," we are quick to assign labels. These labels signal judgment, are usually rooted in conscious or unconscious bias, and alienate the learner. I refer to these as "glasses off" assumptions.

"Glasses on," on the other hand, assumes that we're viewing a learner through trauma-informed, culturally responsive lenses. This take helps us see an individual or situation more fully and in more affirmative ways. When we forget to view learners through these lenses, we run the risk of making unreliable judgments. As a result, we choose instructional moves and behavioral interventions that are ineffective, irrelevant, or harmful.

Doing the work to minimize external triggers and enhance students' positive self-worth means we also need to do some tough work within ourselves. Taking a "glasses on" approach is one of the ways to go about this. Remembering to wear our lenses takes practice and patience, and this exercise is a good place to start.

Each student profile in Figure 4.2 is based on a learner I've had in my own classroom—a student I was unfortunately too quick to evaluate and label. Ultimately, though, each of these students became a teacher to me, pressing me to evolve my personal and professional abilities. I hope you'll also grow from their teachings.

You can complete this strategy on your own. Optimally, however, you'll implement it as a team or schoolwide professional development exercise.

Here's who's empowered:

- Teachers and educators in a professional learning setting or as independent learning

Here's what you'll need:

- Printable cards, divided. Each set should have
  — One instructions card
  — One "glasses off" card
  — One "glasses on" card

Here's what you'll do as a group exercise facilitator:

1. Divide participants into small groups (four or five per team is ideal). Divide teams so each receives an equal number of "glasses off" cards (Figure 4.2). If working with many participants, one card for each team is fine.

2. Distribute the following to each group: one instructions card (face up), up to three "glasses off" cards (face up), and corresponding "glasses on" card(s) (face down).

3. Participants should read the instructions card and then read their first "glasses off" card. Teams will evaluate the situation from a "glasses off" perspective—that is, from a lens that is neither trauma-informed nor culturally responsive. Invite groups to brainstorm all the "glasses off" labels that may be attached to the student or the student's family from the situation (e.g., *troublemaker, lazy, uninvolved, attention-seeking*) and the possible ways a "glasses off" teacher might be inclined to react to those behaviors.

4. Next, participants put their trauma-informed, culturally responsive glasses on, so to speak. Invite them to view the corresponding "glasses on" card, which includes the student's backstory. Teams should discuss how this shift changes the teacher's perspective. The following questions can prompt discussion: *How does this affect the teacher's viewing of the student? In responding to the student's behaviors? How might these changes affect the student's long-term socioacademic success?*

5. Invite participants to think about and share examples from their own professional practice. For example, when or where did they operate from a "glasses off" approach? Encourage honesty since this is about growth. How will this strategy inform your future interactions with students, especially RAEMs?

Here's what you'll do if you're completing the exercise on your own:

1. Read the first "glasses off" card (Figure 4.2). Think about the situation and student at the center from a "glasses off" perspective (taking a lens that is neither trauma-informed nor culturally responsive).

Consider brainstorming all the labels attached to this student or the student's family (e.g., *troublemaker, lazy, uninvolved, attention-seeking*) and the possible ways a "glasses off" teacher might be inclined to react to those behaviors.

2. Put on your trauma-informed, culturally responsive glasses. Read the corresponding "glasses on" card, which includes the student's backstory. Think about how this shift changes the teacher's perspective. *How does this affect the decisions the teacher will make in viewing the student? In responding to the student's behaviors? How might these changes affect the student's long-term socioacademic success?*

FIGURE 4.2

Glasses On/Glasses Off Activity

1. Read one of the "glasses off" cards. List or discuss ways in which the student might be viewed or labeled by teachers and/or students.

2. Read the corresponding "glasses on" card for the same student. Discuss how perceptions of students' behaviors can be reframed from a trauma-informed lens.

"Glasses Off" Profile 1: Farhiya (Somalia)

Farhiya is a very sweet girl until something doesn't go according to her plan, which is often. When Farhiya doesn't get her way, she becomes aggressive and often threatens teachers and other students. In moments of rage, she overthrows desks, destroys classroom displays or materials, and physically assaults other students. In addition to her temper, she is the tallest student in the class, and other students fear her. Usually, Farhiya's classmates just do whatever she tells them to do in order to avoid her inevitable anger. Farhiya struggles the most with adults. If confronted about her behavior, she ignores or loudly curses at them, slams doors, or becomes physically violent. When confronted with potential consequences, she screams, "F--- you. I don't care!"

"Glasses On" Profile 1: Farhiya (Somalia)

These perceptions may have been generated and need to be reframed: *bossy, controlling, dangerous, defiant, scary, out-of-control, mean, rude*

Backstory: Farhiya was the youngest of four children in Somalia. After the family resettled to the United States, her mother had three additional siblings with a new husband. Farhiya wasn't the youngest child anymore. In fact, she is now the oldest child in the home (and the only child from the previous marriage), since her older siblings are married. Farhiya's stepfather works many miles away at a meatpacking plant and is gone for weeks at a time. At home, Farhiya is the boss. She translates bills and represents the family at doctor's appointments and other engagements. She also helps to mother her younger half-siblings, even as she works through the deep resentment that came with them replacing her. By the time Farhiya gets to school, she is exhausted and snaps easily. Farhiya feels as if she doesn't belong at home or at school.

continued

FIGURE 4.2 (*continued*)

Glasses On/Glasses Off Activity

"Glasses Off" Profile 2: Mathis (Democratic Republic of Congo)

Mathis is a very shy student. He is smaller than other students his age, exhibits a stutter, and seems awkward in social contexts. Mathis doesn't engage with other students much or contribute to class discussions. He frequently falls asleep in class. He doodles and draws pictures while his teachers talk. During periods of work, Mathis becomes easily frustrated. When this happens, he shuts down. Sometimes he buries his head in his arms and refuses to participate. Often, he runs into the hallway. When he does, he is often found hiding in corners, lockers, or the boys' bathroom. Twice, Mathis has made it out of school and has to be chased down by school security.

"Glasses On" Profile 2: Mathis (Congo)

These perceptions may have been generated and need to be reframed: *lazy, distracted, self-defeating, stubborn, risk factor*

Backstory: Mathis came from the Congo with his mother and older brother. Both Mathis and his mother are HIV positive, and Mathis spends many hours during the week at the children's hospital where he was diagnosed as a "failure to thrive." Mathis is just beginning to understand what the disease means for him, and he resents it. Mathis adores his brother but struggles to understand why he is exempt from the struggles Mathis and his mom endure. Between the refugee camp, transition, and hospitalization, Mathis is considered a student with limited or interrupted formal education (SLIFE). He is self-conscious of his stutter, his limited English proficiency, and his perceived lack of intelligence. Art is one area where Mathis excels and takes comfort. Other students note his talent and often ask him to illustrate their favorite characters.

"Glasses Off" Profile 3: MawOo (Myanmar)

Everyone in MawOo's class considers him the "sneaky" one. The moment an adult is out of sight or earshot, the assaults begin. He kicks or trips his classmates while they walk in line down the hallway. He slams other students' lockers while they are trying to reach inside. He hides other students' pencils, flicks his elbow partner during carpet time, and has been caught with classroom belongings in his pockets. When accused, MawOo denies all involvement and shows no remorse. Substitute teacher days are the worst, as MawOo pushes every limit of behavior management. MawOo is bright but spends much of his class time focused on others. When he does concentrate, he is capable of nearly grade-level work. However, he consistently receives very low scores due to his lack of focus, incomplete grades, and missing work.

"Glasses On" Profile 3: MawOo (Myanmar)

These perceptions may have been generated and need to be reframed: *bully, sneak, lazy, risk-factor, nuisance*

Backstory: MawOo is used to not staying in one place for too long. His family has been in transition his entire life. He has already lived in four countries prior to resettlement in the United States. MawOo transferred to his current school from another district and had lived in another state prior, all by the time he began 3rd grade. MawOo doesn't see much value in maintaining friendships. In fact, it seems much more practical to push people away. Consequently, he's become an expert at it.

"Glasses Off" Profile 4: Rojina (Bhutan)

Rojina needs to be the best at everything she does, especially when it comes to her schooling. She works hard and excels in class. She also requires constant reassurance of her value, worth, and positive performance. When teachers are working with other students, she interrupts to ask for her work to be evaluated. She is usually the first one to complete a task. When she does, she yells, "Finished!" She becomes visibly upset and teary if a teacher fails to compliment her work or if another student surpasses her scores. Award ceremonies (a schoolwide practice) are especially challenging. If Rojina does not receive an award, she melts down in tears and disconnects for the remainder of the day—or even an entire week.

"Glasses On" Profile 4: Rojina (Bhutan)

These perceptions may have been generated and need to be reframed: *perfectionist, needy, people pleaser, brown-noser, suffocating, egotistical*

Backstory: Rojina comes from a family of academics. Her father ran a school in Nepal after they relocated from Bhutan. Rojina's family has incredibly high expectations for her and anticipates her college graduation and eventual professional success. They view their move to the United States as a tremendous educational opportunity for their children, and they expect nothing short of excellence. Rojina's father waits for each assignment to come home. The higher the grade, the higher the level of approval Rojina receive from her parents. As a child, Rojina lost her only two siblings and both of her grandparents. She left her remaining family and friends behind in Nepal. She carries an enormous sense of guilt about this. Rojina is also aware of everything her parents went through just to move to the United States. She desperately wants to make it up to them in some way, and she sees the best way as through her academic success.

3. Think of a student from your own professional practice. When or where did you operate from a "glasses off" approach? Be honest about your growth. How might this strategy inform your future interactions with students, especially RAEMs?

Senait and I spent her 3rd grade year together. She'd been at our school for half an academic year and had managed to establish a good relationship with her 2nd grade teacher. However, in that time, Senait had also made quite a reputation for herself. So when I saw her name on my roster, I already knew who she was, and I had a few predictions for how our time together might go.

Senait was perceived as strong-willed. She had strong ideas about, well, basically everything. Even in her emergent English (her first languages were Tigrinya, Amharic, and Arabic), she had little trouble communicating this. The adjectives that floated around Senait were *bossy, stubborn,* and *aggressive.* She also demonstrated an entire array of transition shock indicators.

Even during the initial back-to-school weeks, Senait's presence in my classroom was enormous. I had no trouble seeing where some of those labels came from. But I got glimpses of other characteristics, as well, such as Senait's powerful mothering instinct, her ability to relate to outliers in the classroom or school and bring them into the fold, and her ability to creatively solve problems in multiple contexts. I also saw a hint of her softer self underneath this tough shell of externally constructed badges.

Ultimately, Senait and I developed a strong partnership and had a dynamite year. Six years later, just before her 9th grade year, I sat down with Senait to ask about her early experiences in U.S. schools. Here's what she had to say:

> I was a little shy. I didn't know where to go. The school was really big and I didn't know the language, and I didn't have any friends yet. It was a lot of new things. Everything in America was new. For example, it was hard for us to go buy food. We didn't know what the money meant. We thought $50 was like a dollar. We didn't know these things yet, and I didn't learn it in school until after.
>
> I wasn't experienced in going to school with a teacher who spoke English. It's a lot different in my country. There, if you don't listen, you are punished. Also, in my country, we didn't have any homework. You do all of your learning at school. I had to learn what to do with homework.
>
> I didn't know any English, and it was hard for me to communicate. I wanted my teacher to know that when I started learning more English, I was like a translator for everything. I don't have brothers or sisters. It's just me and my mom. My mom got sick a lot in our country and in America. I took care of her. In America, I had to be the translator for the doctors and everyone. Now she's doing better. She has a job here now, so that's really good.

I don't have any brothers or sisters. It made it harder because I was alone a lot. I was also really worried that people would bully me. I was bullied a lot when I went to school in Eritrea, so I thought people would bully me here, too. My teacher saw that I didn't have a lot of clothes and that me and my mom didn't have any coats. She came to our house with coats and clothes and a lot of food. That was really helpful. My mom was so grateful.

I had a friend, Arsema. She spoke my language. It was easier having her by my side. She came about six months after me, so I knew just a little bit more English. I helped her with math. I started speaking more after I had Arsema. Playing with the kids outside really helped me learn English, too.

If I could ask my first teacher to change one thing, I would want her to help me not be so shy. And I would tell other newcomers from my country: Please don't be scared. There are teachers and students who want to help and be your friend.

How do you imagine Senait's labels throughout her time at school might have changed if her instructional team had had more insight into her life? For what it's worth, few of us in the building would have ever imagined that Senait felt shy! How might we have better capitalized on Senait's strengths and funds of knowledge that she was carried around with her every day?

As it turns out, Senait has become incredibly adept at channeling her unique life experiences and skills in productive ways. She is a remarkable tutor for younger children, an outstanding student council representative, a diligent learner, and a multilingual, multicultural asset to her school community. Moreover, Senait is pushing forward with hefty goals for high school and beyond. She remains strong-willed but has learned to negotiate compromise. Perhaps the fact that she's "spicy," as she calls it, is her own secret ingredient for resiliency.

Strategy 3: Hand of Connectivity

There are several variations to this strategy, each with a shared goal of facilitating students' ownership over their space. This is the version I employ most consistently. It calls for students to learn to identify places and people that signal safety and well-being. The choice component of this strategy is critical as it honors intrapersonal agency and hands control of the situation back to students.

Here's who's empowered:

- Students, with the guidance of adult facilitators

Here's what you'll need:

- Paper and writing/drawing utensils

Here's what you'll do as a group exercise facilitator:

1. Ask learners to trace one hand on a piece of paper.
2. Invite students to identify key people *at school* they trust and feel safe around and then record these people in their fingers. At least one of the responses should be an adult. (Keep in mind that not everyone will be able to fill all five spaces, especially early in the year.)
3. In the palm area, students should record a safe space where they feel comfortable going in the school building. This place should be a physical location where they feel calm and can recenter. It should be a place where they feel free of fear, judgment, bullying, distractions, and discomfort. (Again, not all students will be able to name such a place, particularly if students are still unfamiliar with the school building.)

This strategy can be accomplished individually, but it is most effective when students share their responses in a protected and supportive space. A group context may also remind students of other "safe" people or places as they listen to their peers' responses. Hand of Connectivity also works well as a verbal activity (e.g., learners physically touch each finger and their palm with the opposite hand as they name the various components).

Hand of Connectivity helps students consciously define safe people and spaces in the school environment. It is also an opportunity to explore elements that are *not* present on the hand maps. Is the lunchroom mentioned? The front office? The homeroom? The hallway? Why or why not? Are students able to identify peers they consider safe and trustworthy? What about staff? Are you listed on the fingers? Someone else in the building? No one?

In my own experience, this is precisely how we identified specific areas of the building where bullying was taking place (and where mechanisms of saving face had deterred students from calling it out individually). Immediately following implementation of this strategy (or as the year progresses), make a dedicated effort to help students fill up their hands. Remind students that they are agents of control, backed by the support of adults at the school.

Strategy 4: Mirror

This strategy facilitates reciprocity and connection-building. It also helps introduce and create comfort around new sets of conscious-level cultural norms, specifically those related to eye contact and personal space.

Here's who's empowered:

- Students, with the guidance of adult facilitators

Here's what you'll need:

- A willing partner (or, if facilitating, students arranged in teams of two, preferably with someone with whom they do not already have a close relationship)

Here's what you'll do:

1. Determine which partner will be the "driver" and the "passenger." The driver will lead the first round of the exercise.
2. Sit or stand close to your partner and put your hands in front of you. Turn your palms to face your partner as though your hands were flush to an invisible wall. If personal distance considerations are necessary (for trauma mitigation, culturally responsive indicators, or both), ask, "Is it OK to come into your space?"

3. The driver will then initiate the activity by moving their hands slowly along the invisible wall, making smooth, connected movements. The passenger should copy all the driver's movements, mirror each gesture as closely as possible, and notice cues that will help him/her/them antici- pate the driver's motions. As partners develop more synchronicity, they may incorporate movements of the head, torso, or legs. As connectivity increases, partners may be able to move toward making and maintaining direct eye contact.

4. After an established time (one to three minutes is ideal, working upward to build stamina), reverse roles with your partner. The passenger becomes the driver and initiates a new interaction.

Strategy 5: DBT House with Emergent Multilingual Considerations

DBT House is an exercise in art therapy. Art is widely recognized as an effective trauma-informed intervention (Hane, 2016; Malchiodi, 2015; Van Lith, 2016). It has shown exceptional promise in working with refugees and those who have experienced political violence (Kalmanowitz & Rainbow, 2016; Knefel, 2015).

School-based art activities can be used to help mitigate transition shock in the classroom. They introduce opportunities to root down, practice nonver- bal expression, and connect with others in student-paced ways. Activities can include drawing, painting, drama, music-making, creative movement, sculpt- ing, weaving, and collage-making.

Artistic expression is unique in its ability to bypass speech-production areas in the brain and construct wordless somatic paths to expression. The actual process of making art is a predominantly right-brained activity. As the right brain is stimulated and strengthened, left-brain connectivity (the link to language acquisition) can begin to repair. Miranda Field (2016) of Regina University explains, "Research has shown that the non-verbal right brain holds traumatic memories, and these can be accessed through the use of symbols and sensations in art therapy. Communication between the brain hemispheres can be accomplished through the use of art therapy and may assist in the processing of the trauma" (p. 65).

Making art can help students engage with sensory stimuli in safe contexts and can promote feelings of security, belonging, grounding, and validation. A creative output engages students in organizing, expressing, and making meaning from traumatic experiences. It encourages the reconstruction of one's sense of efficacy and the notion of "being present" in the new context. It also provides learners with the option of creative choice and the ability to process trauma on their terms, thereby reducing the likelihood of emotional overload and helping to restore power.

In working with RAEMs, in particular, it's worth pointing out that art is a culturally responsive activity. In fact, "Art is an integral piece in many cultural healing practices [and] creating images of art can act as a bridge between Indigenous and non-Indigenous, self and collective, and art therapy and research" (Field, 2016, p. 65).

The DBT House is a nonintrusive, art therapy–centered strategy that is helpful in learning important background information about students, their thinking patterns, and potential triggers—without prodding or stimulating existing trauma. DBT is an acronym for dialectical behavioral therapy skills. This strategy was developed in the 1970s by Dr. Marsha Linehan, an American psychologist and cognitive behavioral therapist. Today, it is widely applied in clinical settings and resonates with our work in several important ways (Linehan, 1993; Linehan et al., 1999).

Foremost, it touches on each of the four pillars in approaching transition shock. Additionally, it speaks to multiple aspects of culturally responsive teaching. Implementation can be scaffolded and supported to effectively engage learners regardless of age or level of English language acquisition. I have personally implemented this strategy with very young children, teens, and adults, representing nearly 60 unique first languages. I love that DBT House can be implemented in a whole-class setting without singling out stress-affected individuals. The completed houses (or isolated elements within them) can be used in a variety of ways to facilitate healthy discussion, connection, empathy, and creative solution-seeking.

Because different house sections correspond to separate pillars of trauma-informed care, we'll dive deeper into this strategy over the following three chapters. Right now, we'll focus on the construction of the house. Then we'll take a few moments to begin analyzing the elements that align to connection. Finally, we'll return to the house and explore where it meets up with the three remaining pillars of care.

This strategy invites participants to construct a house. We've included a template (see Appendix); however, I always prefer to have participants design and draw their own houses. This step can be revealing by itself. My own students' drawings have included houseboats, huts, apartments, mud homes, traditional urban homes, tents, homeless shelters, and treehouses, and they've appeared inviting, disheveled, or straight out of a storybook.

Let's get started.

Here's who's empowered:

- Students, with the guidance of adult facilitators
- Educators, in gaining a deeper understanding of their students

Here's what you'll need:

- Paper
- Pencil, markers, or crayons
- DBT house template *(optional; see Appendix)*

Here's what you'll do as a group facilitator:

1. Introduce the strategy from a trust-building, goal-setting, or solution-seeking perspective. Ensure access to paper, writing utensils, and a private workspace.

2. Engage participants by saying, "Today, I am going to ask you to draw a house. This house represents you and your thoughts. I will give you instructions as you build your house. Please listen as you draw and write. Please respect your neighbors' privacy as they work. When you are finished, I will collect your papers and keep them safe. Let's begin. Try to use as much of your paper as possible to draw your house. Your house needs five items: a roof, a door, a window, a chimney, and a billboard or

sign. You can place the sign on the roof, in the yard, hanging from a window, or in any other location you like."

3. Pause and give participants enough time to complete their houses. (Note that some students will need extra support for this process. It may take an entire class period to construct the house if students are unfamiliar with features such as window, door, roof, and chimney. It may also be necessary to display a sample house during this process.)

4. When all the houses are ready, begin to guide participants through the DBT House prompts. While participants are working, remind them that they may find a directive or part of the house that resonates or feels uncomfortable and to be aware of those areas as they come up.

— **Floor:** On the floor of the house, write the values that govern your life. (Note: As you walk students through this strategy, it may be necessary to paraphrase directives based on participants' age and language level. For example, when differentiating for younger students, I might say, "Write down things that are important to you to be a good person or to live a happy life. Use words that tell about what you think it means to be a good person.")

— **Walls:** Along the walls, name anything or anyone who supports you. (Write names or words for people or things that are helpful to you.)

— **Roof:** On the roof, name the things or people that protect you. (Write names or words for people or things that keep you safe.)

— **Door:** On the front door, name the things you keep hidden from others or that you are afraid of. (What are the things about yourself you don't like to tell other people? What stresses or fears get in the way of your day?) It may be helpful to invite participants to "write these ideas in your mind" or mark them as symbols if they are too uncomfortable to write down.

— **Chimney:** Coming out of the chimney, write down ways in which you blow off steam. (What do you do when you are sad, mad, or frustrated or when you have too much energy?)

— **Billboard:** On the billboard/sign, name the things you are proud of and want others to see. (What are you proud of? What do you feel that you are really good at? Is there a skill or quality you use to help others?)

— **Window:** In the window space, name a dream, goal, or vision you have for your future. (This is an additional component I like to add that is not included in traditional DBT house practices. I've found that it directs students toward ongoing momentum and allows a space to share dreams and hopes in a safe setting.) I'd like to make one note in advance. As we'll see later, there are only two areas on the DBT House—the billboard and the window—that we might consider sharing out in the classroom, depending on the context and level of peer trust established.

5. Review the house parts, elaborate on their significance, share student examples, and discuss critical "look-fors" and "ahas." (We'll walk through these together as we view student examples!)

Here's what you'll do if you're completing the exercise on your own:

1. On your paper, draw the outline of a house. You can use as much of the paper as you need. Make sure your house has the following:

   — A roof

   — A door

   — A window

   — A chimney

   — A sign or billboard somewhere on or near your house

2. Along the floor or foundation of your house, write some of the values that govern your life. For example, what is important to you in achieving happiness, feeling fulfilled, or being a good person?

3. Along the walls of your house, name the people or things that support you.

4. On the roof, name the people or things that protect you.

5. On the door, write a goal for heart growth (such as emotions, behaviors, or thought patterns) you'd like to change or develop this school year.

6. Coming out of the chimney, write how you get rid of stress or blow off steam.

7. On the billboard/sign, name something you are proud of and want others to know about you.

8. In the window space, name a dream, vision, or goal you have for the future.

Typically, clinical DBT Houses add another layer of complexity. Participants build on the initial exercise by dividing the structure into four sections, or levels of the house. These layers explore the following:

1. **Level 1:** Behaviors you are trying to gain control over or areas of your life you want to change.

2. **Level 2:** Emotions you want to experience more often, more fully, or in a healthier way.

3. **Level 3:** All the things you are happy about or want to feel happy about.

4. **Level 4:** What a "life worth living" would look like for you. (In other words, what is the goal or ideal outcome?)

You may find this extension helpful. However, I don't tend to engage students to this degree. I find that the basic house structure provides just the right amount of information useful for gaining a deeper level of understanding about them as individuals. If you choose to continue, I'd recommend reserving this process for older students (i.e., high school and adult) or students with advanced levels of English proficiency.

I'd like to take a moment for an important note on the door. The original version of the DBT House exercise is this: *On the door, name something you're afraid of or embarrassed about—something you usually keep hidden from others.* I will say that I used this version with students for many years and found it incredibly insightful.

However, the tremendous number of potentially retriggering events that have marked the 2019–2021 school years have led me to reconsider this prompt. Returning to the idea that trauma roots us in the past and power restoration moves us into the future, it's become critically important to me that I "walk the walk" in every aspect of my practice. In short, I began to question the purpose of the door. *What was I committing to do with the information I received? How could I ensure privacy and confidentiality (especially if my duty to report trumped these promises? Most important, was this prompt contributing to power interruptions?*

Please note that the student examples you'll find in this book represent that earlier version. I've left them alone and included this explanation as a way to say *We're all still growing in this.* I think you'll also see how and why the original door space could be useful in certain contexts. Trained school counselors or psychologists may still opt to explore the original DBT door. However, for those of us working to serve students in traditional classroom settings, I hope you'll follow me in this new, more power-restorative direction.

Exploration of DBT Houses is a layered process, as the various areas tie together pillars in approaching transition shock. Therefore, we'll return to the DBT House in later chapters to address the dynamics relative to each pillar of care.

Here, we'll look closely at the floor (foundation) and the walls, both of which highlight connection. When working with students, my eyes always gravitate toward the walls first. What am I looking for here? Actually, I'm looking for myself. That sounds self-centered, doesn't it? Let me explain.

I want to see evidence that the student feels some type of connection at school. Is my name (as someone who works closely with that student every day) written on the walls? If not, then darn it, that's my goal for the entire year. Often, I'll spot the name of another adult at the school—the vice principal, librarian, literacy interventionist, school counselor, or basketball coach. I'm good with that discovery, too. As long as one or more adults from the school appear on the walls (or in the protective "roof" space), I know we've got some traction. If not, then I'm asking some questions: *Why might this be? How can we meaningfully build trust to become beacons for support and/or protection?*

I'm also looking for family members and peer relationships. This activity is sometimes my first indication that a student is struggling with making connections. For example, a learner might present in class as outgoing and charismatic but may not name a close, supportive bond with peers or adults in school. Sometimes, though, these names (or their absence) aren't enough to draw meaningful conclusions, and it's necessary to put different elements of the map together to get a clearer picture or spend more one-on-one time with the student to develop a deeper understanding.

Now let's take a peek at the floor of the house. What sorts of values drive your students? Are specific elements of conscious or collective unconscious culture revealed? Can you see any of these values represented in the learning environment or curriculum? How can you leverage these foundational pieces in the classroom?

All this will make more sense as we explore some student examples. Let's begin with a few that are especially relevant to the pillar of connection.

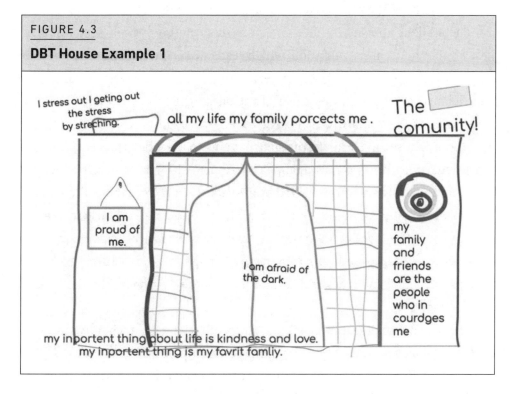

FIGURE 4.3

DBT House Example 1

Take a look at the house in Figure 4.3. It was created by an 11-year-old boy originally from Kazakhstan. The student drew a large rectangular-shaped building, which could be a single-family home or an apartment complex, in blue marker. Centered in the picture is a tall *mashrabiya,* or horseshoe arch. In addition, he included a short chimney, a hanging sign, and what appears to be an "evil eye" amulet (and/or possibly a window). He also added other patterns and shapes throughout the drawing.

One thing that stands out here is that the student identified his supportive factors (what he labeled, with misspellings corrected here, "the people who encourage me") as "The [student's name] community." The use of the word *community* signals a probable network of supportive elements in place. Along the foundation of the house, he wrote, "My important thing about life is kindness and love. My important thing is my favorite family." Family is also highlighted in his roof (protect) space. Perhaps people from school exist within the student's community, but it would still be helpful to name and/or build out viable supportive and protective relationships at school.

The student appears to have an established method of self-regulating, as indicated by his chimney notation, which reads, "I get out the stress by stretching." Adding to his repertoire of strategies for dealing with stress will likely be beneficial. The door indicates a fear of the dark, which is age typical. Nothing is recorded in the window, which suggests an opportunity to partner with the student in goal-setting. Finally, the sign, hanging to the left of the door, reads, "I am proud of me," hinting at what appears to be a healthy sense of self-concept.

Figure 4.4 shows a house created by a 7-year-old girl from the United States who speaks Spanish at home. The student drew a rectangular house with a triangular roof. The image contains a door, one window, a heart-shaped sign, and a long chimney. A large mailbox sits to the lower right of the structure. The house is drawn in pencil and black marker, aside from the writing on the roof (blue) and door (pink).

The foundational features include "my brother's heart, my family, my dogs, shelter." Along the walls, she wrote, "my mom, my brother, Ms. Park, Jaylin, Khadija, Ms. El Yaafouri." From an outside perspective, the connect features of this house appear robust and healthy. The map acknowledges family, pets, shelter, friends, and teachers. This may suggest that the child enjoys strong foundational properties and access to diverse circles of support. Her sign simply reads, "me," hinting at the probability of a positive self-concept.

FIGURE 4.4

DBT House Example 2

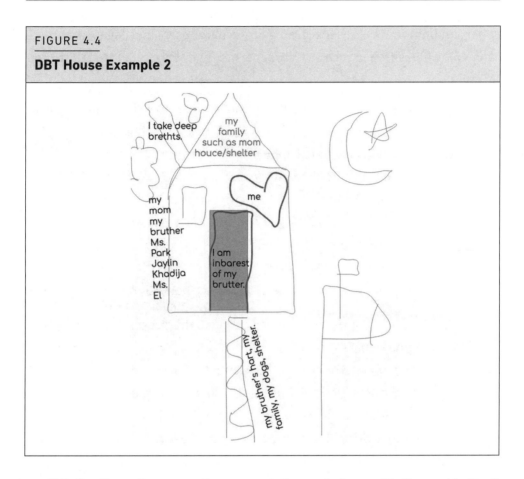

"My family, such as mom," appears on the roof, along with "house/shelter." The student practices deep breathing (as indicated on the chimney), a seemingly age-appropriate stress response. Her door reads, "I am embarrassed of my brother." The year I taught this student, her younger brother, who has Down syndrome, began attending school, and the student was struggling with the questions her classmates were asking about her brother's perceived differences. Her brother is mentioned elsewhere on the map positively, however, including the mention of "my brother's heart."

Strategy 6: Identify Your Space

Chapter 3 identified the four *R*s of self-regulation: root, resource, reach, and reduce. Strategies 6 and 7 belong to the first group; they are all rooting (or grounding) practices. This strategy is ideal for early language learners. In moments of heightened reaction, students are invited to walk through the following steps:

1. Name **five** things to look at. (*window, desk, Mrs. El Yaafouri, book, highlighter*)
2. Name **four** things to touch. (*paper, knee, shoelace, pencil*)
3. Name **three** things to listen to. (*buzzing light, Eh Nar's pencil-tapping, Mrs. Park's voice*)
4. Name **two** things to smell. (*my lotion, Mr. Than's coffee*)
5. Name **one** positive quality about yourself. (*I am a really great soccer player*)
6. If, after completing this exercise, the anxiety persists, repeat the process.

Students may also learn to guide peers through this process. For example, in my classroom, the signal for Identify Your Space is a "gimme five" hand (hand held up with fingers outstretched, like reaching to give someone a high five). This gesture symbolizes that the process should be underway. We may do this as a class, or students may be cued to jump in solo. Often, I'll catch students guiding one another through this process, even outside the classroom on the playground or in the lunchroom.

Strategy 7: S.O.S

S.O.S. mirrors Identify Your Space but is more appropriate for older students and more advanced language learners. This strategy was initially introduced by researchers Julian Ford and Eileen Russo (2006) as a tool for self-regulating post-traumatic stress disorder and substance abuse disorders. Here, it is adapted for a classroom setting. Like Identify Your Space, this strategy helps students root down, diffusing and reframing the problem. Again, if we reach the final component and the emotional energy level is still elevated, we return to the beginning and start again. S.O.S. is three parts:

1. **Slow down:** Reenter the present moment. Observe what is happening in your mind and body. Count to 10, close your eyes, practice relaxing one body part at a time, or take three deep breaths.

2. **Orient yourself:** Focus your mind's energy on just one thought. That thought—an image, an emotion, a goal—is whatever is most important to you at this moment. Focusing on just one thought turns down your brain's alarm.

3. **Self-check:** Take a moment to assess the level of stress you're feeling, as well as your level of personal control (i.e., your ability to think clearly). Put it on a scale of 1 to 10. Are you at a 4 or higher? If so, return to the beginning and start the process again.

Note that S.O.S. provides greater choice and agency. For example, students are prompted to choose a stress-alleviating method that appeals to them, and the second step is open-ended. Considering this element of personal choice, I find that S.O.S is especially effective with older students or students who have developed a sense of mastery over the more concrete Identify Your Space process.

Where Do We Go from Here?

In this chapter, we

- Recommitted to building relationships with our students.
- Developed an understanding of how transition shock can create challenges for making friends and developing reciprocity in relationships.
- Learned a series of strategies aligned to the pillar of connection.
- Gained a deeper understanding of how culture and language influence our approach to mitigating transition shock.

We've taken our first steps in clearing a path for students that leads toward power restoration. Let's continue this forward momentum as we move into the next pillar, protect.

Protect:
Cultivating Trust and Safety

We've taken the important first step of curating authentic relationships with and among our students. Now we'll begin working on the second pillar in approaching transition shock. Protect prompts us to focus on cultivating safety and trust.

Trust is central to safety. It includes trust in oneself, peers, family, and adults; trust in one's surroundings; trust in the process of learning, failing, and growing; trust in the future; and so on. "With any kind of trauma, trust is the biggest issue we're working toward," writes Maggie Fazeli Fard (2019). "Strength is a manifestation of trust in yourself" (para. 37).

This second pillar is a natural next step, especially when we consider that the central difference between connection and relationship is a bond of trust. Making this leap requires an element of vulnerability. As we progress into richer levels of connection, we enter into the expectation that we are willing to expose a bit more of our authentic selves. This can be unsettling—even terrifying—for many of us.

Transition shock can make the prospect of opening up to others even more anxiety-producing (Mind for Mental Health, 2020). In fact, a trauma-affected brain has become programmed to reject vulnerability at all costs. The entire limbic system, including the amygdala and hippocampus, are hard at work "protecting" the affected individual with its hard-wired response system. These reactive processes, by their very nature, are designed to *shut out* (Rosenthal, 2019).

Trust in one's environment is equally as important. Transition shock becomes magnified in settings that are unstable, unpredictable, disorganized, chaotic, overstimulating, or understimulating (NCTSN, 2019). Students with displacement or refugee histories, for example, often face power interruptions related to a lack of environmental trust. Chronic and pervasive pre-emigration threats (including war, migration, exploitation, and border confinement) combine with post-emigration hurdles (harmful migration policy, discrimination, racism, economic struggle). For many, the persistent instability creates a breakdown in environmental or situational trust, leading to power disruptions (Nickerson et al., 2020).

On the other hand, controlled settings—which reinforce a sense of safety— help reduce anxiety, promote redirection, and return agency to the individual (Wyman et al., 1999). Safety is a dynamic quality that builds on trust. Here, we'll focus on physical and psychological safety. Physical safety involves a trust that the external environment will remain relatively stable and predictable, with a minimal threat of impending danger. Psychological safety refers to an internal state of relative calm in which the amygdala's alarm is deactivated and the individual is open to some level of vulnerability.

In short, connection is built on trust, and trust forms the cornerstone for safety.

Risk Factors for Transition Shock

To help kids reclaim their protect power, we need to understand how and why these types of power interruptions occur in the first place. We call these *risk factors*, which are circumstances or situations that can make a person more susceptible to transition shock—or that exacerbate existing anxieties (Brown, 2017). Risk factors are not direct causes of transition shock but can contribute to it. Broadly speaking, the more risk factors a person has, the higher their probability for experiencing power disruptions (SAMHSA, 2019).

Let's explore some examples. In the following sections, the first set of factors is representative of all populations. The second set considers risk factors associated with newcomer populations (and, specifically, those with histories of documented or undocumented refugee or asylee status) (Brown, 2017; Centers for Disease Control and Prevention [CDC], 2009; Kreuzer, 2016; Promising Futures, 2019).

Risk factors for transition shock across all student populations include

- **Socioeconomic factors:** poverty and economic disadvantage; social bias, racism, and inequitable access to opportunity; social isolation of family/ethnic community; community violence, persistent historical/intergenerational trauma
- **Home-life factors:** history of violence, abuse, or disordered substance use in the home; history of mental illness in the home; disorganization/instability; poor parent-child relationships; family dissolution; structural impermanence
- **Individual factors:** mental or physical disability (which may add stress or anxiety); individual disposition, personality, and brain chemistry; prior history of education; prior history of trauma; existing (or nonexistent) plan for care
- **Access-to-care factors:** access to basic needs (e.g., healthy foods, clean water, affordable housing, high-quality healthcare, hygienic supplies); access to well-paying jobs; access to equitable education; access to community resources; access to dependable transportation

Risk factors for transition shock for newcomer populations include:

- **Conditional risk factors:** poverty; malnutrition; early birth/low birth weight; perinatal and infant complications and/or exposure; family stability/instability; academic success/perceived success; history of physical or emotional abuse
- **Pre-transition factors:** persecution; war or violence; flight; loss of stability; loss of loved ones and pets; loss of property; loss of family business/income; insufficient medical care; previous exposure to trauma; family discohesion; degree of prior education

- **Post-transition factors:** degree of culture shock; views of stress and coping; attitudes about the countries of origination and destination; mental or physical disability (which may add stress or anxiety); experienced racism, discrimination, or consequences of inequitable policies; linguistic maneuverability

- **Access-to-care factors:** access to equitable health care; access to equitable education; access to heritage culture communities and support groups; access to affordable housing; access to resettlement resources; access to translation services; access to high-paying work opportunities and financial sustainability

Protect Factors for Transition Shock

Let's now move to protect factors, at the opposite side of the spectrum from risk factors. Protect factors have insulating properties and form a sort of safety net around an individual's locus of control (SAMHSA, 2019; Trauma Survivors Network, 2018).

Protect factors do not exclude a person from experiencing a traumatic event or events. Rather, they serve to support healthy coping mechanisms and bolster resilience. In effect, they blunt the impact of trauma on an individual's limbic system and help diminish stress-related overwhelm (Child Welfare Information Gateway, 2015).

These "buffers" hold particular promise for newcomer populations. A recent study looking at resettled refugee youth in Australia found that "children with four or more protective factors are at low risk of poor social-emotional well-being" (Zwi et al., 2018, p. 1). That's big news! And it's a solution we can make decided moves to be a part of, every day.

Gadson came to the United States as a 6-year-old. He arrived from Mali as an unaccompanied minor to receive medical treatment. His is one of the most harrowing biographies—child or adult—I've had the privilege of knowing. In his short life, Gadson endured war, malnourishment, abuse, the loss of a leg, parental absence, and resettlement to a foreign country.

Gadi, as he wished to be called, also proved remarkably resilient. He credits much of this to his mom, Kelli (who, Gadson will tell you, is "the one who always believes in me"). Kelli volunteered to act as his foster guardian prior to his arrival in the United States, not knowing that just a few years later, she and Gadi would be legally declared family in front of a judge, friends, and family.

For Gadi, 2nd grade meant starting school in a new country and in a new language. Halfway through the year, he received (and sometimes struggled to manage) his first prosthetic. Nevertheless, no other student in the school came bouncing down the hallway with half of his enthusiasm. His animated smile and laughter proved contagious. Within weeks, everyone in the building knew the boy.

I had the honor of welcoming Gadi into my 3rd grade classroom the next school year. He applied himself earnestly to school and made rapid progress. He didn't sit out of any activities—not a rigorous content lesson or a strenuous gym class. Gadi would stumble over his newly acquired language and fall over because of his prosthetic, but in seconds, he was back up, picking up exactly where he left off.

Just before 5th grade, Gadi was accepted into a prestigious school of arts and sciences where he'd be able to develop his love and talent for drama alongside his academic studies. In the days before his big move, Gadi took time with me to reflect on his early experiences as a newcomer student.

> I remember that I was not a very happy person when I first came to America. I did not know anybody in my school or in town. I didn't speak any English or type or write. I didn't even know how to read. I only knew two words in English: "no" and "yes." So, if you asked me what my name was, I would reply, "No" or "Yes!" I also remember when I met my friends and my teacher, Ms. Stash.

The first thing I really wanted my teacher to know was that I didn't like being alone. The second thing was that I was very emotional, and I still am. I cry when I do something wrong, and I always think that I am in trouble.

My biggest worry about coming to America and starting school was that my friends here would not like me for who I am. I wanted my classmates to know that I wanted them to be my friends, but I couldn't tell them that in their language. I wanted them to appreciate that I liked and believed different things than them. I wanted them to like me just the way I am.

Mostly, I think the U.S. schools are very nice. When I was in Africa, I never really liked my school. My teacher would hit or whip me when I did anything wrong—even though it was usually my little cousin who got me in trouble! The one thing that bugged me about school here was when everyone kept on talking and playing so that I couldn't learn what the teacher was teaching me.

My teacher here was so kind, though. I wouldn't change anything about my first teacher, Ms. Stash. She made math fun. She challenged the students with fun games so we could get used to having her around. Telling us stories (mostly chapter books) helped the students visualize the word and help get the word into our smart brains.

The advice I would give to other newcomers is to try their best to fit in. And not to worry, as long as they work hard and think smart.

What risk factors does Gadi appear to present? What protective factors appear to be present? In what ways might these protective factors help counter Gadi's adverse life experiences? Do we need to know the details of Gadi's "door" in order to advocate for more protective factors embedded throughout his learning day? How might Gadi's experiences have been different if he'd had a different teacher in those first days?

"There is a fine line between protective factors and risk factors," explains Dr. Asa Don Brown (2017). "Protective factors will *always* encourage personal growth, maturation, independence, stability, and the ability to thrive, while risk factors deteriorate a person's ability to feel secure, safe, and effectively manage his or her life. *Essentially, the greatest risk is a person's incapability of thriving and proving resilient"* (para. 7). With that in mind, we can sort protective elements according to those forces that are hardest at work in shaping students' lives: home, school, and the community (O'Connell, Boat, & Warner, 2009).

Home

The quality of students' home lives can influence their ability to be present at school (literally and figuratively) and open to learning new things. Research links academic achievement and home-based protect factors (CDC, 2009). Here are some examples of what that could look like:

- Nurturing caregivers, safe boundaries, structure, fair and reasonable discipline.
- Access to basic needs, including adequate housing, healthy foods, clean water, and medical care.
- Financial stability and a commitment to the family's health and well-being.
- Connectedness to extended family, friends, social networks, and community resources.

Other home, school, and community factors that contribute to educational achievement and resilience include

- Using personal narratives about the value of education.
- Emphasizing education as the means of social mobility.
- Providing words of encouragement and moral support.
- Placing a high value on education.
- Monitoring participation in both academic and nonacademic activities.
- Communicating clear and realistic expectations regarding academic performance and providing learning resources at home to meet those expectations.
- Using positive parent-child relationships as an inspirational tool to succeed academically and personally. (O'Connell et al., 2009)

School

Protective classrooms and schools are places where students can experience a developed sense of belonging, safety, and freedom to show up as themselves. They are places with

- A healthy school culture and climate, inclusive curriculum, highly qualified teachers, and equitable access to robust instructional programming.
- A learning environment that is free or mostly free of violence, bullying, and discriminatory policies.
- Equitable access to translation services and mental health supports (including trauma-informed care).
- Healthy adult role models (especially those who reflect the diversity of the students).

Community

Aspects of community play a significant role in resilience outcomes for individuals faced with adverse life experiences. Examples include

- An established sense of cohesiveness or "village mentality."
- Few incidences of crime or violence.
- Equitable access to adequate health care, social services, community groups, houses of worship, and fair socioeconomic opportunities.
- Just and nondiscriminatory public policy, law, and legal system (in which racial profiling, racism, and noninclusive practices are not tolerated).

The more protect factors an individual has exposure to, the higher the likelihood he or she is to realize power restoration (O'Connell et al., 2009). Features of protection are built into a majority of social groupings (see Figure 5.1). If we can capture and capitalize on the mechanisms that already exist within our students' networks (and help our students recognize and draw from them independently), then we can enable resilience. Ultimately, though, the school, as an instrument of the community, should be intentional in its efforts to expose, enhance, or invent new protect factors within the broader social organism it belongs to.

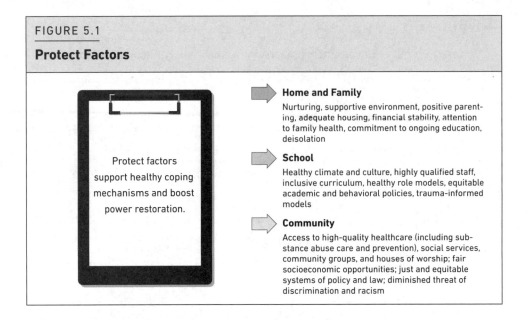

FIGURE 5.1

Protect Factors

Protect factors support healthy coping mechanisms and boost power restoration.

Home and Family
Nurturing, supportive environment, positive parenting, adequate housing, financial stability, attention to family health, commitment to ongoing education, deisolation

School
Healthy climate and culture, highly qualified staff, inclusive curriculum, healthy role models, equitable academic and behavioral policies, trauma-informed models

Community
Access to high-quality healthcare (including substance abuse care and prevention), social services, community groups, and houses of worship; fair socioeconomic opportunities; just and equitable systems of policy and law; diminished threat of discrimination and racism

Parent Engagement as a Protective Factor

Home-school partnerships, including parent engagement, are generally power restorative. Overall, kids get better grades, make healthier decisions, and demonstrate more prosocial behaviors when parents are engaged at their child's school (CDC, 2019).

Of course, something's missing here. There is no uniform rule for how we should expect our students' families to engage in the school experience. As classrooms and campuses, we have plenty of ideas about what that *should* look like. But keep in mind that our "visions" for parent engagement are heavily influenced by individual frames of reference. Because the dominant frame of reference in education is a white middle- and upper-class one, it's easy to misinterpret or understate parent engagement in schools. This occurs frequently in RAEM settings, where intricate social and cultural dynamics are at work.

As part of a 2012 study, researchers interviewed parents and teachers to better understand certain tensions that exist between the two. They concluded that, overall, both parents and teachers believe home-school partnerships are integral to student success. However, "differences emerged as to how teachers and parents constructed and interpreted involvement and operational processes supporting partnerships and the significance each group placed on different aspects of collaboration between parent and teacher" (Ludicke & Kortman, 2012, p. 1). In other words, there's a lot of gray area around who's expected to do what.

What does this mean? Well, for one, it means we must take a more expansive view of parent and family engagement. From a culturally responsive perspective, it also means we must consider various social norms and beliefs about the roles of parent and teacher. Teaching in Tanzania, for example, I quickly learned that educators don't question the role of the parent at home. Likewise, parents don't question the role or decisions of the educator. Teachers are considered "honorables" in the community. To second-guess a person in this position comes across as an insult of their capabilities. When families transition to a new setting (especially where a different set of social norms and values are present), initial mismatches are likely.

Supporting *all* students leads us to shift how we create and grow bonds between the school and our students' homes. Let's once again narrow our focus to concentrate on RAEMs. Here are some conversations we should be having:

- What does engagement look like for our newcomer parents and caretakers?
- What sociocultural components enhance or deter home-school partnerships (e.g., viewing the teacher as an expert, lack of trust in the school system, concerns over immigration status, different views about what the content of instruction should be, not wanting to intrude)?
- What expectations do we currently hold for what optimal parent engagement looks like? What is the root of these assumptions? What biases can we identify and dismantle regarding these expectations?
- Where can we replace deficit thinking with asset-based thinking concerning home-school partnerships and parent/family engagement?
- How can we reenvision our approach to family engagement to ensure they are culturally affirmative and build on existing funds of knowledge at work within our students' homes?

> Here's Rujan:
>
> I recall that I willingly took time to finish my homework as soon as I got home from school. I would then eat and go play until 10 or 10:30 p.m. at times. It is this fine balance that was critical to my individual success. Perhaps, it is this discipline that was equally of importance. I asked my brother this question about me, and the first thing he described about my younger self was my calm demeanor and willingness to go to various clubs at [our apartment complex] for homework help. I tend to think that little of my success is based on my actual character; for me, it is and will always be in large part a credit to the people around me who continue to push me and serve as a driver for my actions.

Protect: Into Practice
Strategy 1: DBT House, Revisited

Let's return to the DBT House introduced in Chapter 4. Recall that the roof space, where we direct students to name the people or things that protect them, speaks directly to this idea of cultivating an environment of safety and trust. What specific people or places from the school are named here? Have you, as the student's teacher, been named as someone who has earned the student's trust as a protector? Does someone else on your team show up?

As long as someone from the school is named in this space, I'm satisfied. I can work to add new folks or places as time goes on. Once again, if I'm not a presence in the child's life as a protective agent (and *especially* if no other site-based protectors are listed), I am committed to getting myself there. That becomes my most important goal in working with that student for the year—even ahead of any academic accomplishments.

This circles back to the idea that when students feel safe and supported, they are better able to learn. So how do we know if students are feeling safe and supported? We ask them. In the case of the DBT House, the approach is less direct, which helps reduce the anxiety students feel in interrogatory situations and may help students "save face."

We can look for other clues on the roof, too. What other aspects of the student's reality exists (or does not exist) there? Are family members present in this space? If so, who are they? Are friends or community organizations visible? What about physical structures? Who or what is not here?

What else can we notice? In the context of my newcomer students, I've seen all kinds of things show up in the roof space. I've seen siblings or foster parents in place of birth parents, faith-based figures and institutions, security cameras, case workers, weaponry, and money make appearances in this space.

When I first began implementing this strategy with RAEM students, a variety of service members appeared in the roof space, including police officers, firefighters, and case workers. However, in recent years, these figures have disappeared from the DBT maps completely. This, it seems, underscores the urgent need for repairing some of these badly damaged bonds (or establishing genuine connection where none existed in the first place). For example, law enforcement presence in the school or community for positive reasons—such as attending students' award ceremonies, engaging in honest and constructive dialogue with student groups, or participating in volunteer community events in the neighborhood—may be an essential first step in establishing (or reestablishing) trust as a person of protection. It's important to note that caution and thoughtful consideration are advised here. In the absence of historical trust or context, such encounters can actually be retriggering.

Let's turn our focus now to the door space of the DBT House. Remember, it's here that we've committed to a more power-restorative prompt. Instead of recording something they're embarrassed of, afraid of, or keep hidden from others, students are invited to write a heart goal. That is, they should focus on a thought, an emotion, or a behavioral pattern they'd like to change or develop during the school year.

Let's sit for a moment with the original version: *something you tend to keep hidden from others.* The purpose of the door, in this case, is not to draw out underlying student trauma but to provide more insight into how we—their teachers—can best serve the whole student. Typically, the items that show up on the door have nothing to do with a direct adverse experience but may nonetheless require attention and care from a practitioner's perspective.

This space is important, even for those who choose to leave it blank. The prompt sends out a signal that vulnerability is welcomed and celebrated within the safe space you have created. Students may not be ready to bring this information to the table, but it opens a door, so to speak, for open conversations in the future. In the hours, days, or weeks after students complete their houses, I often take time to share one of my own door elements. When our students recognize our own humanity—as well as our ability to forge a resilient path—we invite healthy, productive relationships. The two student samples included in this chapter speak to this version of the prompt, which I used in the classroom for nearly 10 years.

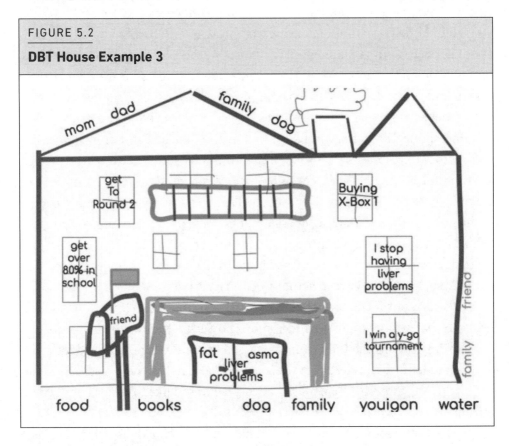

FIGURE 5.2

DBT House Example 3

Take a look at the house in Figure 5.2. It was created by a 12-year-old boy originally from Mexico. The student drew a large house or apartment building, which takes up the entirety of the page (on a horizontal layout). The entire image was drawn in pencil. There are two separate roof peaks with a chimney between them. The student included a number of windows, many of which contain writing (goals), and a balcony stretches across the uppermost windows.

Two joined front doors are centered and framed by a structural border. A mailbox features prominently and is positioned to the left of the doors. This is the space the student has used for his billboard.

A number of features stand out. On the roof space, mom, dad, family, and dog are named. This suggests a clear opportunity to add to this area, especially around friendships and school personnel. Moving to the door, the student has written, "fat, asthma, liver problems." In the classroom, this student was easily distracted and typically showed very low levels of energy. As a teacher, I'd gotten on him repeatedly for his "lack of focus." Until he drew his DBT House, I had no knowledge of his underlying health issues. One of his life goals (as evidenced on a window) is to "stop having liver problems." Clearly, this changed my entire approach in working with this student.

On the floor, the student hinted at areas of high-level interest (which may be utilized to drive motivation and learning). Along the walls, he named family and a singular friend. His billboard (the mailbox) indicates that he is also proud of that friend. In this case, prosocial behavior interventions and friend-making accommodations were put in place.

Figure 5.3 shows a house created by a 13-year-old girl originally from Venezuela. The structure is a rectangular house or apartment building, drawn as a three-dimensional figure. The front of the building is marked by two large doors, framed by a pair of pine trees. Three windows, one large and two small, can be seen on one side of the structure. The drawing also includes a chimney and a large sign, which hangs just above the doors. The student wrote her name in several places, followed by a string of exclamation marks.

The roof space, the area of protection, appears healthy with multiple people named. Interestingly, the student included herself in this space, perhaps indicating some level of confidence in her ability and responsibility to self-protect. However, there is a notable absence of any school-related factors, suggesting room for purposeful initiative on the part of the teacher(s) and staff.

Friendship and family form the foundation of this student's house. One wall includes a number of supports, including friends, grandparents, cousins, and siblings. Looking at these indicators, we see that this learner appears to have well-established connect features, including a strong friend/family network.

Once again, however, there appears to be a clear opportunity to add school-based supports to the map.

FIGURE 5.3

DBT House Example 4

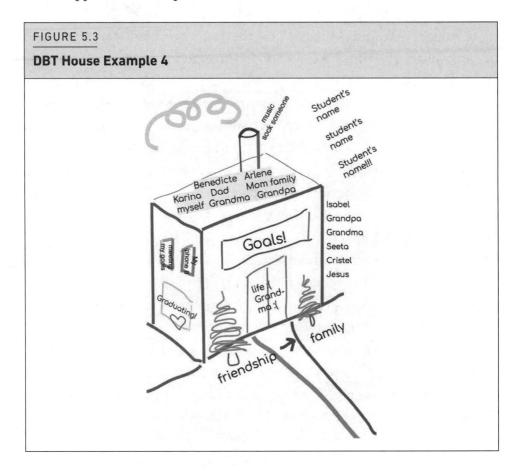

The door indicates a loss of a loved one. It also includes the word *life* and a sad emoji. Without drawing more information from the student, it may be worthwhile to offer regular check-ins or opportunities for release, such as journaling. The billboard and windows on this house stand out. The former reads, in large print, "Goals!" The latter, "meeting my goals," "my iPhone 8," and "Graduating!" Clear goal-setting has been linked to resilience, so this is certainly encouraging to see!

Now let's consider the new prompt. Once again, if you are specifically trained to help young people address whatever appears on their doors, you may choose to keep with it. As for the rest of us, asking students to think on a heart goal further minimizes the risk of a trauma trigger (or "spark," as you'll read about in Chapter 8). It also paves the way for creating an actionable plan with manageable steps toward overcoming an undesirable emotion, thought, or behavioral pattern—or boosting an emotional well-being habit they'd like to see more of!

I transitioned to implementing the heart growth prompt in early 2020. Of course, at that time, we were collectively in the thick of the COVID-19 pandemic and at the height of the social justice protests and racial reckoning brought on by the death of George Floyd. Even though most of our interactions were virtual throughout this period, the responses to the revised prompt were transformative—with incredibly power-restorative outcomes. Here are a few of the insights participants recorded on their doors during this unprecedented period:

- When I start to panic, it's like a snowball, and soon I can't stop it. I want to learn how to catch myself before the panic gets so big.
- It's hard to make friends because I don't trust anybody. And now we don't even go to school at school with other kids anyway. I want to have a friend this year.
- I get in a lot of trouble when I'm mad. I don't always want to be mad. It just happens.

Wondering how we made these into action plans? For the first student (high school), we focused on SEL skills (specifically, mindfulness), and she tracked her process using her own variation of the worry scale, which she created based on a template of the original. (See Strategy 4 in this chapter.) We also utilized a PearDeck check-in where she could anonymously share where she was and comment directly to a teacher if she needed words of encouragement.

The second learner (middle school) benefitted from a concentration on reciprocal behaviors. We also embedded conversations into our shared reading on what it means to be a good friend and what those qualities look like. Then we worked toward sustainable partnerships in class, ultimately building up his window of tolerance for trust.

Finally, in working with the third learner (2nd grade), we had talks about righteous anger—or being mad for a purpose. The Communities for Just

School Funds (2020) describes it this way: "Righteous anger has long been used as a tool to fuel movements that have and continue to propel our nation forward towards justice. To tell students to not harness their anger is to tell them their rage isn't warranted" (para. 12). Rather, says Audre Lorde (1981), "Anger is loaded with information and energy," and when "focused with precision, it can become a powerful source of energy serving progress and change" (pp. 8–9).

As an instructional team, we took a hard look at the disciplinary reactions to the student's anger. In place of dismissive or punitive measures, we worked with the student to help her identify where and how her anger energy could be channeled in positive, productive ways—and we celebrated with her in the moments those shifts were realized. In the meantime, we focused on building up her power-restorative toolbox with strategies such as Identify Your Space (Chapter 4) and Modified Talking Chips (Chapter 6). As the months progressed, she became more adept at recognizing her own power for good in a situation, and she began exercising empowering choices more frequently.

Strategy 2: List-Group-Label

This is a strategy I implement frequently as an instructional support for language learners (Taba, 1967). It is a semantic mapping tool that effectively activates background knowledge and draws from students' personal experiences. It is also an extremely versatile strategy and can be employed across all content areas and language levels, in all stages of learning, and in a variety of constructs (i.e., independent, small group, whole class). In this case, we'll apply it in a trauma-informed context.

The strategy is three-part. First, students brainstorm as many words as they can relate to a topic (list). Then they sort those words into categories, based on shared characteristics, and name each category to reflect the items housed within it (group). Finally, they reflect on their practice and provide reasoning for their sorting and labeling choices (label).

In this case, we invite students to investigate elements of safety and calm in their academic environment. This is a way of building the Hand of Connection or the connect/protect elements of the DBT House. Those strategies are, in a way, diagnostic. They help us establish a baseline of care based on an individu-al's needs at a given time and in a given context. Here, students are encouraged to analyze features of safety and calm as they apply directly to them. The pro-cesses of sorting, naming, and reflecting on the items allows students to "sit" with their thinking, seek out patterns, and process (and expand on) the infor-mation in a deeper way.

From a culturally responsive lens, semantic devices such as this one high-light traditional recall and call-and-response inclinations. In addition, this particular prompt functions as a form of problem-based learning (How can I feel safe and calm at school?), which lends itself to culturally responsive teach-ing. "This is because, when presenting a relatable real-world problem for your students to solve, two cultural connections will typically occur" (Guido, 2017, para. 44). The first is a cultural link, either explicit or implicit, and the second involves the unique cultural perspectives that influence one's approach to solv-ing the problem.

Here's who's empowered:

- Students, with the guidance of adult facilitators

Here's what you'll need:

- Chart paper or letter-sized paper with or without premade template (see Appendix)

Here's what you'll do:

1. Introduce the focus topic. In this case, elements of safety and calm within the school. (See Figure 5.4 for a completed example.)
2. Invite students to brainstorm as many words as they can that relate to the topic.
3. Have students examine the items they came up with and sort them into categories based on similar characteristics or other identifiable relation-ships (e.g., people who make me feel safe, things I do to feel calm, places I go to feel calm). Three or four groups are ideal.
4. Have students think of an appropriate name for each categorized group.

5. Invite students to reflect on their finished charts. Can they explain why they grouped items in a certain way? Can they justify the group names? Would they change anything about the way they moved through the process? Did anything feel uncomfortable or stand out to them?

6. Remind students to add to this chart when they begin to feel overwhelmed.

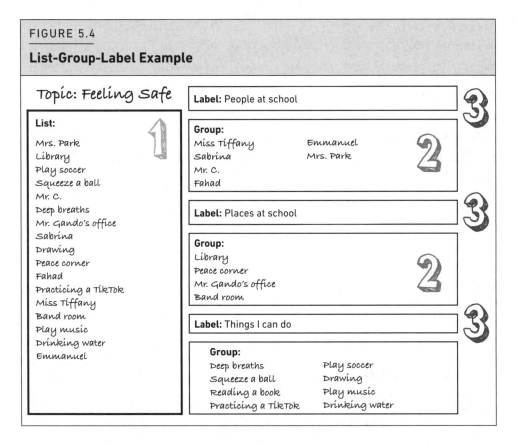

FIGURE 5.4

List-Group-Label Example

Topic: Feeling Safe

List:
Mrs. Park
Library
Play soccer
Squeeze a ball
Mr. C.
Deep breaths
Mr. Gando's office
Sabrina
Drawing
Peace corner
Fahad
Practicing a TikTok
Miss Tiffany
Band room
Play music
Drinking water
Emmanuel

Label: People at school

Group:
Miss Tiffany   Emmanuel
Sabrina   Mrs. Park
Mr. C.
Fahad

Label: Places at school

Group:
Library
Peace corner
Mr. Gando's office
Band room

Label: Things I can do

Group:
Deep breaths   Play soccer
Squeeze a ball   Drawing
Reading a book   Play music
Practicing a TikTok   Drinking water

This tool can also be used to help students observe, identify, and name how their mind and body respond to the brain's alarm system. Helping students understand the human brain and how it works can be incredibly powerful. Taking the time to explain the physiology of the brain in relation to stress serves several purposes, including the normalization of stress and anxiety as protective human functions. As students develop an awareness of these functions and the cues that lead to them, they are better equipped to step in before the limbic system has an opportunity to hijack the reasoning brain. Next, we can explicitly teach about the fight-flight-freeze-submit responses and invite students to recognize key physiological indicators for each. (One particularly useful resource is located at www.innerworldwork.co.uk/wp-content/uploads/2017/04/What-Survival-Looks-Like-At-Home-Quick-Printout.pdf. It is a cheat sheet for reactive indicators with straightforward recommendations for countering them.) Ultimately, once students have "met" and named their own patterns, they can begin to identify which strategies work best for them—and better inform us, as adults of trust, how to guide and assist them in restoring their awesome power.

Strategy 3: Permanence and Detachment Cards

Transition shock disrupts processes and capacities related to . . . *transition*. Individuals experiencing interrupted power spend more of their time living in survival brain than learning brain. Remember, there are some key things with which survival brain struggles: chiefly, ambiguity and anticipating and managing transition. Because survival brain is hyperfocused on perceived threats, it's difficult for an individual to experience trust and flexibility from this space.

I first implemented this strategy in the hope of countering the anxiety my students demonstrated year after year in the days leading up to winter break. Permanence and detachment cards serve as bridges across periods of interruption such as vacations and holiday breaks. Here is the central message the cards deliver:

I am not going anywhere.
I (and we, as a class) will be here, excited to see you when it's time to return.

The cards are a tangible reminder of the connection and trust you have built together and as a class. They are a small token on which students can focus when they feel overwhelmed by unknowns. After implementing these cards, I've seen class anxiety levels (as gathered through daily individual and whole-class check-ins) decrease markedly.

Here's who's empowered:

- Students, with the direct support of adult facilitators

Here's what you'll need:

- Printable cardstock or paper sheets with 4–16 blank cards per page, depending on how large or small you'd like them to be. Alternatively, you can use a selection of traditional note cards.

Here's what you'll do:

1. Decide what you will say to your students. Be as specific as possible. For example, if school will be closed Monday and Tuesday, write, "I look forward to seeing you on Wednesday, March 15 at 11 a.m. for English class! —Ms. K" (see Figure 5.5).
2. Print a sheet of cards and cut them out (or handwrite note cards) to give to students. Share these with students in advance of the interruption (say, on Friday afternoon before an extended weekend or before lunch in preparation for a guest speaker arriving that afternoon). Distribute cards to *all* students, even if you are only targeting one or two for permanence and detachment mediation.
3. For those students who appear to struggle with separation, take the time to add an additional thought or signature (e.g., I might draw a few images that remind them of power-restorative tools they have in their toolbox, such as Circle of Control). The extra step in personalizing a card goes a long way.
4. Remind students what and when the interruption is. Frequent reminders can help diminish the level of ambiguity and subsequent manifestations of stress.

For students who face challenges with navigating transition, any kind of unanticipated shift during the school day can prove triggering. Therefore, it can be helpful to distribute these cards to individual students in advance of a transition. I've employed them before a change in schedule, such as a school performance or our weekly library visit. They've also been incredibly useful before fire alarm, lock down, and tornado drills.

As an example, a 3rd grade class will be hosting a docent from a local museum at 2:15 p.m., in the middle of what is typically their math period. First thing in the morning the teacher posts a whole-class note (or distributes cards to the handful of learners for whom they are part of an intervention plan), reminding students of the event later in the day:

Hey team! Remember, we have an exciting afternoon today! Our guest speaker from the museum will be here at 2:15 to talk with us about landforms. Awesome!

Before lunch, the teacher repeats the message, and half an hour or so before the event, a few more notes are delivered:

Countdown to transition! 😊
We'll make our transition to the guest speaker in 30 minutes.

FIGURE 5.5

Example Permanence and Detachment Card

In addition, permanence and detachment cards can be useful when transitioning to new periods, subjects, or activities during the school day. The same concept can be embedded into virtual instruction tools, such as SeeSaw, ClassKick, or GoogleSlides. For example, when using PearDeck, I'll insert what I call "heads up" slides to the presentation to indicate that a transition is on the way:

Learners, it's almost time to stop working on your atoms project and start writing your reflections.

1. Be ready to transition in 8 minutes.
2. You'll need your writing notebook and a pencil.
3. Listen for the transition cue.

In PearDeck, I'll also invite students to signal that they've understood the information and are prepared for the transition by sliding an object toward a "thumbs up" or "yes" portion of the screen. Sometimes, it should be noted, students do not engage in the interactive component, or they drag their object to the "thumbs down" or "not ready" position. This may be a helpful tool in better supporting students who need more time or extra support during the period of transition. As with any facet of instruction, the better equipped we are to meet our students where they are, the lower the opportunity for anxiety and stress to set in, and the greater probability of learning success.

Permanence and detachment cards are also meaningful as students make their transitions to the next grades (or on to graduation). In this case, the cards may be presented as an offering of safe keeping. The central message should be *"Our time together is safe, protected, and remembered. I'll still think of you and be expecting great things from you, even after you've moved from this shared space."* As for specific messaging, I lean into something like this:

I look forward to hearing about your adventures and accomplishments. We'll always carry pieces of our time together as we continue our journeys!

Personally, I prefer to follow this up with a district-approved way of maintaining communication with students (in-network school email, for example) or, for new graduates, a Padlet (or similar site) where members of the group can continue to post updates and communicate with you and their cohort.

Strategy 4: Worry Box

This strategy helps students learn to temporarily "contain" unruly thoughts and fears so they can be processed in more manageable chunks. Students are responsible for creating and employing their own worry box and for evaluating the intensity of the worries they place in the box using a number scale. As you'll see in the exercise, sometimes a student's worry tips the high end of the scale. Or maybe it's a persistent worry—one that falls on the lower half of the scale but doesn't seem to go away.

We encourage students to share these weightier concerns to a teacher's worry box (which only the teacher can access). Of course, getting learners to a place where they feel they can safely share their worries is a process that takes time and requires trust. (It's also worth noting that this a process that *builds* trust.) When a student has submitted a concern to the teacher's worry box, it is an acknowledgment that they are brave enough to practice placing some of their burdens with others, to begin conversations about their needs and goals, to ask for help, or to initiate self-advocacy. In both cases—learning to manage stressors or learning to ask for help—worry boxes can be incredibly power restorative.

Here's who's empowered:

- Students, with the guidance of adult facilitators
- Educators, as they learn more about their students

Here's what you'll need:

- Printable worry box templates with scales (or a large class-created scale) *(see Appendix)*, empty tissue boxes, or small mint tins (one per student)
- One shoe box or other similarly sized container
- Decorative materials (e.g., markers, paint, stickers)

Here's what you'll do:

1. Preface this activity with a conversation about worries, a read-aloud in which a character deals with a worry, or another appropriate lead-in.
2. Explain to students that they will construct a worry box. The purpose of the box will be to "capture" their worries. Each box will be unique and should reflect the person who made it.
3. Discuss connection, community, and trust. Each person's box is special, sacred, and private to them, unless they choose to share a worry with a friend.

4. Engage students in the process of constructing their boxes from the template. Alternatively, if using tins or other premade containers, invite them to choose one they feel is right for them. Then allow time for students to personalize their boxes using paint, markers, stickers, or other materials.

5. Once the boxes are completed, share the student instructions with the class and invite them to practice. If necessary, model the process yourself first.

6. Until this practice becomes a habit, remind students that their worry boxes are available to them if they need to capture a concern.

7. Remember to frequently check the teacher's worry box and respond to students as needed (see student directions).

Student Directions:

1. Write your worry on a piece of paper.

2. Place your worry on the worry scale so the number on the scale matches the strength of your worry.

3. Place your worry inside your worry box. When you close the lid, your worry is captured inside. You can always come back to it later if you need to.

4. At the end of the day (or the next day), come back to your box and pull out a worry. Where on the worry scale is it now? Is it a smaller worry? Is it still a worry at all? If it's not, take the worry out, think about how it was resolved, and then toss the worry away!

5. If your worry has grown, take it out of your box and place it in your teacher's worry box. This will let your teacher know that you'd like to work on solving your worry together.

In the classroom, I use simple templates for this strategy: a repurposed three-dimensional cube template from our math curriculum (for the worry box) and a visual 1–10 scale with an increasing number of stacking blocks (for the worry scale). Students have smaller desk-sized versions of the worry scale, and we keep a few full page–sized copies in our Restore Your Power space.

For hybrid and virtual learning (or even as an in-person learning alternative to the original exercise), students can create a shared Google folder or design a worry box slide deck. For example, in SeeSaw, we create an entire folder of Restore Your Power resources and tools. PearDeck offers several mental health "check-in" slides where students drag a slider (which appears anonymously on screen) along a gradient from the green zone of 1 ("I'm in a good space and can focus right now") to the red zone of 10 ("I can't manage my emotions or behaviors right now").

If using tools such as these, it may be useful to occasionally invite all students to mark one of their worries on the scale (they wouldn't need to reveal what the worry is). This serves two purposes. First, it allows students to recognize that they are not alone in having concerns, which can lend to a sense of community.

Second, if the scale is filled with 7s, 8s, 9s, and 10s, that's a sign that it's probably time to stop and have a conversation outside the content-learning agenda. If students are consistently entering class in survival mode, then even our best instructional efforts are compromised. We're better off stopping, restoring student power, and facilitating a shift into learning brain.

Finally, remember to check the teacher's worry box regularly and promptly address shared concerns. Usually, I'll acknowledge, verbally or in writing, that I've received their worry. Lately, I've been having students add one of three numbers to their note when they submit it. (1 = Just wanted someone to know; 2 = I could use a check-in; 3 = I need a hand now!) I'll also use these cues when conversing directly with students. This helps maintain boundaries and continue to build trustful partnerships.

Strategy 5: Descriptive Pairs

In Chapter 3, we identified the four *R*s of self-regulation: root, resource, reach, and reduce. Strategies 5 and 6 belong to the second group; they are all resourcing practices. This strategy allows students to practice identifying facial expressions and body language and associating those indicators with probable thoughts or feelings. RAEM students who have experienced transition shock may have a difficult time "reading" these external cues and correctly interpreting their intended meaning (Passardi, 2018). This challenge is twofold. First, individuals in survival mode typically struggle to evaluate the human condition and misinterpret important messages communicated through facial expression and body language. To further complicate the matter, these cues can carry vastly different meanings when viewed through separate cultural lenses.

First, let's take a look at how this strategy can be implemented in a classroom setting. Later, we'll explore relevant and overlapping cultural reference points.

Here's who's empowered:

- Students, with the guidance of adult facilitators

Here's what you'll need:

- Preplanned "play boards" (for whole-class engagement) or play cards (for two-person engagement). Play boards should have emotion words or pictures (e.g., *pleased, confused, frustrated, jealous, excited, nervous, furious*).

Here's what you'll do:

1. Have students work in pairs. Partners should sit back-to-back, with one partner facing the play board or holding a set of play cards. (For a deeper level of language support, vocabulary can be "chunked" into categories, as shown in the example that follows.)
2. The partner facing the board (or holding the cards) describes the facial expressions and body language that correspond with a particular emotion *without saying the actual emotion word.* (For example, "Someone's eyebrows scrunch together. He is not yelling. He is thinking a lot, but he doesn't know what to do.")
3. At any time, the other partner can interject with a guess. If the response is correct, the pair moves on to the next word. If the response is incorrect, play continues with further descriptions.
4. When all the emotions on the play board (or all the play cards) have been completed, have students switch roles and repeat.

Traditionally, this activity is used as a best-practices strategy for language development. (It's one of my favorite academic language strategies in the emergent multilingual classroom.) It may be helpful for students to establish a level of mastery with this activity by introducing it with a less abstract topic before diving into the emotions.

Figure 5.6 includes some cues I've used to practice this strategy with adult teachers in a professional development context. Since the goal is to describe an item without revealing the target word, a player describing *photosynthesis* might say, "Plants. Sun. The leaves soak up sunlight. They convert it into energy by. . . ." The partner might interject at this point with a reasonable guess or guesses.

Note that the vocabulary becomes progressively more challenging and requires the participants to rely on deeper levels of content vocabulary. Thus, we assume that "students" have already interacted with this vocabulary in class and/or are approaching the material from the same cultural/geographical orientation as the instructor.

As a reminder, it's worthwhile to keep our conversations on culturally responsive pedagogy in mind while moving through this exercise with students. Several key points from that section are especially relevant here, including these:

- Individual reference points can influence communication.
- Various cultures (and even cultures within cultures) utilize, view, and respond to social cues such as gestures, facial expressions, and body language in different ways.
- We're careful not to overgeneralize about how a student will interact with social cues based on a presumed cultural affiliation.

Strategy 6: *Quat Esmak* ("The Power of Your Name")

The Arabic term *quat esmak* translates as "the power of your name." Though I now speak the Lebanese dialect of Arabic, I didn't know a word of it when the idea for this exercise came about. The inspiration for the strategy was a student named Noor. She was part of one of the first waves of Syrian refugees to be resettled in Denver.

FIGURE 5.6

Example Descriptive Pairs

Partner A:	Partner B:
Beyoncé	Batman
Eagle	Rollerblades
Lacrosse	Shaquille O'Neal
Metamorphosis	Photosynthesis
World War II	NATO
Gender Inequality	Justice

I've had many students with this name, both in classes before and after this one. Nevertheless, it hadn't occurred to me to ask about the name. Noor didn't say much for the first few weeks she was in class. Then, one day during a small-group reading center, she leaned across the table and informed me, "My name means 'light.' I quickly realized this wasn't just about Noor's name and what it meant. It was about Noor acting on her power to initiate conversation, trust, and relationship.

Some nine years later, we named our first son Noor. Our youngest son is named Joud Kareem ("kindness" and "generosity"). In most cultures, names are filled with meaning. They might hold hopes for the newly welcomed children, or they might describe the child's physical attributes or the conditions on the day of birth. Even in the United States, where names tend to be much more inventive, many people have some story about where their names come from and what they mean.

In education—in multilingual education specifically—one of the most effective things we can do to signal respect in the classroom is address students by their preferred and correctly pronounced name. Our names are directly tied to our sense of identity. The way we choose to call ourselves—by birth name, nickname, or chosen name—is typically the first thing we share with others. It is the first piece of interpersonal exchange and the first step toward vulnerability.

It may be surprising to learn that names can play an important role in mitigating transition shock, as well. As it turns out, there is something incredibly grounding about hearing and writing something as familiar as one's own name.

This makes sense. For most of us, our given name has remained a constant throughout our lifetime (with the exception of changing nicknames). Transition shock, meanwhile, is anything but constant. Indeed, trauma is a direct product of the extraordinary. By recognizing and focusing on one of the most dependable aspects of ourselves, we can better position ourselves (or our students) to invite grounding.

Returning to my conversation with Noor, and recalling what I'd already learned about the grounding that can come from recalling one's own name, I set out to bring these components together as a writing assignment. The goal was to expand the toolboxes of two learners in the class whom I recognized may benefit from grounding tools. In the process, I'd have an opportunity to learn about all of the students in the class. It's an exercise I've turned to every year since both to practice grounding and to strengthen classroom connection and trust.

Optimally, we move beyond simply learning our students' names. We can elevate them to be at the very heart of the classroom community. However, before we get too far ahead of ourselves, let's explore students' names as they directly relate to newcomer students. Names that are different from what we are familiar with require more attention to teach and model. Still, it is a relatively small adjustment with a tremendous payout: working toward gaining students' trust via the on ramp of respect. By contrast, when we fail to get it right—or change it to suit our own sense of convenience and ease—we send our students a message that is power diminishing.

I'll add an important note to this exercise. We're not asking students to tell the complete history of their names. The difference seems subtle, but it looms large in the context of trauma-informed practice. Asking an individual to focus on the history of their name can, in some case, be triggering. That is, it can call on memories of a time, place, or person at the heart of their power interruption.

Asking learners about the power of their name puts them in the driver's seat. With that in mind, we should ask

- What name would you like to be known by (nickname, middle name, shortened name, birth name, newly chosen name, gender-preferred name)?

- What aspects of your name do you draw strength from?
- What does your (chosen, not necessarily given) name say about the power you have and the determination you have to achieve your dreams in the future?
- What language makes you happiest to see your name in?
- What about your name can you hold on to or return to when you're feeling overwhelmed?

When I first got to school here, it was really hard for me to understand anybody. It was really confusing. School is a lot harder in Guatemala. I feel like the things they teach you in 1st grade in Guatemala are the things they teach you in 3rd or 4th grade here. The teachers are harder, too. A lot harder. There, the teachers can hit you if you talk too much or you forget your homework. Here, they say, "It's OK, don't do it next time."

I wish my first teacher in America knew that she could call me Isabel. But I didn't know how to tell her that in English. On the computer, it always said Manuela Isabella. Manuela came from my grandpa's name, Manuel. But my grandma started calling me Isabel. I wanted other people to call me Isabel because I miss my grandma and I can't see her anymore. Now all the teachers and kids at school call me Manuela, even though I still want to be called Isabel because it's special to me.

—*Manuela/Isabel, age 11, arrived in the United States at age 9 from Guatemala (first language: Spanish)*

When it comes to the social-emotional aspect of self-regulation, we can coach students to rely on their own names as an entry point for minimizing unhelpful or overwhelming stimuli. My favorite way to go about this is to simply *ask* students about the power of their names. We talk about the power to choose exactly what you'd like to be called in our classroom and at school, regardless of the formal names I have on my roster. We have a conversation about the power that can live in our given and chosen names—and how we can lean on this power when we're feeling overwhelmed. We also talk openly about the history of names. I explain that students can share the history of their names if that's where they find power. However, I emphasize that I'd really like them to focus on what strengths and power their names give them moving into the future.

Here are a few straightforward responses, composed by 3rd grade RAEM students:

My name is from Nepal.

First, my uncle gave me my name.

When I see my name in Nepali, it makes me proud
to know two languages.

When I remember I know two languages, I feel like I can learn
lots of other things, too.

I hope you learned about where my name came from.

Let me tell you about my name Mohamed.

It's a name for a lot of people in my family.

Some of the people with my name live in America.

Some of the people with my name live in Syria.

My name is my power to bring America and Syria together.

Have you ever wondered about my name?

My name came from Nepal. It is Jamuna.

My Nepali mom got my name from the river.

Next, the meaning of my name is a Hindu and Muslim name, and
another meaning is "divine water and beautiful life to the world."

Last, it is a good name for me. It comes from the names of
the rivers Ganga and Jamuna. So it is special to me and
my sister Ganga.

I hope you like to learn about my name.

My name is from Burma and Thailand.
First, my parents and Allah gave me my name.
Next, my name means "white light pure."
My name makes me feel like I am bright like the sun and strong.
I hope you learned where my name is from.

My name is from Congo.
Nobody has a name the same as me.
Then I remember nobody else is like me and I feel
special and proud.
I don't have to be like everyone else. That's my power.
That's my name.

Figure 5.7 includes a few examples of naming traditions as relayed to me directly by my students and their family members (and verified by experts in the Colorado Refugee Network Service Provider community). As with cultural cues, keep in mind that the examples represent a nonexhaustive introduction to the world of naming traditions—and many variations and exceptions are likely to exist within each culture. You'll want to do your own homework and learn more about the naming traditions for students in your classroom.

Where Do We Go from Here?

In this chapter, we

- Rooted down into the importance of establishing trust with RAEM students.
- Defined and analyzed risk factors and protect factors.
- Highlighted classroom practices and activities that bolster protect factors.
- Employed SEL strategies that are aligned to this pillar of care.

Newcomer students often have unique sets of risk factors that may be less common among traditional student groups. Increasing and enhancing positive risk factors in our students' lives is a powerful way to push back against the negative impacts of transition shock. Next, let's determine how respect amplifies our efforts to connect and protect—and how this growing energy feeds our students' intrapersonal power systems.

FIGURE 5.7

Naming Traditions

Many Arab cultures (e.g., Syria, Iraq, Libya): Naming is systematic. The first name is a personal one; the second is the name of the father; the third and fourth relate to the name of the grandfather and specific clan. Names are connected with *Al* or *El,* meaning "of" (e.g., son of, grandson of). It is common for women to maintain their maiden names after marriage. Individuals are quickly and easily tied to a country, town, family reputation, and religious affiliation by their name. Even two Arabic-speaking individuals in the United States can immediately know much about each other (including region and religion) simply by reading the "code" of the name.

Many Spanish-speaking cultures (e.g., Mexico, Ecuador, Venezuela, Guatemala): Individuals may have one or two first names. The second is considered a composite first name, not a middle name (the second first name is often in honor of a family member, regardless of gender). Typically, two last names are also present—the first being the first surname of the father, the second the surname of the mother. Married women may leave their names unchanged, replace their second surname with the husband's first surname, or add the husband's first surname, separated by a hyphen or *de.* First names may be reserved for close friends and family.

Many Swahili-speaking cultures (e.g., Kenya, Tanzania, Uganda): At the time of birth, an elder gifts a baby with his or her first name, which is based on appearance: the *jina la utotoni* ("childhood name"). As the child grows, his or her parents determine an adult name they wish for the child to grow into: the *jina la ukubwani.*

Many West African cultures (e.g., Nigeria, Ghana, Benin): Children are often named according to circumstances at the time of birth, including the day or time of year, appearance, weather, place of birth, or presence of complications or unusual events.

Many South Asian cultures (e.g., India, Nepal, Bhutan): Names are often indicative of family and religion. For example, Singh indicates Sikh roots. Muslim names do not include a surname and use connectors such as bin or binti ("son/daughter of") to attach the father's first name to the child's first name. Hindus may also use the father's name ahead of their first name, or they may have a first name and surname.

Many Hindi cultures (e.g., Nepal, India): Children are often named according to auspicious astrological features present at the time of birth. Families may include ethnicity or caste determinants in the surname.

Burmese culture (Myanmar): Names do not reflect a surname or family link; each person's name is exclusively his/her/their own. Names are divided into syllables and pronounced in full each time they are stated. The syllabic increments may produce confusion in the West, as our tendency is to break down and order names to include a surname.

Many East Asian cultures (e.g., China, Korea, Vietnam): Traditionally, names are recorded with the family name first, followed by the given name(s).

Inuit culture: Children are often named after a living elder. These two individuals will no longer refer to each other by the relation descriptor (e.g., grandmother, grandchild) but rather by the term *sauniq* ("namesake").

Respect:
Engaging Student Voice, Choice, and Collaboration

We've made it to the third pillar of care, respect. This section incorporates student voice, choice, and collaboration as viable tools for mitigating transition shock and fostering resilience. Respect is not an automatic feature. It develops over time and as an extension of the first two pillars of care.

In the classroom context, this is my favorite pillar. By the time we've made it here, I know that the most complex efforts in welcoming students—getting to know their unique needs and making moves to build and earn trust—are well underway. During this time, many students begin to reveal more of themselves, form interactive alliances, and venture into positive risk-taking. This is where our work starts to pay off!

Think for a moment about the basic tenets of respect. What comes to mind?

Often, we lean into versions of the so-called "golden rule": *Treat others the way you wish to be treated.* In other words, listen well, practice empathy, treat people with kindness, learn to compromise, and be willing to grow as a human.

It is also inclusive of *self-respect:* the idea of recognizing and valuing one's intrinsic worth. Self-appreciation and respect are concepts many of us struggle with, regardless of our exposure to trauma or adverse childhood experiences. However, when transition shock *is* at work within us, it may further restrict our ability to sit with ourselves in grace.

Respect requires trust in the process. It means not always knowing the outcome but staying on the path anyway. It means taking responsibility for your surroundings, tools, and property (and that of others). It means acting with integrity, even when nobody's watching. It signals a willingness to try to see the bigger picture.

Values of Respect and RAEM Populations

Those who work with RAEM students are often alert to other, less frequently celebrated aspects of respect. For example, we are acutely aware that respect ties to race, bias, and how we (explicitly or implicitly) evaluate and interact with people. In addition, we know that respect plays a role in the high (or low) achievement expectations we have for students and how we view the funds of knowledge that exist within our students' homes and communities.

And we haven't even touched on culture yet.

Think back to Chapter 2 and our discussion of culturally responsive teaching and learning. Now imagine all the ways that respect intersects with culture. Most fall into conscious-level culture—those values that are directly taught and modeled by parents and family members and that are generally adhered to throughout a society (Hammond, 2014).

Our earlier example of making eye contact with adults is appropriate here. Depending on the context, both making and avoiding eye contact can signal honor. Respect for time and personal space are also part of conscious culture. In the United States, these values are highly revered and protected, but this is not the case in much of the world. The role of elders, an aspect of the deeper collective unconscious, shapes how young people learn to treat and communicate with their living and deceased ancestors. This aspect of respect carries over into how students and their families might regard various stakeholders at the school. Differences such as these can influence the ways in which students are perceived as respectful or disrespectful in a given situation (Kreuzer, 2016; Zhou, 2007).

Students' various cultural reference points and lived experiences *belong* in the classroom and school. This energy, when validated and valued, fosters student voice, choice, and collaboration.

Here's Rujan:

Truth be told, the rigor of American education is subpar compared to the standard back home. In Nepal, your chance at a better life is through education, so there is a sense of respect and admiration for it. In America, it is a rather stark contrast; it is merely a default prerequisite for everyone. Americans seem to have little to no awe or longing for it. It is simply just there for everyone to do. Unfortunately, this is not true for everyone in Nepal. Hence, education in my first few years hardly ever presented a daunting academic challenge I thought I could not overcome. I had seen greater rigor back home.

How Respect Influences Trauma

Remember, power-restorative practices intentionally manipulate the external environment to reduce anxiety and promote characteristics of empowerment. Respect, when it is authentically embedded in our classrooms, schools, and instructional practices, lends "an atmosphere that promotes safety for the trauma survivor" (Huxley, 2018, para. 7). Respectful environments are poor soil for anxiety and trauma to grow.

Newcomer students, in particular, can have wildly diverse interpretations of and expectations for respect. Here's where Geneva Gay's warnings about misaligned cultural reference points shine through. If our outgoing *respect* messaging doesn't match students' incoming receptors, problems arise (Gay, 2014 , 2018). When this happens, we face challenges drawing our students in and effectively communicating with them. Furthermore, we may be adding to, or retriggering, existing traumas by agitating features of culture shock, misunderstanding, uncertainty, disconnectedness, and exclusion. In short, we may be inadvertently sowing a habitat that feeds trauma.

Here's an example. Historically, U.S. school systems follow an Anglo-Western reference point and have determined that speaking "out of turn" is disrespectful behavior. However, many newcomer students take a different view. From their cultural reference points, conversations are fluid, dynamic, and emphatic processes. Respect looks like animated participation and sounds like overlapping interjections. These behaviors signal engagement and say, "Hey, I'm listening to you and following along." *This* is respect.

When these opposing cultural reference points collide, what generally happens? At first, the student probably gets a few gentle reminders to raise their hand before speaking. After all, *this is how we do things here in this space.* Those reminders become firmer. Then consequences are introduced, which are initially mild but progress toward disciplinary actions and opportunities to reflect on the "disrespectful" behavior.

Meanwhile, these harmful interactions can stir up underlying trauma, diminish feelings of self-worth, and nullify a sense of safety within the school (Mayworm & Sharkey, 2014). Research informs us that students who experience at least one behavioral infraction serious enough for disciplinary action are less likely to graduate from high school (Gregory et al., 2016). They are also more likely to disengage from learning entirely (Marchbanks & Blake, 2018), and that's before we factor in any existing transition shock.

But what if there were a better way? What if there could be room for both sets of reference points? If we can accomplish this, we can achieve power-restorative instruction that includes culturally and linguistically diverse populations.

Defining Student Voice, Choice, and Collaboration
Student Voice

The Glossary of Education Reform (2013) defines *student voice* in education as "the values, opinions, beliefs, perspectives, and cultural backgrounds of the individual students and groups of students in a school, and to instructional approaches and techniques that are based on student choices, interests, passions, and ambitions" (para. 1). Historically, student choice plays out in student-led government. However, the concept has grown in recent years regarding purpose, access, and channels for expression.

What are we likely to see in classrooms and schools with a high level of student voice? Learner contributions (that are acknowledged by adults), sharing feedback, identifying problems and solutions, and advocating for one's needs are all examples of student voice (Benner, Brown, & Jeffrey, 2019). We might also see learners engaged in democratic seminars, student journalism, student-led conferences, personalized learning, and youth-led participatory action research (Center for American Progress, 2019).

Voice can appeal to broader academic concerns, such as curriculum design or building operation. In a class setting, student voice (if effectively solicited and implemented) can influence nearly every aspect of instruction (Wallach, Ramsey, Lowry, & Copland, 2006). It can shape the way a space is used and how students interact and learn within it. Increasing student voice is particularly important for historically marginalized populations, including students from Black, Latinx, Native American, and low-income communities, and students with disabilities (Anderson, 2018; Benner et al., 2019).

Student Choice

What is student choice? Student choice refers to the quantity and quality of opportunities youth have to make self-constructed decisions that influence their learning lives.

Wolpert-Gawron (2018) adds, "[Student choice] redefines the position of teacher from knowledge authority to learning guide" (para. 8). This is so powerful, isn't it? If we, as practitioners, can assume the role of learning guide, then our students' voices naturally rise to the forefront of our instruction. But why is this so important?

Wolpert-Gawron explains, "Student choice builds ownership in the learning. Student choice allows students to display their learning in the way that they feel best represents their knowledge. Student choice enforces true differentiation" (paras. 5–7). Student choice invites other benefits, too. It increases student engagement and investment, flexibility, adaptability, student effort, task performance, and overall learning gains (Marzano & Pickering, 2010). Agency through choice builds on students' existing strengths and draws out innovative ways of negotiating new content understanding.

Student choice can also solicit the types of SEL gains that directly support a trauma-informed environment. In this context, incorporating student choice is a purposeful strategy to help youth regain a sense of self-control within a setting or circumstance (and in the larger picture, over their lives). "Trauma-informed practices use strengths-based approaches that are empowering and support individuals to take control of their lives and service use. Such approaches are vital because many trauma survivors will have experienced an absolute lack of power and control" (Sweeney, Filson, Kennedy, Collinson, & Gillard, 2018, p. 324).

When presented to students in manageable and nonthreatening doses, choice sends a signal that says, "Hey, I trust you to make reasonable decisions on your own. You have the agency, autonomy, and capacity to do this." As individuals practice making choices in controlled settings, they become more confident in their power to make bolder decisions and to do so in new contexts. Restored self-control enables better intrapersonal choice-making, too, such as deciding which coping skills are necessary for a given scenario.

Student Collaboration

Collaborative learning is the process of engaging in prosocial exchanges to problem solve, explore, or aspire to a common goal. Cornell University's Center for Teaching Innovation (2020) explains, "Collaborative learning can occur peer-to-peer or in larger groups. Peer learning, or peer instruction, is a type of collaborative learning that involves students working in pairs or small groups to discuss concepts or find solutions to a problem" (para. 1).

Moreover, we're talking about a critical 21st century skill. "Collaboration is key to successful teams and projects," write Vander Ark and Liebtag (2018). "It is sometimes thought of as a 'soft skill' but in high-performance organizations, collaboration is the result of the intentional design of culture, structure, and tools, and the cultivation of individual mindsets and skill sets" (para. 3). Prosocial, student-owned learning opportunities offer a wide range of benefits. They promote higher-level thinking and the development of SEL skills, including leadership. They expose students to diverse perspectives and ideas, along with real-world challenges. Collaborative schools also have higher retention and engagement rates (Ronfeldt, Farmer, McQueen, & Grissom, 2015).

Meanwhile, collaborative exchange is a culturally responsive practice that speaks most directly to elements of orientation of the self to others (namely collectivism) (Krasnoff, 2016). It can also have aspects of education of the young (such as wander-and-explore approaches) and social standing (such as the idea of saving face).

Newcomer students with cultural backgrounds that favor collectivism may feel more comfortable engaging in cooperative work groups than isolated discovery. When collaboration is introduced and incorporated purposefully, it can serve as an invitation to participate in ways that highlight students' cultural inclinations—rather than detract from them.

Purposeful collaboration can be power restorative, too. When our instruction makes room for students to work toward a common goal or solution as a cohesive team, we may facilitate more than academic outcomes. For example, in Chapter 4, we discovered that transition shock can impair one's ability to establish and maintain relationships. We also introduced recommendations to help students overcome these barriers, including the idea of noncompetition—a prominent feature of healthy collaboration. "People with trauma may have low trust that their needs matter to others. [They] may have few experiences of being considered in decision-making," shares Cheryl Martin (2018). "Collaboration encourages empathy, caring, and a curiosity to seek deep understanding. This perspective softens the fight, flight, freeze response".

From a clinical perspective, the idea of collaboration aligns with the principles of trauma-informed care. The Buffalo Center for Social Research (2015) defines *collaboration* in this context as the process of "making decisions with the individual and sharing power." That is, the trauma-affected person is acknowledged and respected as a key stakeholder in their treatment plan and related choice-making. This further requires an individual to be distinguished from the problem.

As educators, we can work to employ a similar interpretation of collaboration. To do this, we must be mindful that power restoration relies on a network of team players throughout the school, but central to that team is the voice of the student. We must also hold to the truth that learners are not defined by the conditions they are experiencing. Optimal collaboration should

- Identify the goal(s) to be met.
- Recognize individual needs within the group.
- Recognize various interaction styles within the group.
- Focus on strengths.
- Use cooperative language (e.g., sentence stems, preloaded vocabulary).

I'd known Elvina for many years as a paraprofessional in my school building before I learned her personal story of immigrating to the United States as a refugee. Elvina was a licensed teaching peer and my partner in a 2nd grade classroom in my last full year in the classroom. As a teacher and a paraprofessional, it was evident that Elvina had a unique way with students. They *wanted* to learn with her. And they did.

Four years earlier, Thierry had been a student in my 3rd grade class. He'd entered the U.S. school system as a kindergartner and later acknowledged the impact Elvina had on him and his experience. In retrospect, it's astounding that the seemingly small impressions we have on students can be tremendous.

Of my first day of school in the U.S., I remember the hot sun, traffic noises, smelly bus, skyscrapers, unfamiliar faces, the noise of the AC running in a tiny classroom, [and feeling] very scared and uncomfortable. It was hard trying to understand the lesson, but it was harder trying to understand my classmates during classroom activities due to our different accents. I felt like I was in a movie. It was beautiful, and I felt very adventurous. Everything was new and strange. The elevator, vending machines, ramen noodles, and coffee aroma, all in a closed painted room filled with chemicals.

I longed for open space, clear air, and the noise of the jungle.

Schooling here was very different from back home. I love that teachers in the U.S. care and are willing to learn new things even from the students. I love that U.S. teachers have conversations with us—not lecturing. One thing I wish my first teacher in the States knew about me is that [even though] I might not understand English well, I speak three other languages and have an associate's degree in teaching, so

I am not unintelligent. I knew a lot of stuff; I just didn't know the English language.

But getting to know other students was hard. I sounded very rude and disrespectful, but it was just because I didn't speak English, understand this foreign language, and because I am unfamiliar with this culture. So I didn't know better. I wasn't ignorant and rude. I was worried that I would do or say something wrong and offend people, so I kept everything to myself, being as quiet as I could be.

I took English classes for two months then attended Aurora Community College. Because I didn't know the culture and the language well, I felt like an outsider. I didn't get the jokes, the sarcasm, and I could not participate in common-sense conversations about football, pop culture, music, and so on. I felt like I had so much to learn besides education.

If I could ask my teachers to change something, I would ask them to give me background knowledge of something before discussion, so I wouldn't feel very lost and awkward. Also, I think it would be beneficial to study the culture along with the language, because to be able to access the texts, we need to have background knowledge of this culture. For example, not knowing about baseball when a math problem is based around baseball gives us disadvantages to understanding the math problem.

I had a teacher who made me feel welcomed by asking questions about me, my family, and my country and listening to me. I appreciate the teacher going above and beyond, trying to help me learn and understand her lesson. I can see and feel a caring heart through her eyes and smile. That was very comforting! I felt like everything would be OK, even though it was hard to understand and navigate my way through a foreign language. But because of that smile and a caring heart, I had hope.

The advice I'd give to other newcomers is to learn the culture and the language. Practice speaking aloud and make a lot of mistakes. It's OK!

—*Elvina, age 27, ethnic Karen (Myanmar), arrived in the United States at age 18 from Thailand (first language: Karen)*

On the first day of school, I really didn't want to go. I came with my twin brother, Yann, and we were in the same class. My dad would sing in French to me, "Try, try." I didn't want to come at all.

But then, after I started coming, I was really glad I was in school. I remember using the computers a lot in America. I'd never used a computer before. We also had a lot of free time and time to sleep at school. Nobody sleeps at school in Gabon. Also, in America, we eat at school. In Gabon, the kids go home to eat and then come back. I was too scared to tell a teacher on the playground that I wanted to play with the big kids, because in Gabon I always played with my big brothers and their friends, so I liked playing with the big kids more. On our playground, we were only allowed to play with other kindergartners.

When I think about it now, I wish I could have asked my teacher to help me more with reading instead of giving me free time. My reading isn't really great right now, and I wish I read more when I was first learning English.

But my teacher was very nice. She was funny and let us play games sometimes. And there was a classroom helper. She was Asian and she was learning English, too. That made me feel better.

—*Thierry, age 11, arrived in the United States at age 6 from Gabon (first languages: French, Bantu Mbere)*

What pieces of Elvina's circumstances or experiences interfered with productive collaboration? What could have been done to help minimize some of this disconnect? How did having an exemplar in the classroom influence Thierry's voice and choice? What can we gain from intentionally crafting learning environments in which students see reflections and representations of themselves? How might this contribute to a schoolwide commitment to diminishing transition shock?

Respect: Into Practice
Strategy 1: DBT House, Revisited

Let's return to the DBT house we discussed in previous chapters and turn our attention to the chimney. This is the space where we recorded ways we blow off steam or get rid of stress. This is one place where students certainly exercise their choice and voice—and in some cases, collaboration.

What do you notice about how students manage challenge, stress, or adversity? How do they exercise these capacities? Do they lean into healthy anxiety-relieving practices? Are the behaviors harmful to themselves or others? How do they use their voices? By yelling and shouting? Through song or writing? By crying? Do they ask for help? Do they self-advocate (or advocate for others)? Let's look at a few examples:

- "I punch pillows and cry."
- "I eat candy."
- "Play soccer."
- "I write in my diary."
- "Talk to my mom."
- "Hang out with my friends."
- "Take pictures for Instagram."

These all appear to be normative coping behaviors, and some (such as talking to a parent) are healthy prosocial mechanisms. In fact, I can relate to several of them. (Chocolate, anyone?) Most examples are activity-based, appear to promote deescalation, and encourage social reintegration. Several of them even promote deisolation. None seem to be inherently harmful to the student or anyone else.

Now let's take a look at a few other examples:

- "I hurt my sister."
- "Diet."
- "Say bad things."
- "Nothing."
- "Cut myself."

- "Yell at people or kick."
- "Get into fights."

These are the more painful discoveries, and some might be outside your scope of comfort. For most of these respondents, I'd suggest keeping a close watch on their stress-relieving behaviors throughout the year, gradually introducing more productive strategies, and praising students for their positive choices. Some circumstances, however, such as the one mentioning self-harm, require a different approach. It's OK to admit when a situation is beyond our means of care. In fact, it can be *more* harmful if we try to step in without the appropriate training to do so.

The example of a student who mentioned cutting herself is one I encountered at school. In that case, I worked to establish a high level of trust before sitting with her privately. "I noticed in this space that you mentioned hurting yourself. I care about you and would never want to see you hurt. Did you know we have a wonderful adult here at the school who's a great listener and helps many kids understand their problems and feelings? If you ever want to talk to someone, those conversations are always kept private. Would you like me to introduce you to her?"

Take a look at the house in Figure 6.1. It was created by a 14-year-old boy originally from Burundi. The student used colored markers to create a scene that reflects his country of origin (or interim location). Certain features of the house, such as its rounded shape and thatch roof, are consistent with traditional East and Central African construction. The drawing shows the front of the house, which holds a chimney, one window, and a door with a cross hanging above it. To the left of the house is a fruit-bearing tree (possibly mangos or oranges). The student's billboard is to the right of the house. A stone path leads to the entrance, and the student drew a large cloud in the sky.

This student appears to have a toolbox of self-regulating techniques, as evidenced by his inclusion of singing, playing games, watching videos, listening to music, and using WhatsApp. However, most or all of these occur at home, so it may be helpful to incorporate new strategies that are practical in a school setting.

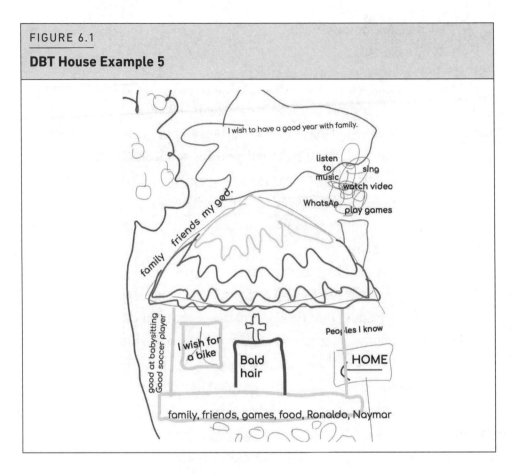

FIGURE 6.1

DBT House Example 5

As indicated on the billboard, the student is proud of his home, which simply reads "← Home." Details such as this make a great entry point for conversing and relationship-building. In the spaces around the house, the student recorded other things he takes pride in: good at babysitting and good soccer player. The ability to identify strengths hints at a positive self-concept. Along the walls, he wrote, "People I know." However, the combined roof an_____d foundation spaces contain family, friends, God, and role models (Ronaldo, Naymar). In the window, the student recorded his wish for a bike. The words in the clouds read, "I wish to have a good year with family." What steps can the school take to encourage or be a part of that vision?

Figure 6.2 shows a house created by a 7-year-old boy originally from Mexico. The student used a blue marker to draw a long rectangular building that consumes a vertical page. The left side of the roof comes to a triangular point; the

FIGURE 6.2

DBT House Example 6

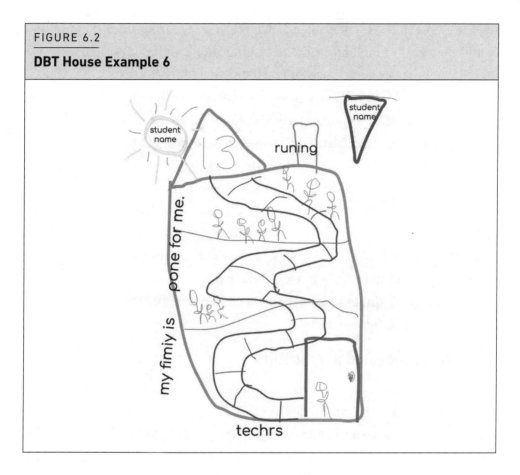

chimney is on the flat right side. Two horizontal lines cut through the home to create three levels. There is a door at the lowest level. Leading directly from the door, a purple staircase winds through the drawing up to the top floor. One stick figure stands in the lowest section, three people can be seen on the second floor, and seven people of different heights (adults and children?) continue the climb up to the last level. At the very top of the structure (in the roof) is the number 13. The student also drew a sun and wrote his name inside it. Hovering in the upper-right-hand corner is a green triangle: the student's billboard. Coming out of the chimney, the student recorded "running" in yellow.

Even though it contains so few words, this map provides plenty of insight. Looking at the roof, my initial thoughts were, "This represents apartment number 13, or 13 people live in the home." A home visit confirmed the latter as well as a reason behind classroom behavior I noticed. This student was having trouble staying awake in class. The student's bed was near the front door at home, and family members came and went throughout the evening. Consequently, we worked with the family to move his bed to the rear of the house.

There is also much cultural value here. First, we see the presence of an intergenerational home, which could indicate strong collaboration and cooperation skills. This was also an industrious family, and vast funds of knowledge existed within the home. Once identified, this underlying wisdom could be called on to enhance learning at school. The walls and foundation indicate that family and teachers are supportive influences in the student's life. The billboard simply includes the student's name—a signal that he is proud of and/or has some level of confidence in himself. Interestingly, the student has not recorded anything in the door, and there are no windows. Although this may simply be related to language or understanding, working with the child to practice setting and striving for short- and long-term goals may be beneficial.

Strategy 2: Scheduled Interactions

Let's return to what we know about "survival brain" and how it perceives ambiguity. "A survival brain is hyper-focused on threat," explains Dr. Jacob Hamm (2017). "It doesn't like ambiguity. It wants clear, hard facts. It thinks in black-and-white terms; it doesn't want anything to be gray at all." As a result, the trauma-affected brain is highly likely to perceive ambiguous or unfamiliar situations as dangerous. The fight-flight-freeze-submit mechanism is well underway by the time the amygdala fires up and shoots off its response message to the hippocampus.

When power is interrupted, peer collaboration can seem like a sea of gray. These experiences can present an extraordinary number of "what ifs." *What if I'm not ready? What if I don't feel comfortable? What if I don't know what to do or say? What if they don't want to work with me?*

On the one hand, research informs us that collaborative activities can promote prosocial behaviors among most people but are especially helpful for trauma-affected individuals (Carello & Butler, 2015). On the other hand, mandatory classroom interaction can produce anxiety. Think back to the Nonnegotiable 4 and recall that routine and predictability are foundational to mitigating transition shock. They both foster trust, and trust enables safety—and when students feel safe, they can learn.

The practice of scheduled interactions is one technique teachers can use to help create more structure, routine, and predictability to peer collaborations. Ideally, this strategy will transform some of the gray areas into more concrete expectations. Essentially, it serves as an anticipation guide for impending social engagement.

In addition to the dynamics of transition shock, newcomer students may face increased levels of anxiety related to the expectations of communicating in a new language. Cultural misalignments compound this stress. To diminish ambiguity and unease, try combining this strategy with purposeful language supports and culturally responsive mindfulness.

Here's who's empowered:

- Students, with the guidance of adult facilitators

Here's what you'll need:

- Targeted learning activity for each learning group. For example, this could be a task or short discovery project aligned to a current topic of study. Remember, we're working to avoid power interruptions. Especially in the initial interaction, it's a good idea to choose activities/topics in which students already have some background knowledge, underlying funds of knowledge, or even mastery.
- Sentence frames, vocabulary banks, familiar cooperative structures

Here's what you'll do:

1. Explicitly teach and model collaborative engagement. The accompanying language strategy Looks Like/Sounds Like/Feels Like is a wonderfully supportive approach.
2. Define *exactly* how collaborative groups function in your environment. When do groups meet? What do they work on? What is the structure? How will students know what is expected of them? How will they know if they've achieved their goal?

3. Within their pairs (or small groups of up to four members), engage students in creating a schedule and calendar for their meetings. Depending on the specific goal, it may also be helpful to have assigned working roles (e.g., recorder, timekeeper).
4. Begin with a schedule that allows for small, bite-sized interactions. Non-academic engagements are a great place to start (e.g., playing a game for 10 minutes).
5. Ensure that appropriate language supports are visibly posted in the workspace, including content-specific vocabulary, sentences frames, or practiced cooperative structures.
6. Ensure consistency with meeting times. Permanence and detachment cards (see Chapter 4) are helpful reminders leading up to scheduled interaction periods (and if there are changes to the anticipated schedule).
7. As students develop agency and build their social stamina, introduce choice by inviting them to schedule new meetings with peers outside the workgroup (or determine the format, roles, or goals within these predictive interactions).

Accompanying Language Strategy: Looks Like/Sounds Like/Feels Like

As a language-supportive content-learning strategy, this can be used independently, in small groups, or as a whole-class exercise. Of course, for our purposes here—restoring power in interpersonal engagements—students work in the scheduled interaction pairs or small groups.

Here's who's empowered:

*   Students, with the guidance of adult facilitators

Here's what you'll need:

*   Large sheet of butcher paper, whiteboard, or other blank canvas
*   Writing utensils
*   Sticky notes *(optional)*
*   Looks Like/Sounds Like/Feels Like template *(optional; see Appendix)*

Here's what you'll do:

1. Divide the butcher paper, whiteboard, or canvas into a two-column, three-row chart (thereby creating six activity areas). Label the rows Looks Like, Sounds Like, and Feels Like (Figure 6.3). Alternatively, use a premade template.

2. Introduce the idea of *collaboration* and provide a reasonable amount of background information. (This strategy is especially beneficial when discussing more abstract or less tangible concepts and can introduce ideas such as *discrimination, integrity,* and *hope.*)

3. Invite learners to contribute to the anchor chart. My favorite way is to provide students with an equal number of sticky notes. Then we move about the room, talking about the topic, and as ideas come up, students place them in the appropriate sections. (PearDeck or a similar app works well as a digital option.)

4. Return to the chart as a class for whole-group discussion and clarify points as needed.

FIGURE 6.3

Looks Like/Sounds Like/Feels Like Chart

Looks like	
Sounds like	
Feels like	

Strategy 3: Guided Choice

As we've seen, choice and flexibility play a remarkable role in mitigating transition shock and promoting resilience. This makes sense because the very nature of an adverse experience signals an absence of personal control over a given situation. Few individuals would choose to have a potentially traumatic experience willingly. Instead, these types of life-altering events tend to occur with little or no consent from the affected person.

When presented with choice-making opportunities in a safe, predictable environment, learners develop self-efficacy and the ability to strategize. By intentionally scaffolding these processes, we enable students to grow as wise decision-makers. And if we lean into culturally responsive cues in the process, we invite RAEM students to make decisions in ways that highlight their existing strengths and tendencies.

One practical approach we can take in the classroom is to offer opportunities for guided choice. A clear advantage of guided choice is that many teachers are already doing it. Reading group rotations, math stations, project-based learning, flexible seating, and choice boards are examples of this strategy. Maybe you've never thought of these instructional components as concrete tools for mitigating transition shock, but they are. Pretty great, right? The academic advantages of these practices are already well known, so now you just need to think of flexibility and guided choice in a slightly different (but complementary) light. What role does (or can) guided decision-making play in activating the pillar of respect?

Here's who's empowered:

- Students, with the guidance of adult facilitators

Here's what you'll need:

- Purposeful section of choices aligned to a lesson, subject, or targeted behavior. Examples include (1) center materials aligned to a science unit of study, (2) an assignment divided into three working parts (of which students will choose the order of completion), (3) three different ways of presenting a final project, or (4) two different types of chairs (such as a rocker and a floor pad) where students can choose to work.

Here's what you'll do:

1. Introduce guided choice with a limited number of options (three is a good rule of thumb). This helps decrease anxiety. For example, you might require that students accomplish three separate tasks or functions within a one-hour class period but have the agency to choose the order they complete the tasks.

2. Expand guided choice by allowing more freedom and autonomy (so long as student expectations are evident and clearly understood). For example, allow students to choose where they sit (or stand) during an activity or task. Some of my students choose to sit in the classroom library; others quietly use the hallway space or opt to work right next to me and solicit feedback as they go. The rest make their way to established workstations or continue working by themselves at their desks.

3. Continue the process of outward expansion by introducing choice in other areas, such as the format for a presentation or as part of a student choice board (both culturally responsive strategies). This encourages students to demonstrate learning in ways that highlight their individual and group strengths. Leave students a reasonable time window to consider and process the potential gains and sacrifices involved when choosing between items or activities. Prompt students to predict probable consequences of unwise choices and reflect on those outcomes when they occur.

4. As students gain mastery and restore intrapersonal power, engage them in brainstorming and naming their choices. Alternatively, invite students to work together to devise a series of choices for the entire class.

Strategy 4: Modified Talking Chips

This strategy continues to restore and grow students' power in exercising flexibility. It opens the door to positive choice-making within a supportive and structured environment as students. The advice-giving dynamic flexes students' funds of knowledge. Meanwhile, using hypothetical problems creates a sense of separation between the perceived problem and the problem solver. This "distancing" helps minimize the risk of stimulating the amygdala's fight-flight-freeze-submit mechanism. This also presents an opportunity to practice choice-making in real time in a way that leans away into learning brain.

This strategy is also culturally responsive. Each learner interprets a picture or scenario from a unique set of cultural reference points. To formulate advice and contribute to the problem-solving process, students access their existing reservoirs of wisdom and make relevant connections to the scenario. The open-ended prompts make way for responses that highlight individual cultural reference points and lived expertise.

From a language-learning perspective, this strategy encourages speaking and listening skills in relevant contexts. It also prompts more hesitant speakers to contribute and enables a more equitable conversation by discouraging one or two individuals from dominating the stream of thoughts and ideas. For RAEMs, it helps regulate the pace of a conversation and scaffold contributions in the instructional language.

Aside from the "You should . . ." stem, it may be helpful to supply students with additional sentence frames (or stems that include options for drawing, diagramming, or labeling their advice). Here are a few helpful suggestions:

- I agree because . . . .
- I disagree because . . . .
- That's an interesting thought, but . . . .
- Could you repeat that?
- Have you thought about . . . ?
- Can I add that . . . ?
- Maybe instead you could . . . .
- Have you tried to . . . ?
- Can I draw you a picture to explain?
- Can I show you on the diagram?

Finally, be sure to model and reinforce clarifying phases, such as "Could you repeat that?" and "Could you tell me more about . . . ?"

Here's who's empowered:

- Students, with the guidance of adult facilitators

Here's what you'll need:

- Images of various people, items, and scenarios (displayed on a white-board, projected in a slideshow, or printed onto playing cards)
- Small items (e.g., craft sticks, paper clips, dice, slips of paper), enough for each student

Here's what you'll do:

1. Arrange students in pairs or small groups of up to four members. Provide each student with the same number of "talking chips" (small items they can handle) equal to the number of people in the group.
2. Display an image (e.g., a basketball, a zookeeper in a lion's cage, a car with the hood raised, a hairbrush and hairdryer, a hiking trail, a packet of seeds).
3. Use a cooperative strategy so one student "owns" the scenario or problem and a second student opens the conversation by offering advice to the other group member(s). That student says, "You should. . . ."
4. Other members respond to this advice with their talking chips. Each time a student contributes one thought to the conversation, they place a talking chip in the center of the workspace. All students must use all their chips, but they must also choose their thoughts wisely. Once they have used all their chips, they must reserve any additional ideas (thereby preventing one student from dominating the conversation).
5. The conversation ends when the last talking chip is used. The students then switch roles and repeat.

Strategy 5: Solution Circle

This strategy exposes students to multiple perspectives while promoting student collaboration and critical thinking skill sets. It's an excellent strategy for culturally and linguistically rich classrooms. It's low stakes, has room for plenty of language supports (including sentence frames, graphic organizers, and interactive word walls), and calls on students' existing funds of knowledge and life experiences.

Solution Circle focuses on perspective-taking—or the concept of putting ourselves in someone else's shoes. Perspective-taking is one element of empathy. In a groundbreaking study, researchers examined markers of empathy among adults who experienced childhood trauma. They found that these folks demonstrated high levels of affective empathy "where we feel in our gut and heart the feelings that others are, or may, be experiencing" and cognitive empathy, which is largely comprised of perspective-taking (Ley, 2020, para. 4).

The same study suggests that perspective taking may be a latent superpower for youth with a history of transition shock. Nurturing these skill sets may have positive benefits for the learner. After all, perspective-taking is highlighted as both a 21st century skill and SEL competency.

Growing cognitive empathy is good for the classroom culture, too. It helps kids see people and situations in more than one light and plays an important role in the process of recognizing and overcoming implicit bias (which is a better predictor of racist and prejudiced behavior than explicit bias) (Edwards et al., 2017). In short, it's an element on which students will rely to become their best selves. Solution Circle gently encourages students to embrace these skills in a way that reduces the stakes of unknowns and minimizes the risk of power interruption.

Here's who's empowered:

- Students, with the guidance of adult facilitators

Here's what you'll need:

- A folder or envelope of some kind
- Paper and/or digital writing/doodling space

Here's what you'll do:

1. Organize students into small groups.
2. Write a problem or puzzle on the outside of the envelope. The problem should be one that could have multiple solutions. Optical illusions and

friendly opinion questions (e.g., Should cell phones be allowed in class?) are a great early place to start. Puzzles can work up in complexity and relevance as students gain confidence and develop language tools.

3. Within their groups, students read the puzzle and brainstorm as many possible solutions as they can. Together, they formulate what they believe to be the most accurate or effective response. If students cannot come to a consensus, they may record the two or three top options.

4. Students place their response(s) inside the envelope and pass it to the next group.

5. Students in the new group should develop a solution to the puzzle without opening the envelope or reading any responses within it. Once finished, they add their response(s) to the envelope. The envelope continues to the next team, and so on.

6. Once each envelope makes its way back to its original group, that team examines all documents within it. Finally, each team should debrief on the exercise, noting the different perspectives and ideas introduced.

Strategy 6: Time Management Challenge

Time-keeping occurs in the frontal lobe, alongside other executive functioning skills, such as organization and planning. In Chapter 1, we learned that a history of adverse experiences could compromise executive functioning. As a result, time management is often an area of growth for students whose power has been interrupted by transition shock (Doyle, 2020; Rodden, 2021).

Let's first talk about the cultural implications for time. As an element of conscious culture, the concept of time varies greatly from one society to another. For example, punctuality, in the way that it is emphasized in the United States (particularly in a school or business setting), is not necessarily prized in other regions.

In the States, a meeting scheduled to begin at 9:00 a.m. means 9:00 a.m. In fact, it probably means 8:55 a.m. But as a college student in Florence, Italy, I recall feeling frustrated by concepts of time. On one occasion, I left my dorm bright and early to make it to a store that opened at 9 a.m. There I was at 8:55, but the store was empty and still closed. Around 9:30, I left to grab an espresso.

The owner casually strolled over and unlocked the door at 10:45, nearly two hours after the store was scheduled to open. There was no explanation, no apology, and no apparent recognition of my look of utter irritation.

Even more confounding to me, punctuality was expected in other social contexts, such as the start of my daily classes. As a result, it took me some time to navigate time norms in my new environment. Overall, the experience of time seemed slower and less urgent in Florence. Though this cultural mismatch initially put me off, the slowed concept of time became one of the things I grew to love about the culture.

Time-keeping cultural mismatches are also likely when working with learners from African, Asian, and Middle Eastern countries and cultures. In Lebanon, we half-joke by saying, *"Kelyoum, boukra."* Everything, tomorrow. Whatever it is, it will be there after today. The future can wait. For newcomer students, time management becomes a component of successful integration. It doesn't mean that a student's time references are "off"; it means that a U.S. reference point may not be a direct match.

Unfortunately, not all educators see it this way. For example, if class begins at 7:20 and a student is dropped off at 7:35, they may be chastised for their tardiness. These interactions can set off a power-interrupting domino effect in which teachers become frustrated with students and issue some type of disciplinary action—a decision that only exacerbates underlying anxiety.

By explicitly teaching the U.S. reference point on time (without discrediting students' existing cultural frameworks) and introducing strategies for adjusting to the perceived normative values, students can become effective at what Geneva Gay has called "cultural border crossing." For students, acquiring this social knowledge can ease frustrations on both sides—and aid in the power restoration along the way.

In addition to promoting cooperative talk and collaboration, the time management challenge helps students learn to organize information, prioritize tasks, and strategize—all of which are essential executive brain functions.

Here's who's empowered:
- Students, with the guidance of adult facilitators

Here's what you'll need:

- Activity Choice Menu board (see Figure 6.4 for examples)

Here's what you'll do:

1. Divide students into groups. (The first time I work through this activity, I cut the group in half, thirds, or fourths, depending on my class size.)
2. Talk through the directions for the activity:

Today, you are going to work with your group to complete a challenge. The challenge's goal is to earn as many points as you can by completing as many activities as you can in a short time.

You'll have 10 minutes to complete the challenge. When the timer starts, the first thing you should do is choose a conductor for your group. The conductor will help guide the team but will not be the only decision-maker.

After you've chosen the conductor, look at the board. I'll post several activities. Each activity is worth points. As a group, you need to decide which actions you will complete and in which order to gain the greatest number of points possible. You probably won't have time to do all the activities, so choose carefully.

Once you've figured out your plan, jump right into the first activity. Move through the menu as quickly as you can, in the order that your team decided on! When the timer stops, you must stop moving and sit down with your group.

3. Take a moment for clarification. With very new-to-English speakers, it may be helpful to post an example set of activities with icons and talk about them together. The goal is for teams to devise problem-solving strategies (and reflect on how well they did or did not work). In this case, it's best not to model the exercise for students before they begin.
4. Once the timer ends, the important work of reflection begins. Invite students to talk in their groups about their experiences. (The Talking Chips strategy works well here, making each student accountable for a contribution.) Here are some reflective prompt ideas:
   — How did your group make decisions throughout the activity?
   — What did the group do well?

— What skills or strengths did you notice in a classmate that you didn't notice before?

— What group dynamics came into play? How did you work through them?

— Would you have done things differently if you were acting solo?

5. Finally, offer the opportunity to reenact the exercise. This can be done immediately or after a few days. Ideally, students should be able to "beat" their previous score once they have had time to reflect on their group strategy and dynamics. As the year goes on, try the activity (using a new menu board) with different student combinations.

FIGURE 6.4

Time Management Challenge: Activity Choice Menu

- Sing the Alphabet Song in unison. (5 points)
- Create a nickname for each group member. (5 points)
- Line up in order of your birthday month/day. (5 points)
- Have every person in the room sign a piece of paper. (10 points)
- Form a circle. Pass an object around the circle using only your elbows. (10 points)
- Write a group poem about today's science topic. (10 points)
- Create a three-part obstacle course and get everyone in the group to try it. (15 points)
- Make a 30-second dance routine as a team. (15 points)

Strategy 7: Sensory Calming Kit

Chapter 3 identified the four *R*s of self-regulation: root, resource, reach, and reduce. Strategies 7 and 8 belong to the third group; they are all reaching (physical desensitizing) practices. Sensory calming kits are self-regulating tools that are unique to the specific needs of individuals. Essentially, they consist of an easy-to-access container and the purposefully selected set of calming resources within it. The contents of a sensory calming kit can vary widely but are likely to include one or more tactile manipulatives.

This strategy can also support culturally responsive teaching and learning when we actively welcome items reflective of a student's identity. This approach empowers students to discover calming mechanisms that also uphold their cultural and linguistic virtues.

Here's what you'll need:

- Small or medium-sized storage containers (e.g., gallon-size bags, small plastic bins)
- A variety of tactile materials and calming tools (e.g., fuzzy craft balls, packing peanuts, pipe cleaners, Velcro strips, noise-canceling headphones, small stuffed animals, books, modeling clay, stress balls, wood blocks or beads, small snow globes, scented cotton balls, resistance bands, puzzle cubes)
- A variety of culturally influenced materials *(optional)* (e.g., beads, mandalas, Kanga material, photographs, books or writing in students' native languages, small rain sticks or egg shakers, woven textiles, milagros charms, leather strips, nazar or hamsa amulets, prayer flags, scarves, small wooden carvings, dreamcatchers, worry dolls, tumbled stones)

Here's what you'll do:

1. Clearly explain the purpose of the sensory calming kit.
2. Begin by offering ownership of the container. Ensure that students write their names on their container; recording one's name holds tremendous grounding power.
3. Explain to students that they will intentionally select items that help them self-regulate and restore personal power. The contents of the kit are not for entertainment purposes. Which items bring a legitimate sense of soothing, calm, happiness, or focus? Provide a wide variety of items from which students can choose, but allow them to bring items from home that have self-regulating properties and reflect their home culture.
4. Help students explain their reasoning. Why did they choose certain items? Why did they leave others behind? Which items are suitable for one purpose (such as concentration) but not great for other reasons (such as improving one's mood)?

5. Have students place the items into their containers. Provide opportunities and reminders for students to access the sensory calming kit until the practice becomes intuitive.

Strategy 8: Crossing the Midline/Bilateral Integration

In school settings, we often talk about the need for occasional "brain breaks." These short activities usually include mindfulness, stretching, and body movement. They are designed to get learners to temporarily set down their cognitive load. However, did you know that these breaks are also a valuable part of the power restoration toolbox?

Most brain break activities involve "crossing the midline" (or bilateral integration), which counters trauma-affectedness. These practices, which can be explicitly taught and modeled in classroom settings, encourage right- and left-brain communication, sensory integration, and emotional regulation. Surprisingly, many children—especially those with trauma histories—find it challenging to complete such tasks and require practice to improve.

Crossing the midline activities engage participants in traversing imaginary lines that divide the human body into quadrants. Imagine two dividing lines—one horizontally across the midsection and another vertically down the center of the body—that render four discrete sections. For example, we might touch our right elbow to our left knee or our left hand to our right foot. These types of movements cross the imaginary dividing lines, and the kinesthetic motion stimulates communication between the two hemispheres of the brain (creating a "crossover" of information and commands). Thus, the physical circuit acts as a stimulus for mirrored brain activity.

Let's loop back to what we've already learned about left-brain/right-brain crossover for trauma-affected students. This type of communication is critical for advancing beyond "stalls" in the right brain that present as a reaction to significant trauma. It is also a viable thread for knitting the language learning process together, as it opens pathways to the left brain (i.e., the hub of language acquisition).

The practice of intentionally embedding bilateral activities into the learning day can be culturally affirmative. For example, challenges or breaks that involve dance "expand the students' awareness of their own bodies as forms of communication—body language—that can often communicate meaning as or more effectively than simply words" (California County Superintendents Educational Services Association, 2017, p. 28). Further, students who are very new to the English language can participate by following the facilitator. This can minimize the language load, thus freeing their focus to tackle the physical task at hand.

So how do we incorporate crossing midline opportunities into the learning day? Brain breaks that incorporate movement are a great place to start. For example, almost any form of dance or coordination exercise naturally stimulates this process (Grasser, Al-Saghir, Wanna, Spinei, & Javanbakht, 2019). Students who are habitual "*W* sitters" (sitting on the knees, with ankles splayed out behind) can be encouraged to shift to a crisscrossed pose. Even asking young kids to congratulate themselves with a self-hug (self-holding with opposite hands on each shoulder) can engage the brain hemispheres in functional communication.

I like to weave bilateral integration into academic activities using a modified "write-the-room." This learning strategy calls for the facilitator to place numbered cue cards throughout the room, with each card holding a different question or problem for students to consider. Students, meanwhile, have matching answer sheets (often in grid form). As learners move around the room reading the cards, they record answers to each card in the corresponding space on their paper.

In our version, I place cue cards in nonsequential order so students have to traverse the room. Alternatively, I "hide" the cards in unusual places so students are encouraged to move their bodies in different ways and on different levels (keeping in mind modifications for all physical abilities). This process effectively integrates crossing midline, stimulates student talk, and energizes desk learning!

Here's what you'll need:

- Time and free space

Here's what you'll do:

1. Choose an action plan (e.g., brain breaks, group coordination exercises, self-hold exercises).
2. Periodically pause between segments of learning to engage students in bilateral integration. Examples include the following ideas:
    — Engaging in sorting activities, using only one hand at a time
    — Crawling while touching elbows to the opposite knees
    — Drawing infinity signs (sideways figure eights) through the air with hands, arms, toes, and heads
    — Playing with cars, trains, or planes in looped, zig-zag, and circular paths
    — Washing (or pretend washing) large objects
    — Hand-clapping games
    — Dancing, ribbon-twirling, scarf-twirling
    — Playing stacking games
    — Tapping right hand to left shoulder (and vice versa); touching right elbow to left knee or ankle (and vice versa); touching right fingers to left toes (and vice versa)
    — Swinging the right leg over the left (and vice versa); swinging upper body to the left and right
    — Tracing
    — Playing Twister
3. Invite reflection when appropriate.

Where Do We Go from Here?

In this chapter, we

*   Explored student voice, choice, and collaboration as central functions of respect.
*   Investigated links among culture, language, and respect.
*   Tethered these ideas to best practices in mitigating transition shock.
*   Highlighted classroom practices and activities that bolster respect factors.
*   Selected SEL strategies that are aligned to this pillar of care.

We're now ready to move into the last pillar in approaching transition shock. We'll take everything we've learned in the previous chapters to this new space where students practice redirecting, reframing, and advocating for their self-restoration. We are moving closer to resilience!

Redirect:
Crafting Sustainability

Over time, students are reminded of their innate power. They also assume greater ownership over their toolkits of restorative strategies. The fourth pillar, redirect, center learners as empowered decision-makers over their behaviors and outcomes.

Why is the agency to redirect counterproductive behaviors so powerful? Well, there are many reasons. First, it builds competency and self-confidence. For newcomers, it also optimizes healthy prosocial integration (Frater-Mathieson, 2004; Kreuzer, 2016). Ultimately, it champions long-term moves toward power-restorative sustainability.

The National Council for Behavioral Health (2019) has identified two indicators for sustainability in trauma-informed programming: (1) making one's changes, gains, and accomplishments stick; and (2) keeping the momentum moving forward for continuous quality improvement. So how can we best support RAEM students throughout these processes?

Making Gains Stick and Maintaining Forward Momentum

Maintaining and strengthening power-restorative gains requires courage, commitment, and flexibility. Courage is necessary to move through fear, rest in vulnerability, and try new approaches. Commitment to the hard work of self-improvement drives forward momentum in the healing process, and flexibility is an asset when setbacks inevitably arise. Here's the three-part "formula" I use with my students to make power-restorative accomplishments stick and keep the momentum moving forward: reiteration, detection, and reflection.

Reiteration

Reiteration returns us to our earlier focus on establishing routine and predictability. Just as reliable structures contribute to a trauma-aware learning environment, they also promote long-term sustainability. Chapter 2 described routine and predictability as bedrocks for safety and trust (the baseline for relationship-building and information-processing). Optimally, we've made moves to establish and maintain regularity and have embedded these structures into the fabric of the school day. Over time, learners—specifically RAEMs experiencing power interruption—can learn to copy the "template" of routine and apply it to other areas of their lives.

For example, a student may develop and use routines to manage their stress in making it home from school on the bus or completing homework. As they gain stability in these areas, they may feel confident in loosening some of the stringency of their routines. These seemingly minor (but significant!) changes signal a growing capacity for flexibility.

Reiteration plays a role outside anticipated day-to-day events, too. It's especially critical in the face of new, unexpected, or unwanted disruptions. "Healing is not a straight line of continuous progress. Just when we feel that things are finally better, we get triggered, or a new crisis comes along," writes Dr. Odelya Kraybill (2018). "It's not realistic to expect to sustain progress made without the stabilizing benefits of a set of routine practices" (para. 11).

Detection

Making gains stick involves learning to identify and respond to the people, places, and things that (sometimes implicitly) provoke power interruption. "Many of the difficulties that trauma-exposed [youth] experience arise when stimuli or situations in their immediate environment trigger upsetting memories, with their associated thoughts and emotions" (Briere & Lanktree, 2013,

p. 97). Trauma reminders (such as certain sights, sounds, or human energies) can produce—sometimes with little or no notice—physical reactions in the body. A trauma reminder is often referred to as a *trigger*.

Now that we are clear on what a trigger is, allow me to share with you that I'm not at all a fan of the word. I find that the term itself is, well, triggering. For one thing, the term has been adopted from mental health dialogue and is now overused (and sometimes jokingly used) in social conversation to denote irritation, offense, or sensitivity. As a result, it's lost much of its intended meaning. Additionally, the actual word can draw other associations (e.g., the *trigger* of a gun, warfare). This may be especially true for newer-to-English learners who often make very literal connections to words and word sounds.

In my classroom, we call this a "spark." When preparing students for sustainability, it can be helpful to talk frankly about what sparks are. The following strategy is one I created to use with RAEM students. It is language adaptive and loosely based on a "trigger identification and intervention" model published by the Keck School of Medicine of USC (2013):

1. Explicitly talk to students about what sparks are. The conversation usually begins something like this:

Sparks are people, places, or things (like sounds, smells, or language) that make you feel especially upset. Lots of things can make up feel upset. A lot of the time, we're able to calm down by ourselves or find a solution to the thing that upset us. But when we experience a spark, we might have a harder time controlling our thoughts, emotions, or behaviors. We probably feel more angry or sad or upset than we do with other challenges. Sometimes, sparks tell us we need to react to a real emergency, like a fire. Other times, sparks are trying to tell our brain there's a real emergency, even though we're not actually in danger. Sparks sometimes surprise us, but we might also notice that sparks happen a lot more when we're doing certain things. If we pay attention to where our sparks are, we can try to stay away from them. You can even learn some ways to help yourself calm down when they do come. If you find sparks in your learning day that you wish to share with me privately, I can do my best to keep those away from our learning space.

2. Invite students to think about a time or times when they felt sparked.

3. Ask students to consider whether this particular spark was a real-time emergency or their brain's alarm working too hard to protect them.

4. Have students reflect on their sparks and think about when they are likely to show up. (For example, Rahul thought about the three times that week that he became very agitated. All three times were on the playground, near the soccer field. All three times, an adult playground monitor had used a loud voice and a whistle to reprimand nearby students, though he'd never been one of the kids in trouble. Rahul loved the playground and didn't usually get upset in other parts of it, so he didn't think the playground was a spark. But we did explore the adult, the loud voice, and the whistle.)

5. Challenge students to think about their Window of Tolerance and what it feels like when they are there (see the next section).

6. Invite students to consider strategies they used (or that could be used) to turn down their brain's alarm and/or expand their Window of Tolerance.

The Window of Tolerance, first introduced by Dr. Dan Siegel (2012), describes a state of functioning (or zone of arousal) in which the limbic system is at relative rest and an individual feels calm, capable, and connected. When a person is within the Window of Tolerance, they may be exposed to stressors but can release them or deal with them in the moment. This is the optimal place to be (National Institute for the Clinical Application of Behavioral Medicine [NICABM], 2019).

Sometimes, the stimulus a person is exposed to—the spark—pushes the brain out of balance and activates the limbic system. Therefore, we can envision the Window of Tolerance as being framed on both sides. The state of hyperarousal is on one side, and on the other, hypoarousal (i.e., understimulation). Overstimulation activates the fight or flight responses, which can feel like panic, anxiety, or rage. By contrast, understimulation mobilizes the freeze submit responses, which can feel like emptiness, numbness, or detachment (Dezelic, 2013). In short, neither zone is a great place to be.

Individuals who have been exposed to transition shock often have a relatively narrow Window of Tolerance (Farrel, 2019). The goal, of course, is to widen it as much as possible. As it expands through awareness and power-restorative moves, the individual becomes better equipped to manage stimuli and spend more of the school day engaged in learning.

Finally, students name specific power restoration strategies they feel confident implementing in these different spark situations. Once its elements are defined, this map becomes an individual sustainability plan: "a set of daily activities a survivor engages in over an extended period for purposes of self-sustenance" (Kraybill, 2018, para. 11). When discussing ownership and accountability, having students define their sustainability plans adds valuable depth and dimension. As students become more resolute in their power, they can redefine aspects of their plans to align with their various stages of growth.

Nouhaila's mornings at school typically went well. She'd participate openly in morning meetings, reading groups, and literacy stations. She'd bounce down the hallway, grinning on her way to "specials." She'd enjoy a giggly lunch with her friends. Even coming back from lunch and settling in was fine. After that, however, it progressed downhill. Quickly.

Nouhaila's afternoons would begin with an episode of crying or hurt feelings. Then the crying would become louder. Before long, the yelling would start—name-calling or her voicing how she hated school. Finally, Nouhalia would begin banging her forehead on her desk. Over and over. She'd become inconsolable until the final bell rang and she got on the bus to go home. Just before leaving each day, though, she'd give me a big hug and apologize for her behavior.

One day, about halfway through the year, Nouhaila wasn't feeling well and asked to stay inside and eat lunch in the classroom with me. So we got to talking about her afternoons.

"I don't know," she said.' "Sometimes everything is fine, and then all of the sudden it's not." We discussed the timing of the day when the episodes got underway. I gave Nouhaila a piece of paper and asked her to brainstorm events, feelings, or frustrations she noticed during those periods. We had been working on web maps in our literacy block, so this was how she began organizing her thoughts.

Something came out of the graphic organizer that surprised me: the lights. We typically turned them off during math since the first part of the instruction was via an interactive whiteboard. I hadn't noticed any apparent anxiety in Nouhaila when we made this change, but apparently, I'd been flipping the switch in more ways than one.

That afternoon, I left the lights on during math. And we made it through. Soon after, I got my hands on an old book light that we stored in Nouhaila's desk. With it, Nouhaila took the reins in exploring (and expanding) her Window of Tolerance. Whenever I dimmed the classroom lights, she'd power up her book light. We also played with various lights around the room, incrementally modifying the level of darkness. Most days were fine; some weren't. But we did push the envelope of what aspects of her power Nouhaila could manage.

Some years later, I worked with Nouhaila again on the middle school musical, which I choreographed. We caught up on our experiences together and what we both learned as a result. Nouhalia's earliest years were in Iraq during wartime. Many of her memories involved hiding in the basement of the building where she lived. She and her family—along with all the other building's residents—would stay in the makeshift shelter for weeks at a time, often in the darkness.

Turning off the classroom lights sparked Nouhaila's brain to recall an emergency situation and respond by protecting her from the perceived threat. Turning off the classroom lights didn't put her life in immediate danger, but her brain had to be reminded of this. Then, as both of us gained a better understanding of what was behind Nouhaila's power interruption, we could get back to restoring it.

Reflection

Reflection engages students in thinking about their goals and their progress toward their goals. However, I'd like to offer another perspective: our role in reflecting students' strengths, positive self-concepts, and goal markers *back at them*. "This is about holding a vision of who my students are becoming, one they can borrow when they feel they've lost their way," writes trauma-informed specialist Tracy Schiffmann (2019). "Trauma-impacted learners who get triggered have momentarily lost their way and need us to reflect back their strengths and the vision they have for themselves" (para. 12). When kids and adolescents have the experience of trusted adults reflecting their strengths and visions back at them, they develop the ability to self-reflect these qualities for themselves. As a result, they are more equipped to acknowledge and hold on to their innate power. As we navigate the learning day alongside RAEMs with transition shock considerations, it's critical to think about how we can invite reflection.

Redirect: Into Practice
Strategy 1: DBT House, Revisited

Recall that the billboard/sign is a space to reflect on and celebrate something we are proud of and want others to see or know about us. And the window sheds light on a goal, dream, or vision we have for the future. Remember, these are the only two places on the DBT House that we intentionally share out in the classroom.

Let's take a closer look. What do you notice about the student's sign? Is it a prominent, "loud-and-proud" fixture? Or is it more subdued? Is it empty? Did the student choose to add a second or third sign? What is it that he/she/they is most eager to share and talk about? What is the student proudest of, and why is it important? Is it possible to capitalize on the student's expertise or confidence in this area?

We can apply a similar thought process when analyzing a student's window. This is a reflective space, and I always feel honored for the opportunity to peek into my students' future visions for themselves. As with the sign, take time to notice the size and appearance of the window(s) and consider ways the existing curriculum enables (or could better enable) a student's long-term personal goals.

In an elementary context, I ask students to share their signs/billboards in an inside-outside circle cooperative structure. Inside-outside circle is a cooperative learning structure in which half of a student group forms a small circle, and the other half of the group creates a larger circle around them. Kids in the inside circle turn outward, and those in the outer circle face inward so each learner is face-to-face with someone else. Students talk with their partners (for newcomers, this usually entails speaking frames or sentence starters). When prompted (I ring a small bell at one-minute intervals for this particular conversation), students in the outside circle rotate one position to the left to face a new partner. A new exchange then takes place, and the process continues.

Following the vocal exercise, we often create a class display of students' responses. This becomes an almost sacred space in the room where we visibly share those things that make us awesome. I make it a point to return to and add to the display as the school year goes on. We also use this wall as an anchor chart for the Identify Your Space exercise.

In settings where a high degree of class trust and respect has been established, I invite students to share their windows. This can be a vulnerable process, especially for trauma-affected students, and many may have already subscribed to a message that they shouldn't dream too big. Sharing one's dream requires an enormous amount of courage, and this honor must be reserved for safe spaces.

As a note, I am careful to view students' signs and windows before inviting them to share their reflections with the larger group. Occasionally, a student's sentiments are not appropriate for sharing aloud, and doing so may further harm the individual. As an example, I've had quite a few students express that they have nothing that they feel proud of. Certainly, it's better to work with students to build up these confidences in advance of any sharing activities. Therefore, these early conversations with students about recognizing their innate powers should occur privately.

Keep in mind that honest responses can help us support students in ways that are better aligned to their unique intrapersonal strengths and opportunities for growth. They can also shed light on classroom, building, or institutional shortcomings that may be poking at underlying anxiety and stress.

Overall, the process of recognizing and publicly celebrating students' accomplishments and goals is a powerful and motivating act. When undertaken as a team, it can accelerate community building and enhance trust. Most important, though, the billboard and window spaces focus students' energy on the present and future, ultimately supporting the goal of restoring their power.

Take a look at the house in Figure 7.1. It was created by a 17-year-old girl originally from Myanmar. Using various colors, the student drew a scene consisting of two separate homes built on stilts (and what appear to be attached sheds or outhouses). The scene also includes a large banana tree, three tables, a sun, and clouds. The main structure has a curved door, two windows, a small chimney, and a hammock.

FIGURE 7.1

DBT House Example 7

One of the tables serves as the student's billboard, which indicates she is proud to be learning new things. Certainly, recognizing and validating this student for her efforts is in order. In this case, it may also be worth considering various funds of knowledge she brings with her into the classroom. In this way, it is possible to demonstrate that she *already* knows many things (including knowledge outside the scope of traditional textbook learning) and can learn a great deal more. The door, however, reveals that the student feels like her grandmother is never proud of her. With this in mind, calling home regularly with good news (and asking Grandma to repay this good news) is a power-restorative strategy.

The house's foundation, roof, and walls indicate strong family ties and the importance of lineage. Even though the student's parents are not named anywhere, the grandparents have a strong presence. As a teacher, this is a reminder to use sensitivity when saying things such as "Go home and ask/tell your parents. . . ." Note that these spaces also don't mention anyone from school, child or adult, so it's worthwhile to help the student grow relationships with others at school, including her teachers, peers, and older-grade mentors.

In her chimney, the student recorded a tendency to yell and slam the door. At school, she employed similar strategies. For example, if she became frustrated with her work, she'd slam her pencil down on her desk or abruptly close her locker. In this case, the student's family had been involved in a devastating car accident (which resulted in a loss of life) when she was 5 years old. Research shows that when triggered, trauma-affected individuals often revert to behavioral patterns consistent with their emotional age when the event(s) occurred (Kreuzer, 2016). Therefore, working toward more sustainable forms of processing and managing stress would be beneficial.

Figure 7.2 shows a house created by a 9-year-old boy originally from Eritrea. This student drew a vertical rectangle on a horizontally positioned paper. The top of the structure angles down to the left. Centered at the bottom of the house is the door. Above it and to either side are two rectangular windows, each with a small circle inside it, giving the appearance of eyes. Above the windows are two broad bands, which look like eyebrows (but may be awnings of some kind). There is writing along the right wall, which has been erased. The chimney, roof, foundation, and one wall contain writing.

The first thing you'll likely notice about this house is its "face." With its intense eyebrows and side-eyes, the energy comes across as anxious, concerned, or even angry. This student demonstrated a pronounced sensitivity to loud noises and unexpected stimuli. Looking at his DBT House, we can see that he is proud of his family because they protected him when the roof exploded. (This student had survived war and transition to neighboring

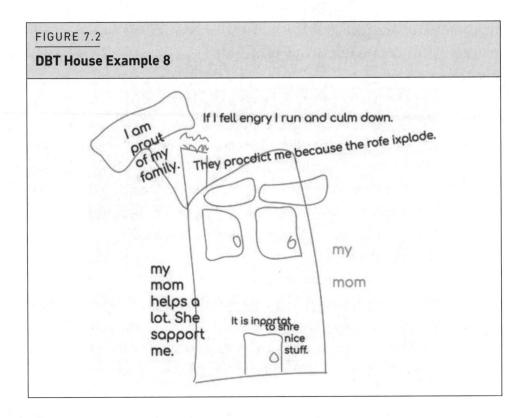

FIGURE 7.2

DBT House Example 8

Ethiopia before resettlement to the United States. In later conversations with a family member, I'd learned that the building in which they had been living in Eritrea had been hit by artillery, causing significant damage to the home, including a collapsed ceiling. This was likely the student's interpretation of the "roof exploding.") In this case, it is necessary to establish a high degree of routine and predictability to minimize the risk of sparking. Additionally, we introduced self-regulating, redirective tools for countering sparks where they did occur (such as a book falling to the ground and making a loud, unexpected thump).

The foundation includes an awareness that it's important to be nice, and the chimney reveals that the student runs to calm down. The student's mother is the only person mentioned by name. Building school supports and protectors, along with positive peer relationships, is a clear focus.

Strategy 2: Black-Out Poetry

Poetry can be an incredibly potent tool for expression. Poetic forms of writing also offer flexibility around form and structure. For language learners, this can impart a sense of freedom and diminished pressure. When the urgency to achieve grammatical perfection is temporarily eased, students can focus on the actual ideas they wish to communicate. Thus, black-out poetry is doubly supportive of English language learners to the extent that it provides a built-in word bank students can manipulate. Black-out poetry is also a fantastic strategy for mitigating transition shock.

From a trauma-informed perspective, black-out poetry redirects student energy, bringing students closer to the "green zone." In this territory, constructive problem solving is within reach, and intrapersonal expression can occur in a language-inclusive way. Meanwhile, it opens doors to talking about one's thoughts and feelings in ways that are less direct and more compatible with culturally responsive features.

Typically, I introduce and model this strategy and then offer it as a choice in the classroom's Restore Your Power area. Students are invited to tear out a page from a book to use for the exercise. This kinesthetic element offers a sort of deviant satisfaction and sensory engagement that students seem to love! In the virtual or distance-learning classroom, black-out poetry can be introduced and implemented by first explicitly teaching the strategy and then making it available as an option in a virtual Restore Your Power folder or during a scheduled period for mindfulness.

Here's who's empowered:

- Students, with the guidance of adult facilitators

Here's what you'll need:

- Texts that can be dismantled, newspapers, other print materials
- Pencils and markers
- Computer-based templates and instructions (e.g., Google Slides) *(optional)*

Here's what you'll do:

1. Choose a print base, which may include tearing a page from a book.
2. Analyze the words on the page. (Language learners may look for words they already know and lightly underline those. It may also be necessary to look up unknown vocabulary.)
3. Map out your poem by circling the words you will use with a pencil.
4. Reread and adjust the draft writing.
5. Use a dark-colored marker to draw lines through uncircled words.
6. Read the poem, which is created out of the remaining white space on the page.

The example in Figure 7.3 comes from the classroom of California high school teacher Angelina Murphy, who describes black-out poetry as "a less intimidating way to engage with writing [that] helps scaffold towards other types of writing poetry." This genre is a powerful testament to the level of emotional depth experienced by our students.

FIGURE 7.3

Black-out Poetry Example

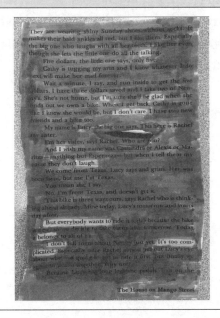

	They talk
	I'm glad I don't care
	I laugh
	But everybody wants to belong
	I don't
	It's too complicated.

Source: Used with permission from Angelina Murphy, Social Justice Humanitas Academy, Los Angeles, CA.

Digital versions of this same strategy can also be used as redirective devices. Several walkthroughs and templates are available online, most of which use Google Slides as a platform for construction (e.g., https://buildingbooklove .com/how-to-create-blackout-poem-using). Magnetic poetry is an excellent alternative for the digital space. I find this especially easy to embed into learning platforms such as SeeSaw and FlipGrid.

Remember, power restoration exercises are not focused on evaluating students' language or literacy skills. Instead, we want to add to their mental health toolkits. As students establish a level of mastery in the art of redirecting unproductive thinking and behavior cycles, they realize greater choice and agency in the process of restoring their power.

Strategy 3: Interactive Self-Portrait

Interactive self-portraits are an art-based means of strengthening intrapersonal concepts of identity. They foster community, empathy, interconnectedness, and self-esteem. They also have reflective qualities; they shine back onto the individual their strengths and visions.

Here's who's empowered:

- Students, with the guidance of adult facilitators

Here's what you'll need:

- Paper (oversized art or construction paper works well) and writing/drawing/painting tools
- Self-portrait template *(optional; see Appendix)*

Here's what you'll do:

1. Introduce the topic of identity. Explain to students that identity is made up of all the parts of an individual's story that she/he/they choose to hold on to. For example, identity can include aspects of one's physical appearance, but it's also made up of less visible attributes (e.g., character traits, likes and dislikes, skill sets, culture and language knowledge, family roles or responsibilities).

2. Have students outline a head, neck, and shoulders. As an alternative, the drawings may include the chest (so it can contain a heart). There is no need to draw facial features (though younger students often add eyes, a nose, a mouth, and other self-reflective qualities).

3. Inside the drawing, students should record pieces of their identity they like, love, or are proud of—or those pieces that define them as individuals. For very young students or very early English learners, prompt with the following: *Think about things you love about yourself. Are you kind or thoughtful? Are you hardworking? Are you a terrific big sister? Are you able to speak two languages? Think of 10 things that make you a wonderful and unique person. When you are ready, write those 10 things inside your drawing.* You may want to prompt older students to record 10–20 words or sentences that reflect these same aspects of their identity. As students write, encourage a variety of fonts and letter sizes. Multilinguals with a more robust command of English may be ready to experiment with word directionality.

4. Explain to students that the next step requires them to permit other students to touch and write on their artwork. This step of granting permission is an important one. Allowing another person to enter a vulnerable student's space can feel overwhelming. Therefore, advance warning and permission are helpful. Some students may not be able to grant permission. In this case, they complete the work on a separate piece of paper.

5. Hang the pictures around the room. Ideally, students' art is oriented so it faces outward. However, students who feel overwhelmed by this may choose to hang their papers so the art is turned to the wall (i.e., the blank side facing out). If this is the case, write that student's name at the top of the page so they can still receive compliments from others.

6. At this point, everyone in the workspace (peers and educators) should walk around the room and visit other students' art (or the paper with a student's name). At each stop, they'll write (emergent multilinguals might draw and label) compliments or strengths they notice in that person. They'll record these thoughts in the outer sections of the paper—in the space around the artistic self-portrait. Here are some examples of

students' comments: *She is very honest. Robert is a great friend. They remembered my birthday. Sabrina is an awesome dancer. I like that he helps his little brother get on the bus. I love their drawing. Khaled always works so hard in math.*

As an alternative, students can create self-reflections of themselves that highlight elements of their identities or stories (see Figure 7.4). In this case, I often use a template of a head and face from the shoulders up. Each student creates the features of their face using symbols that speak to various parts of their identities. For example:

- A learner from El Salvador uses the El Salvadorian flag as one of the "eyes" and a cross for the other.
- A student from Ghana incorporates the continent of Africa as her "nose."
- The border of a Syrian student's "face" is lined with lyrics by her favorite singer, Faia Younan.
- The "smile" of a student from Burundi is actually the story of why he couldn't come out as gay until after he moved to the United States.

FIGURE 7.4

Interactive Self-Portrait Example

Strategy 4: Curiosity/Mindfulness Cards

Curiosity cards guide students to identify external factors that provoke unique internal responses. Then, through art and abbreviated journaling, they consider alternative approaches to the triggering circumstance, event, or feeling.

This type of self-discovery tool is culturally responsive in several ways. First, it supports a wide range of expressive values. This is helpful for students whose cultural reference points favor less direct speech (e.g., smiling and saying "I'm fine" when internally upset). Similarly, it can support frames of reference that recognize distress as somatic symptoms (e.g., stomachaches, shaking, headaches, chest pains).

My favorite and most employed set of mindfulness cards, called Curious Bird Curiosity Cards, are handy in the school setting because they can be used with individual students or small groups. This makes it ideal for both intrapersonal problem-solving and interpersonal conflict resolution. As a bonus, the single cards fit together to form a composite image. This "big-picture" view elicits new perspectives and conversations.

Let's refer back to our understanding of survival brain and learning brain. Recall that students experiencing transition shock are highly vulnerable to the sway of survival brain and may even become "stuck" in this mode of functioning. Remember also that survival brain gets caught up in the details and gray spaces, and it struggles with big-picture thinking. Mindfulness cards are one way to encourage this broader perspective in a guided and protective space.

Here's who's empowered:

- Students, with the guidance of adult facilitators

Here's what you'll need:

- Preconstructed curiosity cards (self-made or purchased)
- A quiet space
- Writing utensils
- Cooperative sentence frames (if working with two or more students together)

Here's what you'll do (with individual students):

1. Lay the cards out for the student. Invite him/her/them to examine the cards and select one that is appealing/attractive. (Alternatively, if you are already aware of a specific need or concern related to this student, it may be helpful to enter the session with only the one card that speaks to that concern.)

2. Help the student consider the card/prompt. Then invite him/her/them to write, doodle, or draw on the card. Avoid directing the session. Instead, allow the student to record thoughts freely and without influence.

3. From here, there are several options:
   - The student considers their response to the prompt and possible solutions (which can be found or recorded on the reverse of the card). They keep the card as a symbolic "closing" of that specific circumstance or event.
   - The student considers their response to the prompt as well as possible solutions. The facilitator holds the card for future sessions, where new cards are introduced (i.e., slowly moving toward the completed larger image).
   - The student considers their response to the prompt and possible solutions before moving on to complete other cards in the series (usually nine) in the same sitting. Once all prompts have been completed, the student solves for the bigger picture by correctly aligning the cards. Now you can view, consider, and talk through other noticings and perspectives together.

Here's what you'll do (with small groups):

1. Lay the cards out so that each is visible. Invite students to examine the cards and select one that speaks to them. If using the whole deck (usually nine cards), each student should select an equal number. If one is left over, reserve it for final thoughts in resolving the issue. If students use only one card each, be sure to use cards that fit together into a bigger picture.

2. Help students consider the cards/prompts. Then invite them to write, doodle, or draw on the card(s). Avoid directing the session. Instead, allow students to record their thoughts freely and without influence.

3. Once students have completed their prompts, help them fit their cards together. What do students notice? Is there anything revealing about where and how the pieces fit together? How do their thoughts and actions affect the bigger picture? When looking at everyone's cards together, what kinds of solutions come to mind?

Strategy 5: Circle of Control

Chapter 3 identified the four *R*s of self-regulation: root, resource, reach, and reduce. Strategies 5 and 6 belong to the fourth group; they are all reducing practices. This self-regulation strategy calls on students to notice what they can and cannot control—and then focus on the former. The exercise, conceptualized by Stephen Covey (1989) and reimagined by Sean Covey, has been adapted and repurposed in various ways. Here, we employ it as a culturally responsive means of reducing social-emotional overwhelm.

Here's who's empowered:

• Students, with the guidance of adult facilitators

Here's what you'll need:

• Paper and writing utensils (or a digital construction space, such as Google Slides)
• Circle of Control template *(optional; see Appendix)*

Here's what you'll do:

1. Draw two concentric circles on the piece of paper (see Figure 7.5) or use a template (see Appendix).
2. Record your name in the center circle. (As a reminder, the simple act of writing something as familiar as one's name initiates grounding.)
3. Move to the space outside both circles. Think about the upsetting situation. In this space, write (or draw) all the things about the event or

feeling that are beyond your control (e.g., how others act, what the weather will be).

4. Finally, in the space between the first and second circles, write (or draw) all the things you *can* control (e.g., how you react, where you can sit, what tools to use). Focus on this space. Breathe deeply. Notice how in control you are. Decide on one of the can-dos that stands out, and act on it.

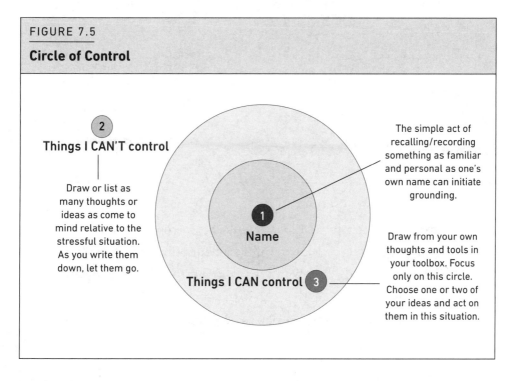

FIGURE 7.5

Circle of Control

Things I CAN'T control

Draw or list as many thoughts or ideas as come to mind relative to the stressful situation. As you write them down, let them go.

Name

The simple act of recalling/recording something as familiar and personal as one's own name can initiate grounding.

Things I CAN control

Draw from your own thoughts and tools in your toolbox. Focus only on this circle. Choose one or two of your ideas and act on them in this situation.

Figure 7.6 shows a personal example. I created this map in the spring of 2020, just after the birth of my second son.

Strategy 6: Zones of Responsibility

This strategy, from a social-emotional standpoint, takes us back to the idea of slowing down. It is one strategy we can use to temper our tendency for "too much, too fast"—that specific combination that can quickly overwhelm the coping mechanisms of a trauma-affected individual. As a tool for diminishing transition shock, Zones of Responsibility helps create clarity and minimize stress by "chunking" personal responsibility into viewable, digestible categories.

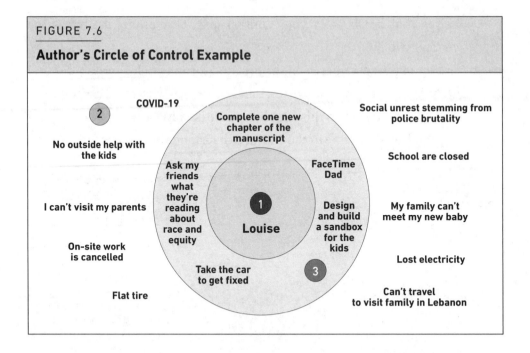

FIGURE 7.6

Author's Circle of Control Example

This strategy supports RAEM students by introducing and scaffolding potentially new vocabulary. It also walks students through an exploration of values, expectations, and responsibilities inherent to (or common within) the new community. Throughout the activity, keep an eye out for those sacred spaces for culturally responsive overlap as they appear in students' organizers.

Here's who's empowered:

- Students, with the guidance of adult facilitators

Here's what you'll need:

- Preconstructed template (ideal) *(see Appendix)* or blank workspace with recording ability (e.g., paper and pencil, Google Slides, Flipgrid)

Here's what you'll do:

1. Introduce and provide background information on categories, if needed (Figure 7.7).

2. Begin with the category of *self.* Invite students to name responsibilities they have at school and home. Encourage thinking around health, hygiene, mental health, setting and achieving goals, building character, and feeling good about themselves. What responsibilities do students identify at home, in the classroom, or in their communities? Encourage students to add as much information to the organizer as possible. Early language learners may have the option of adding words or phrases instead of complete sentences, as the concept (not the language) is the centerpiece of this activity. In addition, I recommend visual cues for each zone and frontloading of meaningful vocabulary.

3. Each horizontal row works together. Once a row has been completed (see Figure 7.7), invite students to stop and reflect on what they notice about that section (e.g., Was one space harder or easier to complete than another? Is there a section you feel you might need to come back to later after more thought?). For young learners, early emergent multilinguals, or students working to grow stamina, it might be worthwhile to pause after the first row and come back to complete the organizer later in the day or the next day.

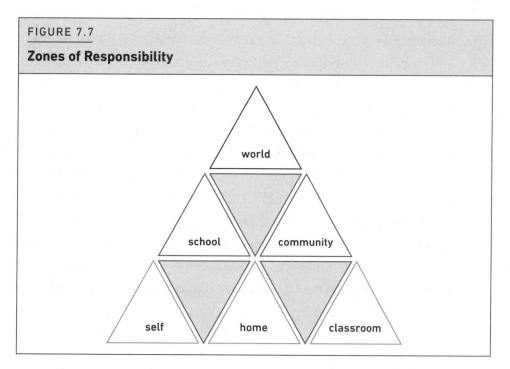

FIGURE 7.7

Zones of Responsibility

4. Continue through the map, in either the same session or subsequent sessions. When finished, zoom out to consider the entire organizer. Where do responsibilities seem balanced? Imbalanced? Manageable? Unmanageable? Where can duties be set down, given away, or picked up? How can we relate to or empathize with others based on our responsibilities? When someone looks at us (or we look at someone else), what parts of the chart are visible or invisible? Why is this important?

5. Invite students to create one discovery statement and one action statement related to the activity. A discovery statement reveals something learned through the activity; an action statement names and describes one positive move or change the writer can commit to related to the discovery statement. For emergent multilinguals, sentence starters/frames are recommended here (e.g., *I discovered that* _____, *To grow my personal power, I will try* _____).

6. *Optional:* In a trusted space, encourage students to share their discoveries. Work together to create a common language that speaks to responsibility. How will students be able to alert you (or one another) when one of their zones of responsibility becomes imbalanced? What is the language for asking for help? How do we offer aid in ways that are perceived as productive and nonjudgmental? What about areas where we don't yet know how to claim responsibility (like in the community or wider world)? Is it possible to create a class responsibility or goal in this area?

7. Keep this anchor chart visible and frequently model practices and language that include features of vulnerability. (For example: *It seems like my cleaning responsibilities in the classroom are out of balance this week. When I spend extra time cleaning up after school, I am late to track practice, which makes me feel like I'm letting the team down. Class, can I share some of these responsibilities with you?*) This strategy is an excellent opportunity to deepen your connection with RAEM students by opening doors to culturally influenced mechanisms of responsibility. Here, for example, are some of the factors I've encountered in the classroom:

- Self:
  - Avoiding any possibility for trouble, especially with law enforcement
  - Adhering to periods of fasting
  - Riding the city bus to school
  - Preserving an observable alignment to traditional gender roles
  - Appropriately covering myself

- Home:
  - Caring for a sibling or other family member
  - Translating for a parent or other family member
  - Attending faith-based classes outside academic schooling
  - Working to send money to a family member in another country

- Classroom:
  - Avoiding trouble or problems
  - Living up to others' expectations to achieve
  - Learning a new language

- School:
  - Attending sports and club obligations
  - Achieving a seal of biliteracy accomplishment
  - Navigating college acceptance/financial feasibility processes

- Community:
  - Maintaining/obtaining immigration and/or citizenship status
  - Adhering to faith-centered duties and commitments
  - Maintaining involvement with cultural community groups, including care of unrelated elders

- World:
  - Following news about the home country or countries where family members live
  - Obtaining travel documents and coordinating travel to reunite with family
  - Learning about environmental care and caution

To close, here are a few discovery and action statements from my classroom:

I discovered that I have a lot of responsibility at home. I can grow my power by being honest with my teachers because they think I'm lazy when my homework is late, but actually, there's just a lot of other stuff going on.

I noticed that talking to my family in Congo is kind of a responsibility, but I never really thought about it like that. I also learned I'm proud to be responsible that way. My action is sometimes I stay up late talking to my family because the time is different in Congo. But then when I come to school, I'm so tired and I get mad easy. I will try to talk to people different days, so I'm not on FaceTime so late one night.

My discovery is I have so much responsibility at school because of class and homework and student council and sports. School is not balanced with everything else. My action is to be less stressed. I can try asking for help and only picking sports or things I love the most instead of trying everything.

Where Do We Go from Here?

In this chapter, we

- Examined sustainability in our efforts to mitigate transition shock in the school setting.
- Established the importance of engaging parents and other stakeholders in the sustainability process.
- Explored school-based strategies for supporting the long-term socioacademic success of RAEM students who may be affected by transition shock.
- Introduced SEL strategies that align with the fourth pillar in approaching transition shock.

We've now considered each of the four elements—connect, protect, respect, and redirect—in depth. In each of these pillars, our goal was to move students from survival brain to learning brain and from power interruption to power restoration. This required a shift in focus from what *has* happened to what *is* happening. We're now ready to concentrate on what will be possible in the future. We're prepared to set our sights on resiliency!

Looking to the Future and Restoring Power

Our students are often stronger than we give them credit for. Youth who encounter significant adversity and receive timely and appropriate interventions are highly likely to overcome transition shock. Most will go on to lead productive, society-enhancing lives.

Often, we hear this referred to as *resilience:* the ability to process, negotiate, and recover from adverse life experiences. Resilience enables a person to maintain intrapersonal and interpersonal stability in the face of disruption, adapt to change, and flourish in spite of challenges. It highlights an individual's agency to maintain or regain the status quo of the brain's internal alarm system.

Positioning Ourselves for Deeper Conversations on Resilience

Let's take a moment to sit with the idea of resilience—and to challenge it.

Resilience appears to be a good thing; it's associated with longevity, lower rates of depression, and greater satisfaction with life (Harvard Health, 2017). Among young people, these same qualities (as measured on resilience scales) link to a reduction of emotional, mental, or behavioral problems; an increase in psychological well-being; and a shield against chronic disease. Among RAEMs (and more specifically within resettled refugee populations), students who demonstrate resilience are also more likely to experience a healthier long-term integration process (Kreuzer, 2016). In short, resilience is what we should be aiming for.

But here's where things get a bit messy. In recent years, the concept of resilience has transcended the clinical setting (where, in the early 20th century, it signaled an ability to overcome childhood trauma). The term spread voraciously to virtually every corner of society—from education to business to the environment. Along the way, the idea of resilience itself has shifted and become exhausted from overuse. It has become politicized and, in some cases, weaponized.

Let's consider four central arguments:

- Resilience, as it is widely applied, suggests a personal responsibility for outcomes that fail to account for factors beyond one's control (Molinar, 2020; Seghal, 2015).
- Resilience is contextual. It is dependent on multiple environmental and intrapersonal variables (Gask, 2015; Heid, 2019).
- Resilience, when regarded as a "have-or-have-not" quality, can lead to victim-blaming (Heid, 2019).
- Resilience can be framed in ways that mask and reinforce inequalities (Seghal, 2015; Suarez, 2020).

The simple fact is that a vast majority of newcomer students are students of color. Even white or white-passing people are likely to find themselves on the cultural, religious, or linguistic fringes of U.S. society. Newcomer families are likely to find housing in or be formally relocated to neighborhoods where crime, gun violence, substance abuse, and racial profiling are woven into the day-to-day experience. They may face labor and housing discrimination or be subject to outright racism, nationalism, or xenophobia.

Educator and YA author Tony Weaver Jr. explains, "There is no amount of resilience that can prepare Black boys to live a life where they can't even bird watch without fear of the police being weaponized against them by someone who deems their existence as a threat" (Weaver, 2020, para. 13). Even though our primary focus here is on serving RAEMs, we can't deny that aspects of this sentiment carry over. RAEMs may not have endured the elapsed sting of systemic injustice as it is uniquely presented in the United States, but there's a good chance they'll encounter its aftershocks (Frater-Mathieson, 2004; Kreuzer, 2016).

Newcomers may encounter any or all of these situations and may be expected to demonstrate some level of resilience throughout. And they do all of this before we've even considered the dynamics that inspired (or necessitated) their relocation to the U.S. states, cities, towns, neighborhoods, schools, and classrooms—*our* classrooms—they now call home.

The problem with resilience became most evident to me while sitting in a high school classroom in Saida, Lebanon, with a group of Syrian refugee students. In our conversations, a common sentiment emerged over and again: *Enough with resilience. We've been through enough. Stop telling us to be resilient, and do something to stop the traumas from occurring in the first place.*

Here's what I'm getting at. Trauma-informed care is long overdue for the same sort of culturally affirmative scrutiny that is already underway for social-emotional learning. The good news is that very similar or parallel considerations will apply. For example, just as SEL programming void of context can be ineffective or problematic, trauma-informed practice must also be responsive to the reality of students' lived experiences. Moreover, trauma-aware programming cannot "cancel out" traumas caused by or exacerbated by deeply rooted social injustices.

Unfortunately, the modern concept of resilience has undertones that are inconsistent with culturally affirmative principles. It's not that there's a lack of evidence supporting the benefits of resilient qualities. Rather, it's that these qualities are too often referenced without context. Therefore, at the risk of falling into the *resilience* trap, I'd like to suggest a different approach.

Moving Toward Empowerment

This is where power restoration comes in. When we talk about restoring personal power, we place students in the driver's seat of their own outcomes. Thus, we center the individual as the architect of their own plan and process for overcoming adversity—encouraged, of course, by the interpersonal and societal structures that support and preserve that person's well-being.

Importantly, this is consistent with students' individual narratives. It's a subtle but effective shift. For one, it moves the focus away from a "right" version of resilience. It also creates a buffer between an individual's personal responsibility to pursue self-work and larger societal responsibilities to counter inequity and injustice.

Power restoration affects each person differently and is reflected in any number of ways. In my years of working with students from some 60 countries across the ECE–12 spectrum, here's what I find boosts resilience the most:

- **Speak directly with students (of any age) about the human brain.** "If we want to empower students, we must show them how they can control their own cognitive and emotional health and their own learning," says Judy Willis (2010). "Teaching students how the brain operates is a huge step" (para. 1). When youth understand how stress influences their thinking and actions, they can balance this awareness with parallel cultural realities. These conversations should be among the first we have in a school year. It is *that* important. After all, as kids and teens learn more about their brains, they will develop greater agency in shaping and controlling them.

- **Practice metacognition, or the practice of "thinking about one's thinking."** This requires helping students "meet" their brains. *How is my brain designed? How does it work? What's its job when I get upset? How does my brain sometimes get in my own way?* Above all else, it is important to teach and remind students of the brain's magnificence and that it can change and be changed over time. The brain itself is resilient. Eventually, students become adept at naming the brain functions or reactions as they occur, and they can issue conscious-level, self-regulatory responses in real time.

- **Explicitly teach, model, and practice power-restorative strategies.** Research informs us that power restoration and resilience can be promoted, if not explicitly taught. In fact, resiliency has been demonstrated to respond positively to scaffolding and survival tools, as made available by adult caretakers, older siblings, or mentors (Daud, Klinteberg, & Rydelius, 2008; Kreuzer, 2016).

- **Encourage students to "own" their outlook for the future.** Power restoration requires forward momentum, but to move forward, we need to know which direction that is. Empowered individuals have learned to distinguish between productive and unproductive paths. They are adept at changing directions when they've moved off course. They understand that sometimes the path itself curves or reverses, and they can be flexible in those moments. Empowered learners set and work toward goals, which is a cornerstone to overcoming adversity.

- **Strengthen problem-solving abilities.** Problem-solving skill sets are incredibly transformative when it comes to power restoration. When students are aware of how stress influences their brain, they are better equipped to seek appropriate solutions within a given situation. Problem-solving can boost social-emotional health, too. Responsible decision-making, remember, relies on an ability to identify, analyze, and solve problems. Consciously and consistently integrated problem-solving opportunities promote SEL skills in ways that benefit resilience.

- **Practice goal-setting.** Kids and teens who set and achieve small, manageable goals build confidence and stamina to go after larger ambitions. Goal-setting is part of the power restoration puzzle. Why? Because working toward healthy intrapersonal and prosocial behaviors is a process. Setting landmarks along that journey helps students get to where they want to be. To support students in becoming effective goal-setters and achievers, I suggest starting with the DBT House. Are existing goals or visions evidenced within the window (i.e., goal, dream, or vision for the future)? Are they able to name a goal or goals? Is the vision a short- or long-term one? If asked to elaborate on their goal(s), can they identify one or more steps they should take in the direction of their vision?

We can also embed micro goal-setting into our daily practice. This practice is especially helpful in power interrupted situations because it breaks goal-setting down into more manageable pieces and builds agency gradually. Micro goal-setting involves shorter-term goals that are digestible and offer concrete markers of accomplishment. Practical examples include

— A reading log to facilitate a goal of reading three pages per day.

— Student responsibility for self-monitoring increments of on-task behaviors.

— Working toward doing 100 sit-ups in a four-minute period.

• **Encourage students to take on the mindset of a champion.** This means being present in their power and self-advocating for their needs and continued growth. Speaking from the TEDxYouth stage, 5th grader Carson Bylow (2018) explains, "A growth mindset is when somebody believes that they can *learn* to be good—that they can learn to get better. They are not afraid of challenges; they continue when things get hard, they know that they have to put effort in to learn, and they learn from criticism. They are also *inspired* by people who do well."

• **Align yourself as an ally in students' journeys to achieve positive life outcomes.** By this point, it should be clear that power restoration is enhanced when students feel a strong sense of belonging, purpose, judgment-free counsel, and community allyship.

Here's Rujan:

I have been very fortunate in my life in that I have parents who understand the importance of letting a child be curious, explorative, and play. They let me do all those things. They valued my education equally as much; to them, it was and still is the case that my academic success is theirs, too. My attempt at a better life and success is also their attempt. These dreams of mine are not just my own; it is theirs too and the generation that came before them.

This may seem like a great deal of pressure, but I never felt it. I never ever felt the pressure to constantly study or do well; it was always a matter of engaging, playing, and being curious about the world.

Additionally, this support paired with the sense of unity in the community (which I understand now) is what helped me flourish.

I am forever grateful to educators like you and community members that unified and made me feel at home. I would not nearly be the man I am today without that. I still remember spending time with you outside of the classroom. As I learn and recall vividly now, these interactions were empowering and powerful. You were not just an educator. You took time out of your schedule to take the initiative to meet us and spend time with my family. That is a boon I could never repay. If there is a model that seemed to have worked in my experience, it is this.

For an educator, it is crucial to understand how students are in the classroom, the values their families live by, and where they are coming from. Perhaps the old adage is correct: It is one thing to acknowledge a person's story; it is quite another to immerse yourself in it. I think familial and community unity is by far the most profound aspect of success.

I remember the joyful moments from classroom environments. These things incentivize students, or at least it did for me, to be curious and put in my maximum effort.

Supporting Students on Their Continued Paths to Empowerment

So far, this chapter has centered the student in conversations around resilient qualities. Now, let's zoom out to consider the bigger picture of education. What is our role—as educators and stakeholders—in promoting sustainable power restorative programming?

We can strengthen our opportunities for combined and lasting success by

- Enabling students as authors of their narratives.
- Engaging caretakers and mentors as trusted stakeholders.
- Encouraging teacher self-care.
- Evaluating our transition-shock mitigation programming.

Enabling Students as Authors of Their Narratives

"Trauma recovery begins the second you emerge from the experience," writes Dr. Deborah Serani (2014). "Your body naturally begins healing; your mind tries to make sense of it all. Your recovery process will be stronger if you can reconstruct what the trauma took away: security and safety, reconnecting with others, and restoring a sense of hopefulness. And one of the most powerful ways toward this reconstruction is through your story—your personal narrative" (para. 5).

Indeed, research highlights storytelling as a powerful mechanism for healing in the aftermath of transition shock (Herman, 1997; Kearney, 2007). Karen Baicker (2020) shares, "[Yale] is currently researching ways that literacy, and the ability to craft and reshape one's personal narrative, can provide a buffer for children facing adversity and build resilience for teachers. Through literature, people can learn that others have experienced and coped with similar adversity" (para. 17).

The process of engaging with one's personal narrative helps organize memories and information in the brain of a person who has experienced trauma (including transition shock). Ultimately, the ability to better categorize and sequence bits of information leads to better outcomes for long-term power restoration (Abramowitz, Tolin, & Street, 2001; Amir, Stafford, Freshman, & Foa, 1998; Gillihan, 2019). Baicker (2020) also adds that "when implemented thoughtfully, storytelling allows the narrator not just the power to retell, but to rewrite their experiences [and] the chance to reclaim and reframe those events in ways that offer hope and healing" (para. 17).

It can also invite sociocultural affirmation when students—particularly RAEMs and students of color—are legitimized as authors of their own stories. For example, Dena Simmons (2017) writes, "While it is important for everyone, regardless of background, to be empowered to author his or her own narrative, this is especially true for people of color and other marginalized groups because, historically, we have had fewer opportunities to have our stories heard" (para. 27). According to Al-Hakawati, a Syrian oral tradition project, "Stories are what we are made of, and if we lose our stories, we risk losing touch with our humanity and our identity" (Cultural Heritage Without Borders, 2020, para. 5).

As a power-restorative approach, we focus these narratives from the present moment onward. After all, although students' pasts are part of their narrative, we're not aiming to revisit life events that may have been power disrupting. Instead, the aim is to stand by kids and teens as they define who they choose to be in the present and future—and create a vision or map for bringing this version of themselves to life.

The process of inviting students to construct, reconstruct, or add to their personal narratives can take on various shapes: storytelling, acting, poetry, multimedia art, performance art, spoken word, or podcasts, for example. Whatever the pathway, we can dedicate specific lessons or periods in which personal narratives are the explicit focus of students' expressive undertakings. As they continue to develop and strengthen their personal narratives, students become better equipped to move toward power restoration, and "when people become the authors of their own stories, they pave the way for social transformation" (Simmons, 2017, para. 28).

Engaging Caretakers and Mentors as Trusted Stakeholders

When we discussed the pillar of connection in Chapter 4, we began engineering a web of support for newcomer students. Let's now concentrate on arguably the most critical group of all: those students' caretakers.

What can we establish as guiding principles when communicating with culturally and linguistically dynamic caretaker groups about transition shock? How do we cross cultural thresholds to build authentic partnerships? Here are some thoughts to consider:

- How are safety and trust cultivated? How do you (or how does your campus) define a welcoming environment?
- Are routine, predictability, and transparency evidenced in the learning environment? How do you know?
- Where are you in the process of being cognizant of your own biases around mental health and trauma? For example, can you name observed behaviors without labeling students *as* the behavior?
- Does your organization reduce isolation by connecting families to appropriate resources? If appropriate, are families connected to other families/ community groups with sociocultural commonalities?

- Do you strive to meet with parents in person and, if needed, arrange for a trained translator? Does your campus resist using children as conversational brokers?
- Does someone from your campus talk to parents about the link between their students' school performance and social and mental health? Is the language direct, clear, and translated, if needed?
- Are mental health terms translated (and is jargon avoided)? (Remember that mental health terms may be unfamiliar, meaningless, or untranslatable for some newcomer parents.)
- Are students' sociocultural perspectives honored in the process of advocating for their care?
- Do you or does your campus champion wraparound supports and refer students for advanced care promptly?

Power restoration is enhanced when students' personal, familial, and cultural values show up in school. Highlighting caretakers' voices can simultaneously bolster our culturally responsive efforts and temper student anxiety. One of my favorite ways to do this is through student-parent notes. This idea came about as I was preparing for a back-to-school night. Our newcomer classroom held a dozen separate primary languages, and I was eager for all our parents to feel welcomed and included in the evening's activities. The problem was that I had no idea how I would overcome such tremendous language obstacles to achieve this. So I asked students for their help, and this is what we came up with.

The students wrote simple notes to their parents and families. As a class, we decided that students would record their sentiments in a language of comfort: either English (and later translate the notes for their parents) or their native language. We then arranged the messages so they were waiting in the classroom for parents when they arrived.

Our campus extended back-to-school night invitations to all family members, so kids attended with their caretakers. Grandparents, older and younger siblings, and extended family members were often in attendance, too. During these events, students took immediate ownership of their letters and were eager to share them. They were equally as excited to ask their adults in attendance to reciprocate the gesture. As a result, our classroom writing station became a hub of activity. We laid out an assortment of writing utensils and stationery. Though shy at first, parents and caretakers took pens in hand to compose notes of love and encouragement. Caretakers, like the students, used the language with which they felt most comfortable.

As parents read aloud to their students in their native languages, the entire tone of the room shifted. Parents of different cultures exchanged knowing glances with one another, and those who shared the same language made room for laughter and conversation. These caretakers all had the same thoughts, hopes, and expectations for their children. Importantly, they mirrored the considerations *I* had for their children:

> I am proud of you. You are a good child.
> Work hard. Try your best. Be kind.
> I am here for you.

Linguistically, I couldn't understand all the notes, but that didn't matter. The messages were not meant for me. The ultimate message was that we were not only on the same playing field—we were on the same *team*.

The notes hung in our classroom for the rest of the year. They provided tangible artifacts of students' heritage cultures and grounded students during moments of anxiety. Indeed, those notes became the most authentic, relevant anchor charts the classroom had to offer. Figure 8.1 includes a few examples of those powerful notes.

Encouraging Teacher Self-Care

No one needs to tell teachers that we picked a challenging line of work. Often, however, the line between effortful and exacting is a thin one. Most of us will spend our careers in education teetering between the two.

The fact is, though, that our students carry a lot with them into the classroom, and teachers tend to care so much about them that it's nearly

FIGURE 8.1

Parent-Student Notes

Dear Mom and Uncle,

Thank you for buying food and for being my family and we are happy.

I love you,

Abdul.

Abdul.

Waxbarashadu aad ayey muhiim u tahay. waa inaad dhageysataa oo ixtiraamtaa oo aad u shaqeysaa. Waxaan filayaa inaad tahay wiil aad u yaab badan.

Baba

(Abdul, Education is very important. You have to listen and respect and work hard. I think you are a very wonderful boy. Dad.)

My dad, you help me to read a book. Mom, when I go to sleep, you read to me a book. And then I like to sleep. Thank you, mom and dad.

Simeon

Na ku penda sana. Una saidia sana. Ulisaidia kulipia ada ya shule. Na sema asante sana ni saidia. Asante sana.

Love, Dad

(I love you very much. You are very helpful. You helped pay for the school fees. And [I] say: Thank you very much. It helps. Thank you very much.)

Thank you to Mom. You are nice to me. When I come to school, you make me a rice.

Ju Be Doh

Ju Be Doh,

သင်ကျိုးစားလုပ်ဆောင် သည် မင်းကျောင်း သွားတက်ပမေ့ငါမလုပ်ခဲ့ ဘူး။ ငါဂုဏ်ယူတယ်

(You work hard. You go to school, but I did not. I am proud. Mom)

impossible to avoid picking up some of that weight. Add in the pressures of planning, preparing, and performing, and it's not at all surprising that a vast majority of U.S. teachers feel overburdened. According to the Centers for Disease Control, more than half of all U.S. children have experienced some kind of trauma:

> Whether you're a teacher, paraprofessional, counselor, or school resource officer, every staff member cares deeply about students. And that means being exposed to the traumas students bring into school every day, including poverty, grief, family problems, racism, and drug abuse. The emotional and physical toll is often severe. Even if they have not endured trauma themselves, educators can begin exhibiting symptoms similar to those of their students—withdrawal, anxiety, depression, and chronic fatigue. (Walker, 2019, para. 5)

We may hear this referred to as *secondary traumatic stress* or *vicarious trauma*, which occurs when "the emotional duress that results when an individual hears about the firsthand trauma experiences of another" (NCTSN, 2020, para. 1). To combat this, teachers must engage in intentional self-care. The process can look different for different people. It can include aiming for enough sleep each night, eating a healthy diet, staying hydrated, exercising, meditating, establishing rituals, engaging with family and friends, enjoying a favorite hobby, and bolstering a set of effective coping strategies. Perhaps most important, students negotiating transition shock should not bear the weight of "healing" broken systems. Instead, their healing should occur within a web of protective factors.

Likewise, we can't expect teachers to resist and recover from secondary traumatic stress in silos. They must be supported by the larger school, the district, and institutional organisms they are a part of. "It's critical that these efforts are school or district-wide," reports Tim Walker (2019), "because an inordinate emphasis on self-care or 'resilience' without adequate supports places too much of the burden on the individual educator" (para. 31).

So what does this look like? Steven Hydon at the University of Southern California recommends a five-step approach, which he describes as listen, protect, connect, model, and teach (Hydon & Marsh, 2005). Karen Baicker (2020) advises schools to consider "regularly scheduled meetings where educators can come together to discuss workplace stress and partake in counseling services; training programs; faculty appreciation events; and other stress-relieving social activities" (para. 13). We might also invest in "increasing the number of social workers, boost support for social-emotional learning, and add mental health services for students *and* teachers" (Meeker, 2020, para. 7).

Perhaps most important, we must become better at talking about secondary traumatic stress and vicarious trauma. As leadership coach L. Sha Fanion (2020) puts it: "When students are traumatized, educators are traumatized too. Thus, we must start talking about educators and vicarious trauma" (para 15).

Evaluating Our Transition-Shock Mitigation Programming

Like other organizational systems, we should routinely evaluate our methods for supporting learners who experience transition shock. Self-assessment calls for data collection and analysis to determine if our trauma-informed programming is effective and equitable.

Optimal power-restorative practice requires us to monitor students' successes and adapt the strategies and cues as needed. Essentially, we must ensure that the methods we introduce are good fits for individual students.

What does that mean? A good fit means the strategy is *not* retriggering and *is* culturally affirmative, consistent with students' lived experiences, and language adaptive. A good fit means students are empowered to experiment with mitigation strategies, fail forward in a safe space, reevaluate without self-admonishment, and try again.

Shifts in the broader educational landscape are necessary, too. To best meet our students where they are, we must be willing to engage in honest conversations about our organization's infrastructure, including leadership, policies, and procedures, as they ignite or diffuse underlying transition shock. Effective models for mitigating transition shock push back against punitive practices and embrace restorative solution-seeking (Ford, 2020).

We must ensure that all team members are equipped with tools for understanding and addressing student trauma. It's also imperative that educators receive comprehensive support in recognizing and managing the secondary stress that may arise through their work with trauma-affected youth (Whitfield

& Kanter, 2014). Finally, we must routinely self-assess our power-restorative programming to determine achievements, gaps, and next steps.

Some trauma-informed self-monitoring and self-assessment rubrics exist online (e.g., the NCTSN's Trauma-Informed Organizational Assessment at www.nctsn.org/resources/trauma-informed-organizational-assessment-information-packet). However, there are several concerns with using these. First, most are designed for use in clinical or social-sector settings, not classrooms. This means that the prompts embedded within the rubrics target deeper levels of care and psychological counseling than what can (or should) occur at school. Second, the goal is to accurately capture an organization's starting point, gains, and growth opportunities. Therefore, the self-evaluation instrument should be customized to reflect the vision and demographics of the organization and its members.

When I work directly with schools and districts, I like to suggest formulating a rubric internally. Ideally, this process occurs within a focus group or committee composed of many stakeholders committed to power-restorative practice. Teachers, administrators, and parents should all be represented. Campus counselors, psychologists, and student health team members should also be a part of this team, along with experts in trauma-informed care (from inside or outside the district), whenever possible.

I find that approaching evaluative rubrics from a backward-design perspective is both powerful and efficient. Where, in the most optimal sense, are you reaching for your RAEM students to be when it comes to establishing or reestablishing their personal power? Entirely eliminating transition shock is not an option, so what might it look like if and when your learners are empowered to employ tools and strategies that minimize the negative impacts of transition shock? What does this entail in terms of building a broader culture, staff training, and opportunities for educator self-care?

Here are a few things to keep in mind as you create a transition shock evaluation rubric for your organization:

- Self-evaluations are a "snapshot" of where an individual or team is along a spectrum of growth toward their goals.

- The assessment process (and the corresponding rubrics used) should be strengths-based.
- Rubric prompts should be carefully analyzed to avoid embedded bias and encourage objectivity.

Take a look at some of the following prompts. Which stand out to you relative to your practice or the aims of your organization? What would you expand, modify, or tailor to your school or student groups?

Prompts for self-assessment:

☐ I have a clear understanding of what transition shock is.

☐ I can explain how transition shock affects the brain and learning.

☐ I understand the relationship between culture and transition shock and can describe some of the ways this plays out within my student groups.

☐ I understand the key differences between trauma-informed practice and social-emotional learning.

☐ I am a protective factor in my students' lives.

☐ I establish and maintain healthy and respectful professional boundaries with my students.

☐ My students feel safe in my classroom.

☐ My students feel safe throughout the school day, including at lunch, passing between classes, and before/after school.

☐ Most or all of my students are experts in at least one power restoration tool/strategy.

☐ I feel safe, protected, valued, and respected at my place of work.

☐ My approach to working with students is asset-based.

☐ I feel confident in my ability to implement evidence-based, power restoration tools and strategies.

☐ I feel confident implementing evidence-based, power-restoration tools and strategies in culturally and linguistically diverse settings.

☐ I can explain how my classroom's power restoration tools and strategies are also culturally affirmative and language accessible.

☐ I know where and how to refer students for mental health care and analysis.

☐ I have access to high-quality training/professional development opportunities related to transition shock, including trauma-informed practice.

☐ I recognize that working with trauma-affected youth puts me at greater risk for secondary traumatic stress, and I have tools to help combat this.

☐ I clearly understand my school's/district's policies and procedures that ensure the privacy of our students, including information about their physical and mental well-being.

☐ I have access to support groups, mental health services, and/or counseling services through my organization.

Prompts for school/district organizational assessment:

☐ Students are centered in our organization's work.

☐ Students' physical and mental well-being is the concern of *every* member of our staff.

☐ Our organization has clear protocols surrounding policies, practices, and strategies related to mitigating transition shock.

☐ Our staff has a clear understanding of what transition shock is.

☐ Our staff can explain how transition shock affects the brain and learning.

☐ Our staff understands the relationship between culture and transition shock and can describe some of the ways this plays out in classrooms and throughout the school/district.

☐ Our staff understands the key differences between trauma-informed practice and social-emotional learning.

☐ Our school/district—and the people and places within it—are protect factors in students' lives.

☐ Our staff establishes and maintains healthy and respectful professional boundaries with students.

☐ Our staff feels safe, protected, valued, and respected in the building and district.

☐ Our approach to working with students is asset-based.

☐ Our staff feels confident in their ability to implement evidence-based, power restoration tools and strategies.

☐ Our staff feels confident implementing evidence-based, power restoration tools and strategies in culturally and linguistically diverse settings.

☐ Our staff can explain how the power restoration tools and strategies they use are also culturally affirmative and language accessible.

☐ We have highly trained mental health professionals on our team. Our staff knows where and how to refer students for mental health care and analysis.

☐ We provide consistent and ongoing professional development and support related to transition shock, including trauma-informed practice.

☐ We recognize the risk of vicarious traumatization that teachers face, and we provide training, support groups, and mental health services to support our staff.

☐ Information related to students' mental well-being is available in the languages represented within the organization.

☐ We have clear policies and procedures in place to protect the privacy of our students, including information about their physical and mental well-being.

☐ We have a framework and timeline for ongoing assessment and debriefing of program success.

Resilience: Into Practice

Let's explore a few final strategies together as we focus on resilience and promise. Each is culturally responsive and suitable across all language domains (and may also be completed in students' heritage languages, if desired).

Strategy 1: Reconstructed Folktales

Folktales are stories that are retold across generations, usually to teach a lesson, explain why something is the way it is, or connect people to their histories. However, the primary purpose of folktales, many scholars argue, is to promote a sense of cultural unity (Samuel, 1997).

Every corner of Earth is a birthplace for folktales. These intergenerational stories can even distinguish one sociocultural group from another. "Folktales help the community to maximize their strengths. They may be as old as the hill, but they contain real issues about life in general and human nature in particular, which people have observed," writes Lakau Mphasha (2017) of the University of Venda, South Africa. "Through the folktales, people gain their cultural heritage, which, to a great extent, determines their further thinking, desires, and attitudes" (p. 295).

Similarly, 10 months of ethnographic fieldwork in Ethiopia showed that Oromo-speaking youth constructed critical social values and connections via their participation in dramatized folktales. Researcher Tadesse Jaleta Jirata (2018) explains, "By presenting children as actors in the re-contextualization of folktales, [we can] argue that participation in a folkloric performance is not a mere play practice for children but is a social and artistic forum through which they acquire survival skills and grow connected to values of their society" (para. 1).

Folktales also model constructive and effective decision-making. By design, characters face conflicts that require difficult decisions and are forced to take action. The decisions they make lead to clear consequences. Consequently, folktales demonstrate the importance of making difficult decisions under challenging circumstances.

When we think about transition shock, the messaging of folktales runs parallel to the narrative of power restoration: resilience can only be born through our encounters with conflict and the difficult decisions we make while moving through it. This strategy invites students to disassemble and reassemble a traditional folktale to reflect their own lived experiences.

Students have the agency to reveal as much or as little of their experiences as they feel comfortable with. They can choose to let the folktale conceal the reminder, even as they may internally recognize and process deeper details of power restoration. Alternatively, they can choose to rewrite the narrative of their own experience to reflect their wishes, intentions, or empowered outcomes.

In my own experience, I find reconstructed folktales to be most effective when they are familiar or based on cultural stories with which students most identify. Then, using the story as a template, students reimagine the characters and details to reflect their own experiences overcoming a challenge or adversity. The process of reconstructing folktales (and simultaneously reflecting on one's own journey to overcome adversity) engages all three aspects of empowerment: knowledge, prospect, and championship. In addition, when we invite students to share the original stories on which their new folktales are based, we open the doors for authentic cultural relevance.

As another option, students could explore a single folktale together and then amend the characters, setting, struggle, conflict resolution, and lesson or moral so it aligns to their own lived social, cultural, and linguistic experiences. In either case, I recommend opening this activity with a shared literacy experience. For example, in my 3rd grade Level 1 newcomer classroom, we'd usually begin by reading the Peruvian folktale "The Fox in the Moon" by Juan Quintana, which explains why some people see the image of a fox in the moon. We'd then ask students to contribute what they know to look for in the moon and the stories accompanying these images. Together, we learned that people see everything from handprints, a tree, a rabbit, a tiger, and the man in the moon. These dynamic retellings set the stage for the activity.

Here's who's empowered:

- Students, with the guidance of adult facilitators
- Educators, as they learn more about their students.

Here's what you'll need:

- Whole-class mentor text or unit study
- Practiced writing system or template for planning and organization (e.g., prewriting planners, storyboards, or structural organizers, including those with sentence frames, where helpful).
- A means of researching culturally relevant folktales, if necessary
- Language supports: a personal copy of the mentor text to scaffold vocabulary and structure; interactive word walls, bilingual dictionaries, or other suitable writing tools; sentence structure lead-ins and/or stems; accessibility to other relevant guideposts, such as transition words

Here's what you'll do:

1. Ensure that students understand the folktale genre through a unit of study, examples in literature, and so on.
2. Invite learners to identify a folktale that exists within their culture or select a folktale from the unit of study with which they identify.
3. Help students deconstruct the folktale by identifying the characters, character traits, conflict, struggle, resolution, lesson or moral, and other central elements.
4. Have students layer their own lived experiences atop the "bones" of the folktale, highlighting ways in which they have overcome a significant challenge and demonstrated power restoration. *(Note: Not all the challenges students face have been or will be defeated. Imaginative resolutions to a dilemma are also welcomed.)*
5. Younger students may feel compelled to illustrate their work. Provide time for them to do so.
6. Encourage students to reflect on their compositions and the challenges they encountered and set out to diminish (either in reality or imaginatively).
7. I usually conduct this activity at the end of the school year. By this time, we've established a high level of trust within the classroom community. To close out the activity (which often runs a week or two), we debrief

together. During this time, guide students to identify and name one way they are empowered or have the tools to restore personal power.

Example: Octavio and OhMar both looked to the mentor folktale "The Fox in the Moon." It tells the story of Fox wanting to go to the moon, which he has been told is made of cheese. He convinces his friend Mole to join the adventure. They ask many friends for help along the way. The friends try and fail, so they tell Fox that his dream is impossible. Eventually, Condor loops a rope to the crescent angle of the moon, and Fox and Mole begin climbing. Mole looks down and crashes to Earth, which is why he lives underground. Fox climbs all the way to the moon—where he can still be seen today.

Octavio writes about his journey of coming to the United States from Guatemala. In his version, he (as the main character) is Coyote, and his brother (the role of Mole) is Rabbit. Coyote and Rabbit ask many people for help getting to the United States, but everyone tells them it's impossible. Then they meet Owl (in real life, their USCIS asylum agent), who can help. Coyote and Rabbit both make it to their new home and stay there together. Octavio's ending reads, "And that is why the owl is good luck in my country, Guatemala."

OhMar's folktale also tells of a bond between herself and a sibling. In the story, her character is embodied by a hummingbird, and her sister is a bumblebee. Hummingbird and Bumblebee are separated in The Big Fight, and they ask for help from many people in their quest to reunite. (In real life, the girls, who are half-sisters with different mothers, were separated in the process of resettlement and had not yet been reunited. Only OhMar and her younger brother were resettled to the United States, along with their parents.) The resolution to OhMar's story is imaginative. Hummingbird and Bumblebee both climb to the moon from separate sides of Earth and meet together there, where they live happily.

Octavio revealed the deeper message of his folktale immediately after reading it aloud to me. OhMar shared her story with me several years later (she was no longer my student). Octavio's power, in his own words: "In a hard time, I keep looking for a way. Plus, me and my brother can do anything together." And from OhMar: "I can go all the way to a new country and learn to speak and make friends."

Strategy 2: Hands of Promise

This art therapy strategy engages students in purposefully envisioning their future selves. Because the future is unknown and filled with ambiguity, picturing the possibility of what it *could* hold may be difficult among students experiencing transition shock. Hands of Promise is one way to scaffold this type of thinking and promote resilience.

Here's who's empowered:

- Students, with the guidance of adult facilitators

Here's what you'll need:

- Blank paper or hands template *(see Appendix)*
- Writing, drawing, painting, or collaging materials

Here's what you'll do:

1. Ensure that students are in a reasonably calm state of being. If self-evaluating on a worry scale of 1–10, a score of 5 or below is ideal.
2. If using blank paper, have students trace two hands on the paper.
3. Briefly explain the concepts and vocabulary related to *past, present,* and *future,* if necessary.
4. Have students begin with the left hand. In this space, they should record words, images, and/or designs reflective of their past or present. Specifically, they should name those things they are willing to set down or leave behind. Next, ask students to consider thoughts, behaviors, or parts of their personal story that no longer serve them or create unwelcome challenges in their lives.
5. Encourage students to thank the completed hand. Each of the words, images, and ideas in this space helped shape them and make them stronger.
6. Then have students move on to the right hand, where they should record words, images, or designs representing features they would like to invite into their lives. What thoughts, emotions, or behaviors would they like to see more of? What outcomes might they expect to see as a result of

thought, emotional, or behavioral shifts? What specific goals, visions, or dreams are they striving toward? How do they feel as they work toward achieving these goals?

7. Ask students to carefully observe the things they included in this space. Then have them enunciate (verbally, in writing, or their minds) one small step they can take *right now* in this future direction.

8. Remind students periodically to return to their hands of promise, either by revisiting their art or by simply studying the hands and recalling what they included on them. When students feel stuck, encourage them to formulate and act on one small step to help their forward momentum.

A 1st grader created the example in Figure 8.2. The left hand prominently includes a picture of the coronavirus and a crying person. Also included are computers and distance learning interfaces. On the right hand, the child indicated that travel (an airplane) and a return to in-person school (the larger building is her school) are elements she looks forward to in her future.

FIGURE 8.2

Hands of Promise Example

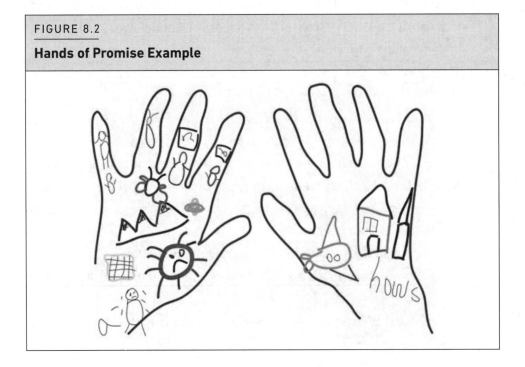

Strategy 3: Wheel of Protection

This strategy works especially well with middle and high school students, but it can be easily modified to meet the needs of younger students. The Wheel of Protection helps students deepen their understanding of protective factors and can be a tool for self-analysis. It also functions as a stakeholder tool to identify students' areas of strength and opportunity. Ultimately, it can help guide an individual's plan to support the power restoration and retention processes.

The process remains the same for any purpose. The inside circle names elements that are a part of the student's life and that he/she/they consider positive, supportive, or uplifting. The outside circle is a space to consider how those elements provide strength, calm, or connectivity.

You'll see that I've included a second wheel here, as well. This one, based on a concept out of Arizona State University, looks more at features of identity (Intergroup Relations Center, 2012). I use this version frequently in professional development settings and when having conversations with older (high school–aged) students about race, ethnicity, and identity. The format is the same, but the process is slightly different, as you'll see in the instructions. Completed self-concept organizers can be used to guide constructive conversations around race, diversity, and inclusion. Additionally, they can provide insight into individual intersections of identity and transition shock. If I'm working through both wheels, I find it useful to complete the Wheel of Self-Concept first.

Here's who's empowered:

- Students, with the guidance of adult facilitators
- Educators, as they gain a deeper understanding of their students

Here's what you'll need:

- Wheel of Protection and/or Wheel of Self-Concept (see Figure 8.3)
- Writing utensils
- Cooperative sentence stems, if engaging in conversation

Here's what you'll do:

1. Introduce the strategy to students as a way to explore the protective and supporting factors that exist within their lived experiences.

2. Have students add information to the wheel. To do this, they'll record aspects of their life they consider positive, supportive, or uplifting in the inner frames. In the outer frames, they'll consider *how* those elements provide strength, calm, or connectivity. For example, looking at the personality traits wedge, one student wrote this in the inner space: "organized, kind, work hard." In the outer frame, they recorded, "My kindness makes a lot of people want to be my friend. The other ones help me do great at school and work toward my goals."

3. Prompt individual or group reflection and conversation. Ask questions such as the following: *Which part of the wheel is most important to you and why? Are there certain categories that stand out to you more than others? Why are some categories less dominant for you? What personal experiences have influenced your responses? What supports are not represented in the wheel? Which part(s) of the wheel have created the most/fewest challenges for you? Which parts of your wheel are most/least emphasized by your family or community group? Do you rely on different aspects in different situations? Which segment(s) are you most grateful for? Why? Which parts of your wheel would you like to explore further?*

4. Remind students that self-awareness, including an awareness of one's own protect factors, is an important indicator for success and well-being at school and beyond.

5. Explain that some protect factors will change over time, based on our experiences and the people around us. Provide opportunities for students to re-create the wheel from time to time and analyze differences as they appear.

For the Wheel of Self-Concept:

1. Introduce the strategy to students as a way to explore their own identities, as well as the cultural identities of others in the classroom.

2. Have students add information to the wheel. To do this, they should record elements they identify with in the inside frames. The outside frames explore how those pieces affect their lived experiences and interactions with others. To more fully engage multilinguals, I have them simply color in these areas as follows:
   — This is an area I don't think about much and doesn't change how most people treat me. (yellow).
   — This is an area I sometimes think about or sometimes changes the way people treat me. (green)
   — This is an area I think about a lot or makes a big difference in how others treat me. (orange)
3. Prompt individual or group reflection and conversation. Here are additional thoughts you may want to have learners consider: *What aspect do other people notice about me first? Which part of the wheel was the hardest to fill out? Which part of my identity do I know the most (or least) about? What part of my identity is most important in my home or community? What part of my identity have I had the best (or worst) experiences with? What part of my identity do I want to grow/celebrate/learn more about? What parts of my identity are my biggest superpowers? Why?*
4. Remind students that self-awareness, including an awareness of one's identity (including all of its unique intersections), is power restorative. Meanwhile, recognizing and celebrating other people's identities is the deepest demonstration of respect.
5. Help students focus on the commonalities of the group. Where can the class come together? If continuing on to conversations about implicit and explicit bias, this is a great launching point!

A Return to Protective Factors

Recall that protect factors are people, places, circumstances, or toolsets that buffer the effects of adverse life experiences. They can help counter risk factors (including transition shock) and improve youth's social and emotional well-being (SAMHSA, 2019). In fact, the Family Resource Information, Education, and

FIGURE 8.3

Wheel of Self-Concept and Wheel of Protection

Wheel of Self-Concept

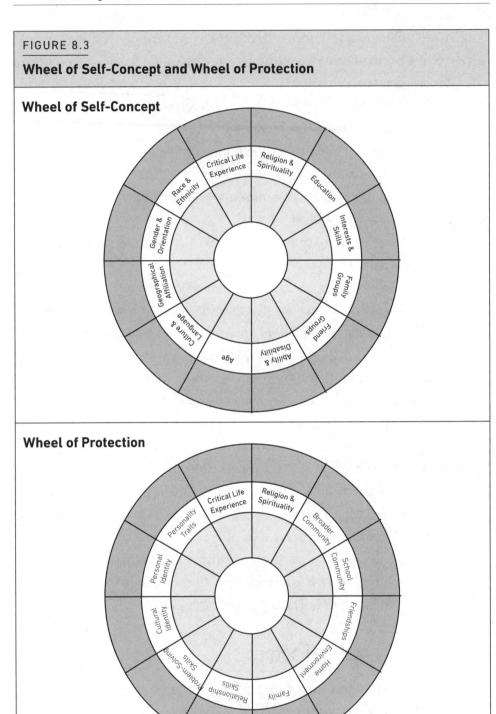

Wheel of Protection

Network Development Service (2020) reminds us that "outcomes for children can be substantially improved by helping children and their families build protective factors" (para. 3).

That's a pretty mighty call to action, isn't it? The fact is, we have nothing to lose by introducing and promoting protective factors in the educational landscape—and we have absolutely everything to gain. There are three critical areas of protection: within the individual, within the family/home, and within the community. Here's a look at protective factors and how they may or may not manifest in students' lives:

Individual

The student

- Demonstrates a sense of purpose
- Demonstrates hopefulness.
- Has a strong and complex cultural identity.
- Has healthy, age-appropriate social and emotional skill sets.
- Is engaged in positive activities.
- Is affiliated with spiritual, religious, and/or cultural value systems.
- Has strong and consistent friendships.
- Engages in a hobby, skill, sport, or personal interest.

Family/Home

At home, there is

- Access to safe, clean, and affordable basic resources, including shelter, food, water, clothing, and medical care.
- Access to parent programming and parenting classes
- Access to adult education and workforce training, including English language instruction services.
- A consistent presence of a nurturing adult or adults.
- A supportive environment.
- Stability.
- A reasonable set of rules or expectations (as well as reasonable consequences).

- Access to consistent employment opportunities.
- Access to physical and mental health care, as well as social services.
- A quiet place and time to work and study.
- A variety of coping strategies.
- A proximal and robust network of relationships with extended family members.
- A solid and consistent set of social and friendship connections.

School Community

Within the school community,

- Students feel safe and welcomed.
- Parents and other caretakers feel safe and welcomed.
- All students, parents, and staff feel as though they are seen, heard, and valued.
- All languages and cultures are respected and viewed as assets.
- Students, staff, and caretakers are referred to by their preferred names and pronouns.
- Staff are well trained on trauma-informed best practices and how to bolster resilience.
- Staff are well trained on culturally responsive and relevant pedagogy.
- The overall environment is trauma-informed and culturally responsive.
- The learning spaces are physically safe and aesthetically appealing.
- There is a wide range of socioacademic resources that are equitably available to everyone.
- There is a clear sense of cohesiveness and interconnectedness.

Greater Community

Within the greater community,

- Children and their families feel safe where they live.
- Students have a safe place to go for recreational activities.
- Students have a safe place to learn or study outside the home.
- People are held accountable for irresponsible or illegal behaviors, including physical abuse or substance misuse.

- Children have access to role models and mentors.
- There is access to mental health and substance abuse services.
- There is a system of accountability against racism.
- There is a system of laws that protect all members of the community equally and fairly.
- There is a variety of faith-based houses and support systems.
- There is a wide range of health and well-being resources that are equitably available to everyone.
- There is a clear sense of cohesiveness and interconnectedness.

Where Do We Go from Here?

The power of resilience—in context—is irrefutable:

> The day in and day out experiences that children have—in particular with caregivers, parents, and educators—have clearly been found to be a very powerful force in shaping children's lives. But *how?* What *is* it? . . . It's fairly ordinary magic. It's not that special. It's how we go about instilling in children an understanding and an appreciation of *How do you deal with a mistake? How do you go about solving a problem? How are you connected to others? Why is it important to help and to have empathy?* These seemingly ordinary qualities make the difference. (Goldstein, 2013)

When we talk about empowering students, it's important to remember that the power isn't coming from us. It belongs to our students, and they've owned it all along. Sometimes that power gets lost in the shuffle of life or blurred out by anxiety, stress, or trauma. Sometimes, after months or years of neglect, it's forgotten about. Sometimes it's stolen or exploited by others. But resilience—in context—is a word that means one's power is never really gone . . . though sometimes it is in the process of being restored.

As we learn to see our students in this way, and encourage them to view themselves in this way, transformation is not only possible but probable.

It's fairly ordinary magic.

Appendix:
Blank Templates

DBT House

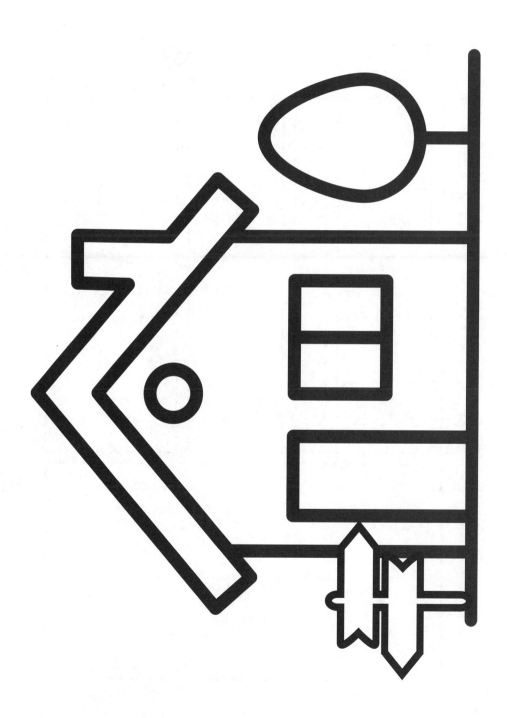

List-Group-Label

Worry Box

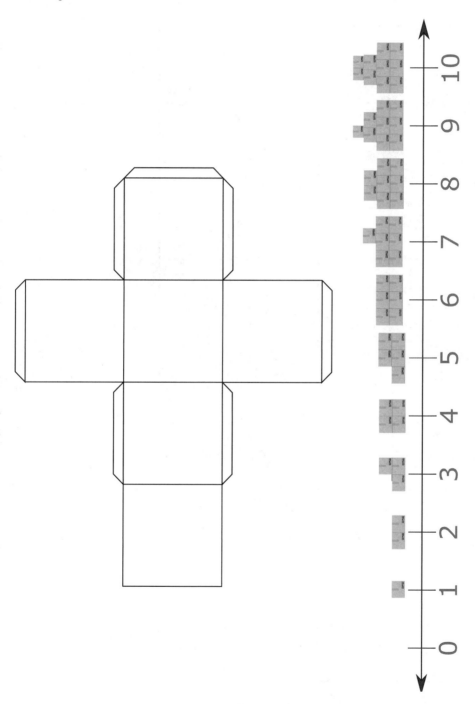

Looks Like/Sounds Like/Feels Like

Interactive Self-Portrait

Circle of Control

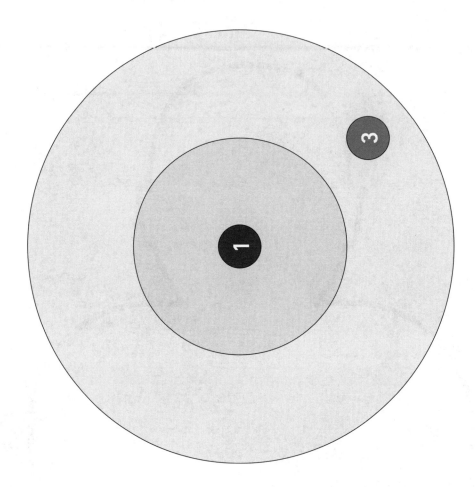

Zone of Responsibility

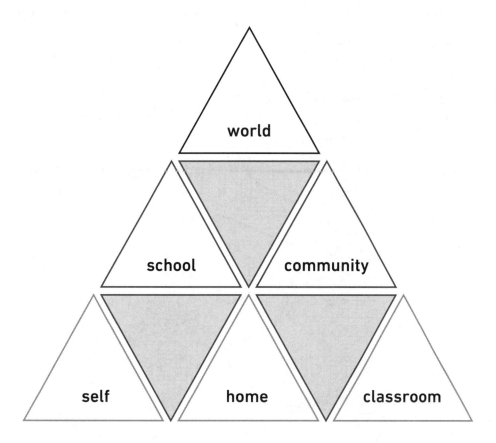

Hands of Promise

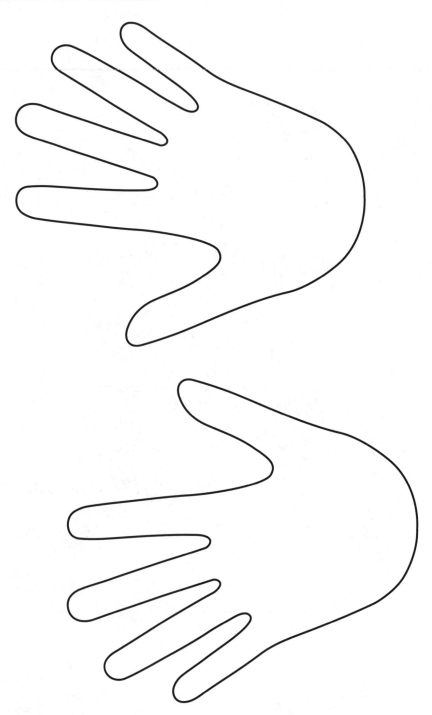

References

Abramowitz, J. S., Tolin, D. F., & Street, G. P. (2001). Paradoxical effects of thought suppression: A meta-analysis of controlled studies. *Clinical Psychology Review, 21*(5), 683–703.

Acharya, B., Basnet, M., Rimal, P., Citrin, D., Hirachan, S., Swar, S., Thapa, P., Pandit, J., Pokharel, R., & Kohrt, B. (2017). Translating mental health diagnostic and symptom terminology to train health workers and engage patients in cross-cultural, non-English speaking populations. *International Journal of Mental Health Systems, 11*(62).

American Psychological Association (APA). (2019). Positive relationships boost self-esteem, and vice versa. www.apa.org/news/press/releases/2019/09/relationships-self-esteem

American Psychological Association (APA). (2012, updated 2020). *Resilience guide for parents and teachers.* www.apa.org/topics/resilience/guide-parents-teachers

American Speech-Hearing-Language Association (ASHLA) (2020). Right hemisphere brain damage (RHD). www.asha.org/public/speech/disorders/right-hemisphere-brain-damage

Amir, N., Stafford, J., Freshman, M.S., & Foa, E. B. (1998). Relationship between trauma narratives and trauma pathology. *Journal of Traumatic Stress, 11*(2), 385–392.

Anderson, A., Hamilton, R., Moore, D., Loewen, S., & Frater-Mathieson, K. (2004). Education of refugee children: Theoretical perspectives and best practice. In R. Hamilton & D. Moore (Eds.), *Educational interventions for refugee children: Theoretical perspectives and implementing best practice* (pp. 1–11). Routledge.

Anderson, M. (2018). A voice at the table: Positioning African-American youth at the center of education reform. Brookings. www.brookings.edu/blog/brown-center-chalkboard/2018/06/19/a-voice-at-the-table-positioning-african-american-youth-voices-at-the-center-of-education-reform

Aronson, J., Fried, C. B., & Good, C. (2002). Reducing the effects of stereotype threat on African American college students by shaping theories of intelligence. *Journal of Experimental Social Psychology, 38,* 113–125.

Arnetz, B. B., Sudan, S., Arnetz, J. E., Yamin, J. B., Lumley, M. A., Beck, J. S., Stemmer, P. M., Burghardt, P., Counts, S. E., & Jamil, H. (2020). Dysfunctional neuroplasticity in newly arrived Middle Eastern refugees in the U.S.: Association with environmental exposures and mental health symptoms. *PLOS One.* https://doi.org/10.1371/journal.pone.0230030

Aupperle, R. L., Melrose, A. J., Stein, M. B., & Paulus, M. P. (2012). Executive function and PTSD: Disengaging from trauma. *Neuropharmacology, 62*(2), 686–694.

Baicker, K. (2020). The impact of secondary trauma on educators. *ASCD Express, 15*(13). www.ascd.org/ascd-express/vol15/num13/the-impact-of-secondary-trauma-on-educators.aspx

Ballantyne, K. G., Sanderman A. R., & Levy, J. (2008). *Education English language learners: Building teacher capacity.* National Clearinghouse for English Language Acquisition.

Bath, H. (2015). The three pillars of traumawise care: Healing in the other 23 hours. *Reclaiming Children and Youth, 23*(4), 5–11.

Beck, J. G., Grant, D. M., Clapp, J. D., & Palyo, S. A. (2009). Understanding the interpersonal impact of trauma: Contributions of PTSD and depression. *Journal of Anxiety Disorders, 23*(4), 443–450.

Benner, M., Brown, C., & Jeffrey, A. (2019). *Elevating student voice in education. Center for American Progress* www.americanprogress.org/issues/education-k-12/reports/2019/08/14/473197/elevating-student-voice-education

Bhopal, R. (2004). Glossary of terms relating to ethnicity and race: For reflection and debate *Journal of Epidemiology & Community Health, 58,* 441–445.

Blue Knot Foundation. (2020). What is childhood trauma? https://blueknot.org.au/resources/understanding-trauma-and-abuse/what-is-childhood-trauma

Bremner, J. D. (2006). Traumatic stress: Effects on the brain. *Dialogues in Clinical Neuroscience, 8*(4), 445–461.

Briere, J., & Lanktree, C. B. (2013). *Integrative treatment of complex trauma for adolescents: Treatment guide* (2nd ed.). USC Adolescent Trauma Training Center, National Child Traumatic Stress Network.

Brown, A. D. (2017). Protective and risk factors associated with trauma. *Psychology Today.* www.psychology today.com/us/blog/towards-recovery/201704/protective-and-risk-factors-associated-trauma

Budde, H., Akko, D. P., Ainamani, H. E., Murillo-Rodríguez, E., & Weierstall, R. (2018). The impact of an exercise training intervention on cortisol levels and post-traumatic stress disorder in juveniles from a Ugandan refugee settlement: study protocol for a randomized control trial. *Trials, 19*(1), 364

Buffalo Center for Social Research. (2015). Infographic. http://socialwork.buffalo.edu/social-research/institutes-centers/institute-on-trauma-and-trauma-informed-care/what-is-trauma-informed-care.html

Bylow, C. (2018). The mindset of a champion. www.youtube.com/watch?v=px9CzSZsa0Y&t=2s

California County Superintendents Educational Services Association. (2017). *Culturally and linguistically responsive arts teaching and learning in action: Strategies that increase student engagement and achievement.* http://ccsesaarts.org/wp-content/uploads/2019/01/CCSESA_CulturallyResp_18_Web_5_2_18.pdf

Carello, J., & Butler, L. D. (2015). Practicing what we teach: Trauma-informed educational practice. *Journal of Teaching in Social Work, 35*(3), 262–278.

Cartier, C. (2018). The storytellers of Syria: Displaced women keep tradition and history alive with folktales. *The New Arab.* https://english.alaraby.co.uk/english/indepth/2018/6/27/keeping-history-alive-syrian-storytelling-in-refugee-camps

CASEL District Resource Center. (2020). What is social and emotional learning? https://drc.casel.org/what-is-sel

Caven, M. (2020). Why we need an anti-racist approach to social and emotional learning. *Education Development Center.* www.edc.org/blog/why-we-need-anti-racist-approach-social-and-emotional-learning

Center for American Progress. (2019). Infographic. www.americanprogress.org/issues/education-k-12/reports/2019/08/14/473197/elevating-student-voice-education

Centers for Disease Control and Prevention (CDC). (2009). *School connectedness: Strategies for increasing protective factors among youth.* U.S. Department of Health and Human Services.

Centers for Disease Control and Prevention (CDC). (2019). Brief: Parent engagement in schools. www.cdc.gov/healthyyouth/protective/parent_engagement.htm

Charmarik, S. (1999). Oral tradition in Thailand: A developmental perspective. Paper presented at the 65th IFLA Council and General Conference at Bangkok, Thailand. Retrieved from the International Federation of Library Associations and Institutions.

Child Welfare Information Gateway. (2015). Promoting protective factors for victims of child abuse and neglect: A guide for practitioners: A fact sheet. www.childwelfare.gov/pubPDFs/protective_factors.pdf

Collins, L. Y. (2021). *Healing from racial trauma: A consciousness journey through autoethnography.* Lewis & Clark College, Graduate School of Education and Counseling.

Communities for Just Schools Fund. (2020). When SEL is used as another form of policing. https://medium.com/@justschools/when-sel-is-used-as-another-form-of-policing-fa53cf85dce4

Conklin, T. (2014). *Social and emotional learning in middle school: Essential lessons for student success: Engaging lessons, strategies, and tips that help students navigate middle school and focus on academics.* Scholastic.

Conner, K. O. (2020). Why historical trauma is critical to understanding Black mental health. *Psychology Today.* www.psychologytoday.com/us/blog/achieving-health-equity/202010/why-historical-trauma-is-critical-understanding-black-mental

Cornell University Center for Teaching Innovation. (2020). Teaching resources: Collaborative learning. https://teaching.cornell.edu/teaching-resources/engaging-students/collaborative-learning

Covey, S. (1989). *7 habits of highly effective people.* Free Press.

Cultural Heritage Without Borders. (2020) Syria. Al-Hakawati: The storyteller. http://chwb.org/syria

Daud, A., Klinteberg, B., & Rydelius, P. (2008). Resilience and vulnerability among refugee children of traumatized and non-traumatized parents. *Child and Adolescent Psychiatry and Mental Health, 2*(1), 7.

De Bellis, M. D., & Zisk, A. (2014). The biological effects of childhood trauma. *Child and Adolescent Psychiatric Clinics of North America, 23*(2), 185–222.

Devaney, E. (2020). How can we ensure SEL is anti-racist? *Children's Institute.* www.childrensinstitute.net /about-us/blog/note-elizabeth-how-can-we-ensure-sel-anti-racist

Dezelic, M. (2013). Window of tolerance: Trauma/anxiety related responses: Widening the comfort zone for increased flexibility. www.drmariedezelic.com/window-of-tolerance--traumaanxiety-rela

Doyle, N. (2020). Trauma-informed management: Four essential skills for a longer term crisis. *Forbes.* www .forbes.com/sites/drnancydoyle/2020/10/30/trauma-informed-management--four-essential-skills-for-a-longer-term-crisis/?sh=6984c4c613c6

Duckworth, A. L., & Seligman, M. E. P. (2005). Self-discipline outdoes IQ in predicting academic performance of adolescents. *Psychological Science, 16*(12), 939–944.

Durlak, J. A., Weissberg, R. P., Dymnicki, A., Taylor, R. D., & Schellinger, K. B. (2011). The impact of enhancing students' social and emotional learning: A meta-analysis of school-based universal interventions. *Child Development, 82,* 405–432.

Dvir, Y., Ford, J. D., Hill, M., & Frazier, J. A. (2014). Childhood maltreatment, emotional dysregulation, and psychiatric comorbidities. *Harvard Review of Psychiatry, 22*(3), 149–161.

Dykshoorn, K. L. (2014). Trauma-related obsessive-compulsive disorder: A review. *Health Psychology and Behavioral Medicine, 2*(1), 517–528.

Edwards, D. J., McEnteggart, C., Barnes-Holmes, Y., Lowe, R., Evans, N., & Vilardaga, R. (2017). The impact of mindfulness and perspective-taking on implicit associations toward the elderly: A relational frame theory account. *Mindfulness, 8*(6), 1616–1622.

Elliot, A. J., & Dweck, C. S. (2005). Competence and motivation: Competence as the core of achievement motivation. In A. J. Elliot & C. S. Dweck (Eds.), *Handbook of competence and motivation* (pp. 3–12). Guilford.

Family Resource Information, Education, and Network Development Service. (2020). Protective factors. https://friendsnrc.org/prevention/protective-factors

Fanion, L. S. (2020). We need to start talking about vicarious trauma in educators. *LinkedIn Pulse.* www .linkedin.com/pulse/we-need-start-talking-vicarious-trauma-educators-l-sha-fanion-ed-d

Fard, M. F. (2019). How movement therapy can heal traumatic stress. *Experience Life.* https://experiencelife .com/article/how-movement-therapy-can-heal-traumatic-stress

Farrel, T. (2019). Practicing the pause: Addressing tensions in widening the window of tolerance. *PACEs Connection.* www.pacesconnection.com/blog/practicing-the-pause-addressing-tensions-in-widening-the-window-of-tolerance

Ferfolja, T., & Vickers, M. (2010). Supporting refugee students in school education in greater western Sydney. *Critical Studies in Education, 51*(2), 149–162.

Field, M. (2016, Autumn). Empowering students in the trauma-informed classroom through expressive arts therapy. *Education Journal, University of Regina, Canada, 22*(2), 55–71.

Ford, D. (2020). Social-emotional learning for Black students is ineffective when it is culture-blind. *Diverse Issues in Higher Education.* https://diverseeducation.com/article/166341

Ford, J. D., & Russo, E. (2006). Trauma-focused, present-centered, emotional self-regulation approach to integrated treatment for posttraumatic stress and addiction: Trauma adaptive recovery group education and therapy (TARGET). *American Journal of Psychotherapy, 60*(4), 335–355.

Fought, C. (2006). *Language and ethnicity.* Cambridge University Press.

Frater-Mathieson, K. (2004). Refugee trauma, loss and grief: Implications for intervention. In R. Hamilton & D. Moore (Eds.), *Educational interventions for refugee children: Theoretical perspectives and implementing best practice* (pp. 12–34). Routledge.

Frey, N., Fisher, D., & Smith, D. (2019). *All learning is social and emotional: Helping students develop essential skills for the classroom and beyond.* ASCD.

Gask, L. (2015). The problem with resilience. *Patching the Soul.* https://lindagask.com/2015/10/12/the-problem-with-resilience

Gay, G. (2002). Preparing for culturally responsive teaching. *Journal of Teacher Education, 53*(2), 106–116.

Gay, G. (2014). Video: Geneva Gay: Cultural elements. *Continuing Professional Studies, Learning for Justice.* www.youtube.com/watch?v=L9--vdDEk6I

Gay, G. (2018). *Culturally responsive teaching: Theory, research and practice.* Teachers College Press.

Gichiru, W. P. (2012). Challenges and prospects of providing critical educational opportunities for Somali refugees in the United States. *Counterpoints, 427,* 49–68.

Gillihan, S. J. (2019). The healing power of telling your trauma story: Six ways revisiting painful memories can loosen their grip. *Psychology Today.* www.psychologytoday.com/us/blog/think-act-be/201903/the-healing-power-telling-your-trauma-story

Glossary of Education Reform. (2013). Great schools partnership: Entry: Student voice. www.edglossary.org/student-voice

Goldberg, J. (2016). It takes a village to determine the origins of an African proverb. National Public Radio, *Goats and Soda.* www.npr.org/sections/goatsandsoda/2016/07/30/487925796/it-takes-a-village-to-determine-the-origins-of-an-african-proverb

Goldstein, S. (2013). The power of resilience: Sam Goldstein, PhD at TEDxRockCreekPark. www.youtube.com/watch?v=isfw8JJ-eWM

Grasser, L. R., Al-Saghir, H., Wanna, C., Spinei, J., & Javanbakht, A. (2019). Moving through the trauma: Dance/movement therapy as a somatic-based intervention for addressing trauma and stress among Syrian refugee children. *Journal of the American Academy of Child and Adolescent Psychiatry, 58*(11), 1124–1126.

Greenberg, M. T. (2006). Promoting resilience in children and youth. *Annals of the New York Academy of Sciences, 1094,* 139–150.

Gregory, A., Hafen, C. A., Ruzek, E., Mikami, A. Y., Allen, J. P., & Pianta, R. C. (2016). Closing the racial discipline gap in classrooms by changing teacher practice. *School Psychology Review, 45*(2), 171–191.

Guido, M. (2017). 15 culturally-responsive teaching strategies and examples. *Prodigy.* www.prodigygame.com/main-en/blog/culturally-responsive-teaching

Hall, E. T. (1977). *Beyond culture.* Anchor Books.

Hamm, J. (2017). Understanding trauma: Learning brain vs survival brain. www.youtube.com/watch?v=KoqaUANGvpA

Hammond, Z. (2014). *Culturally responsive teaching and the brain.* Corwin.

Hane, A. (2016). Art as intervention: Evaluation of a trauma-informed creative arts program for young children. *Wilder Foundation Research Library.* www.wilder.org/sites/default/files/imports/ArtAsInterventionCTC_9-16.pdf

Hanson, H. (2018). On the important of titration for trauma and healing. *The Art of Healing Trauma.* www.new-synapse.com/aps/wordpress/?p=1842

Harvard Health Publishing. (2017). Ramp up your resilience! *Harvard Medical School: Mind & Mood.* www.health.harvard.edu/mind-and-mood/ramp-up-your-resilience

Heid, M. (2019). It's okay if you're not resilient. *Elemental.* https://elemental.medium.com/its-okay-if-you-re-not-resilient-cc74c3f2db26

Herman, J. (1997). Trauma and recovery: The aftermath of violence—From domestic abuse to political terror. BasicBooks.

Henkin, H. (2019). Culturally responsive pedagogy and its relevance in the adult English as a second language classroom. *Master's Projects and Capstones, 955.*

Henry, J. P. (1993). Psychological and physiological responses to stress: The right hemisphere and the hypothalamo-pituitary-adrenal axis, an inquiry into problems of human bonding. *Integrative Psychological and Behavioral Science, 28*(4), 369–387.

Himelstein, S. (2016). Trauma and the brain: An introduction for professionals working with teens. Center for Adolescent Studies. https://centerforadolescentstudies.com/trauma-and-brain

Hochschild, J. L. (2005, Winter). Looking ahead: Racial trends in the U.S. *Daedalus: Journal of the American Academy of Arts & Sciences*, 70–81.

Hollie, S. (2011). *Culturally and linguistically responsive teaching and learning: Classroom practices for student success.* Shell Education.

Honsinger, C., & Brown, M. H. (2019). Preparing trauma-sensitive teachers: Strategies for teacher educators. https://files.eric.ed.gov/fulltext/EJ1209431.pdf

Hoot, J. L. (2011). Working with very young refugee children in our schools: Implications for the world's teachers. *Procedia—Social and Behavioral Sciences, 15,* 1751–1755.

Hummer, V. L., Crosland, K., & Dollard, N. (2009). *Applied behavioral analysis within a trauma-informed framework.* Presented at the Florida Center for Inclusive Communities "Lunch n Learn" Series. Tampa, FL.

Huxley, R. (2018). The Rs of trauma informed care. https://ronhuxley.com/2018/04/25/the-rs-of-trauma-informed-care

Hydon, S. P., & Marsh. D. (2005). *Interdisciplinary dimensions of social work: In law, business, medical services, gerontology, public administration, and education.*

Im, H., Ferguson, A., & Hunter, M. (2017). Cultural translation of refugee trauma: Cultural idioms of distress among Somali refugees in displacement. *Transcultural Psychiatry, 54*(5-6), 626–652.

Intergroup Relations Center. (2012). *Voices of discovery.* Arizona State University Press.

James, M., & Burgos, A. (2020). Race. *Stanford Encyclopedia of Philosophy.* https://plato.stanford.edu/archives/sum2020/entries/race

Jirata, T. J. (2018). Folktales, reality, and childhood in Ethiopia: How children construct social values through performance of folktales. *Folklore, 129*(3), 237–253.

Kalmanowitz, D., & Rainbow, T. H. (2016). Out of our mind: Art therapy and mindfulness with refugees, political violence, and trauma. *The Arts in Psychotherapy, 49,* 57–65.

Kaplan, I., Stolk, Y., Valibhoy, M., Tucker, A., & Baker, J. (2015). Cognitive assessment of refugee children: Effects of trauma and new language acquisition. *Transcultural Psychiatry, 53*(1), 81–109.

Keck School of Medicine of USC. (2013). Integrative treatment of complex trauma. https://keck.usc.edu/adolescent-trauma-training-center/treatment-guide/chapter-11-trigger-identification-and-intervention

Kelley, S. (2018). *Left, right and center: Mapping emotion in the brain. Cornell Chronicle.* https://news.cornell.edu/stories/2018/06/left-right-and-center-mapping-emotion-brain

Kearney, R. (2007). Narrating pain: The power of catharsis. *Paragraph, 30*(1), 51–66.

Khan, K. (2014). How somatic therapy can help patients suffering from psychological trauma. *PsychCentral.* https://psychcentral.com/blog/how-somatic-therapy-can-help-patients-suffering-from-psychological-trauma#1

Knefel, J. (2015). How art therapy is being used to help Syrian children in Lebanon. *The Nation.* www.thenation.com/article/archive/how-art-therapy-is-being-used-to-help-syrian-children-in-lebanon

Krasnoff, B. (2016). *Culturally responsive teaching: A guide to evidence-based practices for teaching all students equitably.* https://educationnorthwest.org/sites/default/files/resources/culturally-responsive-teaching.pdf

Kraybill, O. G. (2018). How to maintain progress after trauma. *Psychology Today.* www.psychologytoday.com/us/blog/expressive-trauma-integration/201804/how-maintain-progress-after-trauma

Kreuzer, L. H. (2016). *The newcomer student: An educator's guide to aid transition.* Rowman & Littlefield.

Kubota, R., & Lin, A. M. Y. (Eds.). (2009). *Race, culture, and identities in second language education: Exploring critically engaged practice.* Routledge.

Ladson-Billings, G. (1994). *The dreamkeepers.* Jossey-Bass.

Ley, D. J. (2020). Surviving childhood adversity builds empathy in adults. *Psychology Today.* www.psychologytoday.com/us/blog/women-who-stray/202009/surviving-childhood-adversity-builds-empathy-in-adults

Linehan, M. M. (1993). *Cognitive behavioral treatment of borderline personality disorder.* Guilford.

Linehan, M. M., Schmidt, H., Dimeff, L. A., Kanter, J. W., Craft, J. C., Comtois, K. A., & Recknor, K. L. (1999). Dialectical behavior therapy for patients with borderline personality disorder and drug-dependence. *American Journal on Addiction, 8,* 279–292.

Linquanti, R., & Cook, H. G. (2017). *Innovative solutions for including recently arrived English learners in state accountability systems: A guide for states* U.S. Department of Education, Office of Elementary and Secondary Education, Office of State Support.

Lorde, A. (1981). The uses of anger. https://academicworks.cuny.edu/cgi/viewcontent.cgi?article=1654&-context=wsq

LSA Inclusive Teaching University of Michigan. (2019). Social identity wheel. https://sites.lsa.umich.edu/inclusive-teaching/sample-activities/social-identity-wheel

Ludicke, P., & Kortman, W. (2012). Tensions in home-school partnerships: The different perspectives of teachers and parents of students with learning barriers. *Australasian Journal of Special Education, 36*(2), 155–171.

Madda, M. J. (2019). Dena Simmons: Without context, social-emotional learning can backfire. www.edsurge.com/news/2019-05-15-dena-simmons-without-context-social-emotional-learning-can-backfire

Mahoney, J. L., Durlak, J. A., & Weissberg, R. P. (2018, November 26). An update on social and emotional learning outcome research. *Phi Delta Kappan Professional Journal for Educators.*

Malchiodi, C. A. (2015). Neurobiology, creative interventions, and childhood trauma. In C. A. Malchiodi (Ed.), *Creative interventions with traumatized children* (2nd ed.) (pp. 3–23). Guilford.

Malhotra, S., & Sahoo, S. (2017). Rebuilding the brain with psychotherapy. *Indian Journal of Psychiatry, 59,* 411–419.

Marchbanks, M. P., & Blake, J. J. (2018). Assessing the role of school discipline in disproportionate minority contact with the juvenile justice system: Final technical report. U.S. Department of Justice, National Criminal Justice Reference Service. Document number 252059.

Martin, C. (2018). Unlock the secret to successful engagement. New York State Care Management Training Initiative. Webinar presentation held on January 15, 2018. Slide deck retrieved from https://docplayer.net/180607870-Unlock-the-secret-to-successful-engagement.html

Marzano, R. J., & Pickering, D. J. (2010). *The highly engaged classroom.* Marzano Research.

Mayworm, A. M., & Sharkey, J. D. (2014). Ethical considerations in a three-tiered approach to school discipline, policy and practice. *Psychology in the Schools, 51*(7), 693–704.

McEwen, B. S., & Gianaros, P. J. (2010). Central role of the brain in stress and adaptation: Links to socioeconomic status, health, and disease. *Annals of the New York Academy of Sciences, 1186,* 190–222.

McHugh, M., & Doxsee, C. (2018). English plus integration: Shifting the instructional paradigm for immigrant adult learners to support integration success. Policy Brief, Migration Policy Institute.

Meeker, B. (2020). Teachers: It's time to talk about our secondary trauma. *Chalkbeat Chicago.* https://chicago.chalkbeat.org/2020/9/10/21429591/teachers-secondary-trauma

Mind for Mental Health. (2020). Trauma. www.mind.org.uk/media-a/4149/trauma-2020.pdf

Mohatt, N. V., Thompson, A. B., Thai, N. D., & Tebes, J. K. (2014). Historical trauma as public narrative: A conceptual review of how history impacts present-day health. *Social Science & Medicine, 106,* 128–136.

Molinar, G. A. (2020). (Re)defining resilience: A perspective of "toughness" in BIPOC communities. *Mental Health America.* www.mhanational.org/blog/re-defining-resilience-perspective-toughness-bipoc-communities

Mphasha, L. E. (2017). Folktales reveal the cultural values of the community (strengths, weaknesses, opportunities, and threats). *The Anthropologist, 19*(1).

National Child Traumatic Stress Network (NCTSN). (2018). About child trauma. www.nctsn.org/what-is-child-trauma/about-child-trauma

National Child Traumatic Stress Network (NCTSN). (2019). Effects. www.nctsn.org/what-is-child-trauma/trauma-types/complex-trauma/effects

National Child Traumatic Stress Network (NCTSN). (2020). Secondary traumatic stress. www.nctsn.org/trauma-informed-care/secondary-traumatic-stress

National Council for Behavioral Health (NICABM). (2019). Bulletin: Trauma-informed primary care (TIPC) sustainability guide. www.thenationalcouncil.org/wp-content/uploads/2019/11/Sustainability-Guide.pdf?daf=375ateTbd56

National Institute for the Clinical Application of Behavioral Medicine. (2019). Infographic: How to help your clients understand the window of tolerance. www.nicabm.com/trauma-how-to-help-your-clients-understand-their-window-of-tolerance

National Research Council. (2004). *Measuring racial discrimination*. National Academies Press.

Nickerson, A., Liddell, B., Asnaani, A., Carlsson, J., Fazel, M., Knaevelsrud, C., Morina, N., Neuner, F., Newnham, E., & Rasmussen, A. (2020). *Briefing paper: Trauma and mental health in forcibly displaced populations*. https://istss.org/public-resources/istss-briefing-papers/trauma-and-mental-health-in-forcibly-displaced-pop

Nietlisbach, G., Maercker, A., Rössler, W., & Haker, H. (2010). Are empathic abilities impaired in posttraumatic stress disorder? *Psychological Reports, 106*(3), 832–844.

O'Connell, M. E., Boat, T., & Warner, K. E. (2009). *Preventing mental, emotional, and behavioral disorders among young people: Progress and possibilities*. National Research Council (U.S.) and Institute of Medicine (U.S.) Committee on the Prevention of Mental Disorders and Substance Abuse Among Children, Youth, and Young Adults. National Academies Press.

Organisation for Economic Co-operation and Development (OECD). (2015). *Skills for social progress: The power of social and emotional skills*. OECD Publishing.

Organisation for Economic Co-Operation and Development. (2018). Social and emotional skills for student success and well-being: Conceptual framework for the OECD study on social and emotional skills. OECD Education Working Paper No. 173. https://www.oecd.org/officialdocuments/publicdisplaydocumentpdf/?cote=EDU/WKP(2018)9&docLanguage=En

Organisation for Economic Co-operation and Development (OECD). (2019). *Social and emotional skills: Well-being, connectedness, and success*. www.oecd.org/education/school/UPDATED%20Social%20and%20Emotional%20Skills%20-%20Well-being,%20connectedness%20and%20success.pdf%20(website).pdf

Parkins, R. (2012). Gender and emotional expressiveness: An analysis of prosodic features in emotional expression. *Griffith Working Papers in Pragmatics and Intercultural Communications, 5*(1), 46–54.

Passardi, S. (2018). *Emotion processing in posttraumatic stress disorder: Emotion recognition, interpretation of neutral facial expressions, and facial mimicry*. www.zora.uzh.ch/id/eprint/161098/1/161098_1.pdf

Pawlo, E., Lorenzo, A., Eichert, B., & Ellis, M. J. (2019). All SEL should be trauma-informed. *Phi Delta Kappan*. https://kappanonline.org/all-sel-should-be-trauma-informed-schools-pawlo-lorenzo-eichert-elias76390-2

Perry, B. (2011). *The boy who was raised by a dog*. BasicBooks

Porche, M. V., Fortuna, L. R., Lin, J., & Alegria, M. (2011). Childhood trauma and psychiatric disorders as correlates of school dropout in a national sample of young adults. *Child Development, 82*(3), 982–998.

Porges, S. W. (2004). *Neuroception: A subconscious system for detecting threats and safety*. https://static1.squarespace.com/static/5c1d025fb27e390a78569537/t/5ccdff181905f41dbcb689e3/1557004058168/Neuroception.pdf

Powers, A., Ressler, K. J., & Bradley, R. G. (2009). The protective role of friendship on the effects of childhood abuse and depression. *Depression and anxiety, 26*(1), 46–53.

Prinz, J. (2020). Culture and cognitive science. *Stanford Encyclopedia of Philosophy Archive*. https://plato.stanford.edu/archives/sum2020/entries/culture-cogsci

Promising Futures. (2019). Protective factors and resiliency. *Promising Futures.* http://promising
.futureswithoutviolence.org/what-do-kids-need/supporting-parenting/protective-factors-resiliency

Rauch, S. L., van der Kolk, B. A., Fisler, R. E., Alpert, N. M., Orr, S. P., Savage, C. R., Fischman, A. J., Jenike, M.
A., & Pitman, R. K. (1996). A symptom provocation study of posttraumatic stress disorder using positron
emission tomography and script-driven imagery. *Archives of General Psychiatry, 53*(5), 380–387.

Rodden, J. (2021). What is executive dysfunction? *ADDitude: Inside the ADHD Mind.* www.additudemag
.com/what-is-executive-function-disorder

Roipel, L. (2021). Resilience skills, factors and strategies of the resilient person. https://positivepsychology
.com/resilience-skills

Ronfeldt, M., Farmer, S. O., McQueen, K., & Grissom, J. A. (2015). Teacher collaboration in instructional
teams and student achievement. *American Educational Research Journal, 52*(3), 475–514.

Rosen, M. (2016). Mapping word meanings in the brain. *Science News for Students.* www.sciencenewsfor
students.org/article/mapping-word-meanings-brain

Rosenbaum, S., Vancampfort, D., Steel, Z., Newby, J., Ward, P., & Stubbs, B. (2015). Physical activity in
the treatment of post-traumatic stress disorder: A systematic review and meta-analysis. *Psychiatry
Research, 230,* 130–136.

Rosenthal, M. (2019). How trauma changes the brain. *Boston Trials.* www.bostontrials.com/how-trauma-
changes-the-brain

Ruixue, J., & Persson, T. (2021). Choosing ethnicity: The interplay between individual and social motives.
Journal of the European Economic Association, 19(2), 1203–1248.

Ruiz-de-Velasco, J., Fix, M., & Clewell, B. C. (2000). *Overlooked and underserved: Immigrant students in U.S.
secondary schools.* www.urban.org/UploadedPDF/overlooked.pdf

Samuel, S. (1997). Cultural unity through folktales. https://teachersinstitute.yale.edu/curriculum
/units/1997/2/97.02.09.x.html

Scafidi, S. (2005). *Who owns culture? Appropriation and authenticity in American law.* Rutgers University
Press.

Schauer, M., & Elbert, T. (2010). *Dissociation following traumatic stress, etiology and treatment.* Hogrefe.

Schiffmann, T. (2019). 10 trauma-informed strategies for navigating classroom behavior emergencies. *The
Trauma-Informed Classroom.* www.tracyschiffmann.com/blog/trauma-informed-classroom-strategies

Schwartz, S. J., Unger, J. B., Zamboanga, B. L., & Szapocznik, J. (2010). Rethinking the concept of accultura-
tion: Implications for theory and research. *American Psychologist, 65*(4), 237–251.

Schweitzer, R. D., Brough, M., Vromans, L., & Asic-Kobe, M. (2011). Mental health of newly arrived Burmese
refugees in Australia: Contributions of pre-migration and post-migration experience. *Australian and
New Zealand Journal of Psychiatry, 45*(4), 299–307.

Seghal, P. (2015). The profound emptiness of "resilience." *New York Times.* www.nytimes.com/2015/12/06
/magazine/the-profound-emptiness-of-resilience.html

Serani, D. (2014). Why your story matters: The healing power of personal narrative. *Psychology Today.* www
.psychologytoday.com/us/blog/two-takes-depression/201401/why-your-story-matters

Shechtman, Z., & Yaman, M. A. (2012). SEL as a component of a literature class to improve relationships,
behavior, motivation, and content knowledge. *American Educational Research Journal, 49*(3), 546–567.

Siegel, D. J., & Bryson, T. P. (2012). *The whole brain child.* Bantam.

Siegel, D. (2012). *The developing mind: How relationships and the brain interact to shape who we are* (2nd ed.).
Guilford.

Simmons, D. (2017). How to change the story about students of color. *Greater Good Magazine.* https://
greatergood.berkeley.edu/article/item/how_to_change_story_of_students_of_color

Simmons, D. (2019). Why we can't afford whitewashed social-emotional learning. *Education Update, 6*(4).
www.ascd.org/el/articles/why-we-cant-afford-whitewashed-social-emotional-learning

Smedley, A. (1998). "Race" and the construction of human identity. *American Anthropologist, 100*(3).

Snellman, A. (2007). Social hierarchies, prejudice, and discrimination. *Digital Comprehensive Summaries
of Uppsala Dissertations from the Faculty of Social Sciences, 32.* Uppsala University Press. http://
uu.diva-portal.org/smash/get/diva2:170901/FULLTEXT01.pdf

Spokane Regional Health District. (2019). Health brief: What is emotional regulation? https://srhd.org/media/documents/What20is20Emotional20Regulation1.pdf

Suarez, C. (2020). The problem with resilience. *Nonprofit Quarterly.* https://nonprofitquarterly.org/the-problem-with-resilience

Substance Abuse and Mental Health Services Association (SAMHSA). (2014). Trauma-informed care in behavioral health services division. www.ncbi.nlm.nih.gov/books/NBK207191

Substance Abuse and Mental Health Services Association (SAMHSA). (2019). Fact sheet: Risk and protective factors. www.samhsa.gov/sites/default/files/20190718-samhsa-risk-protective-factors.pdf

Sweeney, A., Filson, B., Kennedy, A., Collinson, L., & Gillard, S. (2018). A paradigm shift: Relationships in trauma-informed mental health services. *BJPsych Advances, 24*(5) 319–333.

Taba, H. (1967). *Teachers' handbook to elementary social studies.* Addison-Wesley.

Teicher, M., Anderson, S., Polcari, A., Anderson, C., Navalta, C., & Kim, D. (2003). The neurobiological consequences of early stress and childhood maltreatment. *Neuroscience & Behavioural Reviews, 27,* 33–44.

Thiele, R. (2018). Year in review: Burmese refugees struggle with mental health issues. *WMUK.* www.wmuk.org/post/year-review-burmese-refugees-struggle-mental-health-issues#stream

Trauma Survivors Network. (2018). Risk and protective factors. www.traumasurvivorsnetwork.org/traumapedias/777

Treismen, K. (2018). Good relationships are the key to healing trauma. [Video]. www.youtube.com/watch?v=PTsPdMqVwBg&t=385s

Tripp, T. (2016). A body-based bilateral art protocol for reprocessing trauma. In J. L. King Ed.), *Art therapy, trauma, and neuroscience: Theoretical and practical perspectives* (pp. 177–194). Routledge.

United Nations High Commissioner for Refugees (UNHCR). (2020). *Integration handbook: Promoting integration through social connections: Part 1.* www.unhcr.org/handbooks/ih/social-connections/promoting-integration-through-social-connections

University of California–Los Angeles. (2010). Good grades? It's all in who you know: Having friends who attend the same school is key, study shows. *ScienceDaily.* www.sciencedaily.com/releases/2010/06/100603172221.htm

Usborne, E., & de la Sablonnière, R. (2014). Understanding my culture means understanding myself: The function of cultural identity clarity for personal identity clarity and personal psychological well-being. *Journal for the Theory of Social Behavior, 44,* 436–458.

Van Lith, T. (2016). Art therapy in mental health: A systematic review of approaches and practices. *The Arts in Psychotherapy, 47,* 9–22.

Vander Ark, T., & Liebtag, E. (2018). Collaboration: Key to successful teams and projects. *Getting Smart.* www.gettingsmart.com/2018/02/collaboration-key-to-successful-teams-and-projects

Walker, T. (2019). I didn't know it had a name: Secondary traumatic stress and educators. *NEA Today.* www.nea.org/advocating-for-change/new-from-nea/i-didnt-know-it-had-name-secondary-traumatic-stress-and

Wallach, C. A., Ramsey, B. S., Lowry, L. K., & Copland, M. (2006). *Student voice: Tapping the potential of relationships, relevance, and rigor.* Small Schools Project.

Weaver, T. (2020). Antiracism in social-emotional learning: Why it's not enough to talk the talk. *Edsurge.* www.edsurge.com/news/2020-06-16-antiracism-in-social-emotional-learning-why-it-s-not-enough-to-talk-the-talk

Werner, E. (2013). Risk, resilience, and recovery. *Reclaiming Children and Youth, 21*(1), 18–23.

Whitfield, N., & Kanter, D. (2014). Helpers in distress: Preventing secondary trauma. *Reclaiming Children and Youth, 22*(4), 59–61.

Williams, C. M., Tinley, P., & Curtin, M. (2010). Idiopathic toe walking and sensory processing dysfunction. *Journal of Foot and Ankle Research, 3*(16).

Willis, J. (2010). How to teach students about the brain. *Educational Leadership, 67*(4). www.ascd.org/publications/educational-leadership/dec09/vol67/num04/How-to-Teach-Students-About-the-Brain.aspx

Wodzenski, D. C. (2017). *Attachment & trauma: How trauma-related neuroscience and psychology translate to real classroom and early childhood practice.* Psychoneuroeducational Institute.

Wolpert-Gawron, H. (2018). Why choice matters to student learning. *KQED.* www.kqed.org/mindshift/52424/why-choice-matters-to-student-learning

Wyman, P. A., Cowen, E. L., Work, W. C., Hoyt-Meyers, L., Magnus, K. B., & Fagen, D. B. (1999). Caregiving and developmental factors differentiating young at-risk urban children showing resilient versus stress-affected outcomes: A replication and extension. *Child Development, 70,* 645–659.

Zhou, L. Y. (2007). What college students know about older adults: A cross-cultural qualitative study. *Educational Gerontology, 33*(10), 811–831.

Zwi, K., Woodland, L., Williams, K., Palasanthiran, P., Rungan, S., Jaffe, A., & Woolfenden, S. (2018). Protective factors for social-emotional well-being of refugee children in the first three years of settlement in Australia. *Archives of Disease in Childhood, 103,* 261–268.

Index

The letter *f* following a page locator denotes a figure. Strategies are shown in all caps.

About the Author

Louise El Yaafouri is a recent arriver and cultural competency consultant at DiversifiED Consulting. She provides
action-oriented programming, professional development,
and curriculum design in the areas of multilingual education,
trauma-informed practice, culturally responsive pedagogy,
and equity/inclusion work. Louise has also authored a wide
range of materials, including books and magazine articles,
and is a regular contributor to multiple education publications.

As a newcomer educator, Louise was named a Rodel Exemplary Educator,
a distinguished teacher (Denver Public Schools), a Mile High Teacher, and a
Professional Fulbright Educator to Tanzania—where she founded a school
that continues to graduate students each year. She also served as a global mentor to teachers in Kenya's Kakuma and Dadaab refugee camps in partnership
with Columbia University. Currently, she holds board positions at the United
Nations Association of Denver and New America School and maintains vital
partnerships with local and international refugee-serving entities.

Louise is based out of Denver, Colorado, and Saida, Lebanon. She can be
found at louise@diversifi-ED.com and on Twitter @ElYaafouri.

Related ASCD Resources: Trauma-Informed Instruction

At the time of publication, the following resources were available (ASCD stock numbers in parentheses).

Assessing Multilingual Learners: A Month-by-Month Guide (ASCD Arias) by Margo Gottlieb (#SF117076)

Creating a Trauma-Sensitive Classroom (QRG) by Kristin Van Marter Souers and Pete Hall (#QRG118054)

Even on Your Worst Day, You Can Be a Student's Best Hope by Manny Scott (#117077)

Fostering Resilient Learners: Strategies for Creating a Trauma-Sensitive Classroom by Kristin Van Marter Souers and Pete Hall (#116014)

Hanging In: Strategies for Teaching the Students Who Challenge Us Most by Jeffrey Benson (#114013)

How to Reach the Hard to Teach: Excellent Instruction for Those Who Need It Most by Jana Echevarría, Nancy Frey, and Douglas Fisher (#116010)

Learning in a New Language: A Schoolwide Approach to Support K–8 Emergent Bilinguals by Lori Helman (#120015)

Relationship, Responsibility, and Regulation: Trauma-Invested Practices for Fostering Resilient Learners by Kristin Van Marter Souers and Pete Hall (#119027)

Teaching and Supporting Students Living with Adversity (QRG) by Debbie Zacarian and Lourdes Alvarez-Ortiz (#QRG120035)

Teaching to Strengths: Supporting Students Living with Trauma, Violence, and Chronic Stress by Debbie Zacarian, Lourdes Alvarez-Ortiz, and Judie Haynes (#117035)

Trauma-Invested Practices to Meet Students' Needs (QRG) by Kristin Van Marter Souers and Pete Hall (#QRG119077)

For up-to-date information about ASCD resources, go to www.ascd.org. You can search the complete archives of *Educational Leadership* at www.ascd.org/el.

ASCD myTeachSource®
Download resources from a professional learning platform with hundreds of research-based best practices and tools for your classroom at http://myteachsource.ascd.org/

For more information, send an email to member@ascd.org; call 1-800-933-2723 or 703-578-9600; send a fax to 703-575-5400; or write to Information Services, ASCD, 1703 N. Beauregard St., Alexandria, VA 22311-1714 USA.

WHOLE CHILD
TENETS

1 **HEALTHY**
Each student enters school healthy and learns about and practices a healthy lifestyle.

2 **SAFE**
Each student learns in an environment that is physically and emotionally safe for students and adults.

3 **ENGAGED**
Each student is actively engaged in learning and is connected to the school and broader community.

4 **SUPPORTED**
Each student has access to personalized learning and is supported by qualified, caring adults.

5 **CHALLENGED**
Each student is challenged academically and prepared for success in college or further study and for employment and participation in a global environment.

ascd
whole child

The ASCD Whole Child approach is an effort to transition from a focus on narrowly defined academic achievement to one that promotes the long-term development and success of all children. Through this approach, ASCD supports educators, families, community members, and policymakers as they move from a vision about educating the whole child to sustainable, collaborative actions.

Restoring Students' Innate Power relates to the **safe**, **engaged**, **supported**, and **challenged** tenets.

For more about the ASCD Whole Child approach, visit **www.ascd.org/wholechild.**